W9-ADB-688

"Don't Fall Off The Mountain"

"Don't Fall Off The Mountain"

Shirley MacLaine

W · W · NORTON & COMPANY · INC · New York

Copyright © 1970 by Shirley MacLaine. All rights reserved. Published
simultaneously in Canada by George J. McLeod Limited, Toronto.
Printed in the United States of America.

Library of Congress Catalog Card No. 66-10823
SBN 393 07338 6
6 7 8 9 0

To P P P

CERTAIN persons have been excluded from this narrative, in deference to their feelings, and here and there a name has been changed to conceal an identity, but everyone who is included is real and of course the events are true.

KITH OF INFINITY
Hail, O Wind! Salutations!
From a night wanderer seeking light
    searching a mystic land
        from which I have come,
O wind, I am not human:
I am a stranger
    from a different planet:
Is it the same planet from which
    you, O wind, have come?
I breathe as a man,
I see with a man's eyes
    But I am not a man.
O wind, rustling through the forest,
    eager whisperer
    doleful sigher
Forever coursing
    the banks of some invisible river
Borne through the darkness:
Existing only
    in a quasitangible substance
Carrier, uncarried!
Hail, O wind! I greet thee:
Thou alone art the inhabitant of that world
    to which I am akin:
For I am a shadow without body
    come from the unknown depth
    from the unattainable land
Borne by the foam
    carried by the current . . .

Oh epitomiser of purity
   I too am matter:
I am interchangeable,
I am energy, I am one,
I am indivisible and single,
One with all abstractions
Foreign to that earth
   bounded by the impure.
I am kindred to thee, O wind!
I know thee as I know myself.
Thou comest from mine own world

   —"A Poem," by Somtow P. Sucharitkul,
The Bangkok Post, Sunday, September 17, 1967

"Don't Fall Off The Mountain"

One

I WAS BORN INTO A cliché-loving, middle-class Virginia family. To be consistent with my background, I should have married an upstanding member of the community and had two or three strong-bodied children who ate Wonder Bread eight ways. I should have settled down on a clean, tree-lined street in a suburb of Richmond, Virginia, had a maid once a week, a bridge game every Wednesday, and every three years or so a temptation—I would feel guilty about it—to have an affair.

We were taught to respect all material possessions, because it took long, hard years of work to be able to afford such things. Their value was something we should always be aware and proud of. We owned the very table that John Adams (or maybe it was George Mason) ate his wedding breakfast from, and it was our responsibility to uphold cultural tradition and keep the table in perfect condition for our children's children by never putting wet glasses on it. The Chippendale mirror in the dining room was never to be touched (even though it was a fake, as I found out later). The three Wedgwood bowls and the matching plates and ash trays, the antique Chinese vase, the reproduction of "Blue Boy" in the goldplated frame always made me think twice before I invited someone to the house. I was afraid something would get knocked over.

The walls of the house always seemed to remind us that we were a fine Virginia family, and anyone graced with an invitation should conduct himself accordingly. But it was such a plain house, really a plain, modest, middle-class, red-brick house—mortgaged and everything. The big tree in the front yard had to be cut down because one of the branches got sick. I asked, "Why, because a tree's arm got sick, did they have to cut down the whole body?" And they told me the tree doctor had said it was the right thing to do.

So I believed that almost everything that went on around me was the right thing to do. I certainly had loving parents and, it seemed, everything I wanted—I mean up to a point. There were lots of things I wanted, but they weren't "things"; they were feelings.

My father was the autocratic head of the family, well educated, with a portly build moving toward rotundity whenever there were peanuts around. He was a stern man with light blue eyes full of suspicion, the censor of all he surveyed, and the guardian of our safety. He sat in judgment on our actions and behavior. He was some-times terrifying, because he always acted as though he knew not only about the "bad" things we *had* done, but also those "bad" things we were *going* to do. Then there were times when he was so moved with pride for us that his chest puffed out even further than his stomach. His sensitivity was bottomless, but the fear of his own feelings was sometimes too painful to witness.

Mother was a tall, thin, almost ethereal creature with a romantic nature, who found even the most insignificant unpleasantness difficult to accept. In fact, it didn't exist— nothing unpleasant existed; it was a mistake or a mis-interpretation.

While one of my father's primary motivations seemed to be to ferret out a harsh truth, expose it, and gloat over his correct suspicion that it had indeed been there, Mother's was to say, "Ira, you're just tired; you'll feel different in the morning." So many nights and so many mornings rolled around with my trying to fathom the opposing natures of Mr. and Mrs. Ira O. Beaty, and at the same time condition myself to the best approach for survival and level-headedness. I wanted to believe Mother, that nothing bad existed, but it got to be so I knew it just wasn't true. On the other hand, living wasn't always as suspect as Dad said either.

Thank goodness, when I was three, a companion in adjustment and rebellion entered my life. Wrapped in a blanket, he was handed to me to hold. He spent most of his time yelling, and with growing finesse and sometimes astounding precision, he has been doing so ever since. The grownups called him Little Henry, because he looked like the character in the comic strip. Looking at him today, I can't remember when he stopped looking like Little Henry and started looking like Superman. His real name is Warren.

He was my kid brother and we were friends, in fact allies. We had to be, because otherwise we found ourselves battling each other, vying for favor as a result of the competition unconsciously imposed on us by our parents. They probably didn't even know they were doing it, but Warren and I felt it. We would fight each other until an outside force intruded; then we stuck together. Sometimes my allegiance to him would go too far. If some bigger boy on the block started a fight with Warren, I would rush in like Rocky Graziano and finish him off. Warren would look grateful but bewildered, because he really wanted to take the risk himself; and I would lose boy friend after boy friend because I was too "powerhouse" (my nickname after hitting fifteen home runs in a row as the only girl on the team).

Conformity was the rule of behavior in our neighborhood. We were all Baptists. Every single last modest tree-lined person on the block was a white Southern American middle-class Baptist. Oh, maybe there were a few Methodists but not enough to hurt. We lived according to what our neighbors thought, and I guess they were living according to what we thought (which was wishing they would stop thinking what we were thinking).

Mother loved to garden, but someone gossiped over the back fence about the big picture sunhat and the shorts she wore. Warren and I loved to see her out there looking like a walking umbrella, but Dad agreed with the neighbors that she was too conspicuous, so she didn't go out very much after that.

Sometimes I felt I couldn't find Mother. She was under there somewhere, but Warren and I could never really find her.

When I finally quit the ball team and got a steady boy friend, Dad suggested that he (Dick, age fourteen) take a job painting someone else's house instead of ours, because across the street they said it took him six hours to paint my bedroom shutters. So, instead of coming to the house, Dick used to meet me by the creek. It was more fun anyway, and soon I discovered I didn't have to ask my parents one single question about the birds and the bees. I didn't know my mother and father well enough anyway.

Warren used to love model cars, and he could name every car made since the invention of the wheel. Whenever he played with them and forgot to collect them at the end of the day, Dad would come home, feign tripping over one, fall down, and then warn Warren sternly that it was O.K. for that to happen to his own father, but could he imagine how much we could be sued for it if it happened to a stranger on our property? So Warren took his toy cars to his room and finally just didn't play with them any more.

So, because of Dad's sometimes distorted discipline and Mother's insistence that "we were lucky to have such a lovely life really," and the neighbors' twisted frustrations, which permeated even the good times, Warren and I breathed the breath of rebellion into each other. A kind of conniving rebellion to beat the system. It wasn't easy, because the principal of the school we attended was our father, so we were expected to set a good example. How could we set a good example and still enjoy life? It took teamwork. Together we shared the responsibility of being model children. Warren never tracked mud into the house or ate cookies in the living room. I always made beds, did the breakfast dishes, and shut the windows when it rained. In the house we were exemplary citizens, never too exemplary though, or they would suspect. And our parents were proud of us.

Outside we really lived. We emptied garbage cans on other people's front porches, punched holes in tires, set off fire alarms, rang doorbells and ran, stole Twinkies cupcakes and Luden's cough drops from the corner grocery, and crossed busy boulevards with fake limps, sometimes pretending to drop dead in the middle until someone called a cop—and then we beelined it for shelter.

All this was somehow unknown to the stern figure who presided at the head of the dinner table. At the end of the day, we would sit nodding agreement as he complained earnestly that delinquent kids were ruining the neighborhood. At the other end of the table Mother listened with a sad sparkle in her eyes, saying nothing.

After dinner Dad would light his brierwood pipe, the smoke curling about his head and drifting in blue layers up to the fake Chippendale mirror, blending with smells of roast beef and gravy. Presently he would pick up the thread again, expounding on his theory that all kids should be put on ice until they were twenty-one.

Enthusiastically willing to prove him right, Warren and I would retreat to our homework—and blueprint the plan of action for the next day—our new plan of action against the establishment. A small plan and a small establishment, but a promise of things to come.

I was born with very weak bone structure in my ankles. Soon after I learned to walk I began having problems. My ankles turned in so far and were so weak that with the slightest misstep I would fall. So, about age three, for therapeutic reasons, Mother took me to a ballet class. There my imagination took anchor, my energy found a channel. What started as therapy became my life. And I had an outlet for expression.

For the next fifteen years the long lines of girls in sweaty black leotards, straining in unison at the steel practice bar to the beat of the tinny piano, became my challenge, my competition. I needed no urging to join them; I loved it from the beginning. Some of the young ladies were there to lose weight, some to pass the awkward years of adolescence, others to give their mothers an extra two hours at the bridge table. But a few fragile, iron-willed youngsters truly wanted to dance, and dedicated themselves to endless hours of toil, sweat, sore muscles, and repetition. I became one of these—not fragile, but iron-willed.

We moved to Arlington, Virginia, and I went to classes in a big house built on a grassy knoll across the Potomac River in Washington, D. C. The house was renovated into a dance studio and became the Washington School of the Ballet.

Every afternoon during the school week, I spent an hour and a half on the bus going to and from the school. It was run by two expert lady teachers, and it was they who molded my professional attitudes toward my work. The elder was Lisa Gardiner, who had danced with Anna Pavlova. A dignified woman with silver hair, she moved with a stately gait and bearing that reminded me some-

how of Cinderella's horses. She would sit for hours telling
me of her travels with the ballet, and as she talked her
graceful hands floated through the air, her slender pink
nails accenting her words. "If you choose to do something, be sure to do it with your utmost," she would
say to me. "And remember, expect nothing and life will
be velvet."

Her partner, Mary Day, was fifteen years younger
and had tiny feet that could turn out so far they made
a straight line, piercing black eyes, and a temperament
that would have frightened a Cossack. She was an excellent teacher, whose demanding, harsh, and sometimes
irrational perfectionism made each class an event.

These were the women I strove to please, five days
a week, year after year. We were not a professional group,
because none of us was paid for our performances, but
no greater precision could have been asked of profes-
sionals. By the time I was twelve, I was part of what I'm
sure was the best amateur ballet company in the United
States. At various times during the year, we performed
ballets with the National Symphony at Constitution Hall,
and for these occasions we rehearsed far into the night,
after our regular classes. *Cinderella, The Nutcracker, The
Wizard of Oz, Hansel and Gretel.* I always played Hansel
—and every other boy's role, for that matter—because I
was always the tallest in the class.

Rehearsals ended at midnight. I would rush for the
bus, which, it seemed, was always either late or early,
but never on schedule. I'd stumble groggily from the bus
an hour and a half later, and make my way down the
quiet street to a dark and silent house. My dinner usually
was saltine crackers smothered in ketchup and Tabasco,
and with them a quart of ginger ale. I always ate standing up, and then I'd stagger to bed, rarely before two
o'clock. Not surprisingly, my snacks produced nightmares,

and the nightmares were always the same: night after
night I missed the bus.

At six-thirty I was up again for school, ready to start
over—day . . . after day . . . after day, until I was about
seventeen. Rebellious, mischievous days with Warren were
over. I had found a way out, a destiny I could follow, a
life I could make for myself so I wouldn't end up like
every other petty, comfortable Baptist in the community.
I seldom saw my parents, and I didn't see Warren much
after that, either. They were asleep when I left for school
in the morning, because Washington-Lee was so crowded
half the students went on early-morning shifts (six-thirty
bus pickup), and generally asleep when I returned at
night, because the bus trip home took 1½ hours from the
time midnight rehearsals ended.

It was a lonely life, for a teenager especially, but I
had a purpose—a good reason for being. And I learned
something about myself that still holds true: I cannot
enjoy anything unless I work hard at it.

An incident occurred when I was about sixteen that
still blazes in my memory. I came home from a dancing-
school rehearsal distraught because they had taken the role
of Cinderella away from me for our Christmas production. Miss Day and Miss Gardiner said I had simply grown
too tall, and that I looked clumsy.

I remember blurting it out in tears as I climbed the
stairs to go to my room to be alone. Dad was coming down
the stairs. He stopped, and with finger wagging told me
that that should teach me to stop trying to do things I
wasn't capable of. Wasn't this episode proof enough for
me that, if I attempted to go beyond my range, I would
only be crushed? Hadn't he told me many times during
my life? When would I believe him? When would I
understand that if I tried I would only be hurt?

It was like the time I sang "I Can't Say No" a few

years before, at the entertainment assembly program. I had seen *Oklahoma* and fallen in love with the comedy character Ado Annie. I somehow felt I understood the level of her comedy. I put on a silly perky hat with a huge flower square on top and big clodhopper shoes, and when I did it at school everybody laughed—they really laughed. But Dad said I shouldn't be lulled into thinking that theirs was reliable laughter, that a high-school assembly wasn't the world, that I didn't know how to sing, and knew nothing about performing, and just because I had been tickled and moved by Celeste Holm didn't give me the right to take such a standard example of American musical comedy and desecrate it on the stage of Washington-Lee High School. . . . I never sang after that, not even "The Star-Spangled Banner" at assembly. I was too self-conscious. I thought he must be right. He said only people who had been taught things well and had been classically trained had the background to perform and be accepted. Naïve, raw instinct was one thing, but it couldn't compare with traditional education. Only a fool would dare spread his arms wide, exposing his heart, and say— without training—"Here I am, World, I've got something to say." Only a deadhead would believe he could get away with that, because he'd get hurt—and hurt badly. And someone who might realize the pitfalls but say, "Up yours, World, I'm going to say it anyway," would have to be put away. Not only would he be insane—he'd be dangerous. He'd be dangerous because he was willing to be hurt.

I fell on the stairs, that December evening after rehearsal, with my father over me, berating me not only for trying to perform, but for thinking that I could dance Cinderella, and for making a conspicuous ass out of myself as a result. And I cried hard—I cried so hard that I vomited. But the vomit on the stairs didn't stop him;

he went right on driving home his point, that I would only be hurt if I dared to dare. I couldn't move. I looked over at Mother in the living room. Warren wasn't home. Mother sat quietly until finally she said, "All right, Ira, that's enough." But Ira knew that wasn't going to be the end of it. He could see, even though I had dissolved into a little pile of protoplasm, that I would never stop daring. And he seemed to understand that ironically he, in effect, was teaching me to dare because I saw that he was such a spectacular disappointment to himself for having never tried it. A strange clear look of understanding came into his eyes as he realized I didn't want to be like him. He stepped over the vomit and went to the kitchen to fix himself a drink. It was then that I determined to make the most of whatever equipment I had been born with, and part of that equipment was to dare. But mostly I didn't want to be a disappointment to myself.

Two

It was the evening of the *Cinderella* performance. I was dancing the Fairy Godmother, and I stood in the wings after completing my *pliés* and warming-up exercises. The orchestra tuned up, the house lights dimmed, and the audience quieted. The overture began and the curtain was about to open. Before it did, I took a few practice *grands jetés* across the stage. *Snap*—I went down. A sharp pain pierced my right ankle as it doubled under me. Terrified, I looked quickly around to see if anyone had noticed. No one had. Dancers fall down all the time. I looked at the ankle. It was already swollen. I tightened my toe-shoe ribbon to a death grip, and stood up. The curtain went up.

I climbed on point and began to dance. With each movement I seemed to step further out of myself. The pain left me. I began to feel a sense of triumph that gave me strength—not an anesthetized strength as though I had dulled the pain, but more as though my mind had risen above me and was looking down. The dance movements came in an easy flow, and I felt that I was soaring above myself. I knew the pain was there, but I was on top of it somehow. It was probably my first experience in mind over matter. And the feeling was exquisite. On a ballet stage in Washington, D.C., I first came in contact with my potential talent for becoming a mystic!

Two and a half hours later the ballet and curtain calls were over. I asked for an ambulance, and then the pain hit me. I didn't walk for four months.

While I was laid up with my broken ankle I asked

mother to have a talk with me. There had never been many significant talks between us, because I always felt that "significant" subjects would be painful for her. But this talk was necessary, and I would have to stumble in the dark a bit, hoping that I could find part of her that I wouldn't hurt.

I remember sitting with my foot up on pillows on the edge of my bed in my room, gazing at my freckled face in a hand mirror. My face embarrassed me most of the time and I couldn't get a comb through my mass of unruly, tangled red hair.

Mother paused in front of the door. With a glance toward the back yard where my father sat, she entered the room and sat down beside me on the bed.

"What's wrong?" she asked, bracing herself as though anticipating disaster.

"I guess I want to be too many things, too many people," I began, gesturing at the walls covered with the symbols of my restlessness. She looked at the maps, the photographs of famous ballerinas, at the books filled with other people and other places, and at the high-powered telescope I wished would take me to the moon. The familiar sad sparkle filled her eyes.

"But I have to go away from here—away from the schedule, the rigid discipline, the conformity. Perhaps it's been good, and useful, and necessary, but there's so much out there I have to see, and have to do, and have to be a part of."

My words were cutting straight through to her heart, I could see that, and her expression was more than I could bear. She understood only too well. It was something she had wanted to do herself once, a long time ago when her spirit was independent, before she succumbed to being what she thought she *should* be. Her friends told me she had been "delightfully carefree" and that her gaiety had infected everyone she met. I never remembered her that way. I wondered what had happened, and I guess I didn't want it to happen to me.

She changed her position on the bed. "The ballet is stifling you, too, isn't it?"

"Yes," I answered. "I don't know how it started or why, but ballet seems so limited. Miss Gardiner and Miss Day are always telling me not to move my face so much, but I can't help it, and I don't *want* to help it. If the music means laughter to me, my face smiles, naturally. They told me that if I can't control it I should go into movies or something."

"What do *you* want to do to express yourself?" she asked.

"I want to interpret people and what they think and feel. I think I love people, but I don't know very much about them. And I want to be more specific about the way I express myself. I don't want to be a mechanical doll in a mechanical art, and I'm not even sure I want to dance it."

"Have you thought about how you would do it?"

"Well, yes, but I never get very far because I'm afraid."

"Afraid of what?"

"Well, I don't know how to explain it. It's something about being stuck with being me."

"What do you mean?"

"Well, you know how much I love the Spanish dance, for instance."

"Yes."

"And you know that at ballet school it's my favorite class, and you know that I've worked hard at the castanets and the heel beats, and you know that Miss Gardiner and Miss Day think that I'm the best one in the class since Liane left."

"Yes," she agreed. "I think so, too."

"Well, even though it's something I really love doing, I'm self-conscious about it."

"Why?"

"Because how can I expect the audience to believe that I'm a Spanish dancer if I'm really an American girl from Virginia? How can I ever be anything more if that's what I really am?"

Mother folded her hands in her lap, sat up straighter than she had in years.

"Above all, you must know emotions. Study how people *feel*. I believe that is one thing we are all capable of understanding in others. We may not always be able to understand how they live, or accept what they eat, who they pray to, or why they die, but we can all, with a little effort, understand how another *feels*. How does a Spanish dancer feel? She dances to the same music we hear. What does she feel when she hears it? When you can convey what she feels, then anyone would believe you're a Spanish dancer, too, in spite of your red hair and freckles."

I hugged her. She didn't seem trampled on any more.

"May I go to New York? May I go as soon as I graduate?"

All her years of frustration came alive in one moment. The sad sparkle vanished from her eyes. She answered with unflinching certainty. "Yes, it's time. Your father won't like the idea, he'll think you'll get hurt or taken, but then isn't that always the risk? I think you're prepared."

So I was free to try my wings. I remember the morning I left home. Warren had skipped football practice. He sat down at the piano to beat the hell out of it. He used to work everything out on the piano, and this particular morning he was working it out on "Manhattan Towers." He was tall and handsome by now and didn't need me any more to finish his battles. I wondered when I'd see him again. I wondered when he'd decide what he would do with his life. He still had three years of high school to go, three years to be fending for himself. I didn't know then (because he was as shy about his inside self as all of us) that every afternoon while Mom and Dad were grocery shopping and I was at dancing class, Warren was in the basement acting out his soul to every Al Jolson record ever made, and memorizing in detail every play Eugene O'Neill ever wrote. It wouldn't be long before we'd meet again; it would be only a matter of a few years, really—just long enough for us both to get established.

I don't think either of us ever seriously considered that we *wouldn't* be able to make something of ourselves. We *had* to; it was the only way we'd have any respect for ourselves. We *wanted* to live up to whatever our potentials might be. The frustrating spectacle of people who hadn't, who had been afraid to, and were bitterly disappointed in themselves as a result, had been crippling to us in many ways as we grew up; but, on the other hand, their failures and frustrations had been so clear that Warren and I had a precise blueprint of how *not* to be.

And one of the lessons we learned was to judge ourselves, to conduct ourselves according to what *we* thought was best for us, not by what others might think. In the final analysis, we would have only ourselves to answer to; to live inside of. It was *he* whom he didn't want to disappoint. And it was *I* whom I wanted to be proud of.

So I thought, as I left Virginia that day, "He'll do something. And it will be his way, just as I am going off to do something my way." But I knew then that, whatever it was, somehow it would continue to be a joint plan against the established way of doing things. And in a way I secretly thanked Mom and Dad for inadvertently channeling us on such a course.

I arrived in New York at eighteen, wide-eyed, optimistic, brave, and certain I would crash the world of show business overnight. Naïveté is a necessary personality trait in order to endure New York, and a masochistic sense of humor an indispensable quirk.

I took an apartment at 116th Street and Broadway with the money I had saved from babysitting in Arlington. It was a sub-sub-sublet, a fifth-floor walkup in an old brownstone building, where for sixty-four dollars a month I had two tiny bedrooms, a bath, a kitchen, and a view of the Hudson. To release the bathtub drain, I had to take up two of the floor boards and unplug it from underneath. To see the Hudson, I had to line myself up with a half-inch slit between two brick buildings. One of the bedrooms had no closet, the other no windows, and the kitchen was a hot plate and a small, filthy sink.

But the shabbiness wasn't the only reason for the low rent. At night people lurked in the dark shadows of doorways, and doors opened an inch or two as eyes followed me while I made my way up the four flights. The building was crawling with dope addicts.

That first year I had twelve different roommates. They bombed out on half the rent for reasons ranging from unemployment to out-of-wedlock motherhood. One of their problems I shared, the other I didn't.

One roommate departed regularly every night at midnight for cookies and milk. I never saw anyone so fond of cookies and milk. It took her all night to eat them. One morning she showed up wearing a mink coat, and that afternoon she moved out.

My first few weeks in New York were an initiation into the kingdom of bugs. Sleep was impossible. I complained to the absentee landlord about my six-legged companions. He told me to plug my ears and keep my mouth closed.

The exterminator I called was more sympathetic, but he was a thirty-year-old Italian with an appetite for other things. He squirted the bed bugs. He saved the cockroaches until I called him again.

At first I lived principally on whole-wheat English muffins, graham crackers, and honey (for energy). It all tasted of garlic, because the superintendent's wife cooked with so much garlic that nobody else in the building ever had to buy any. Every night, before going to bed, I'd sit watching the cockroach army as it marched across the living room toward the kitchen. I could almost hear them groan as, night after night, they found the same old graham-cracker and muffin crumbs.

Summer was stifling and the apartment a tomb. I would climb up the fire escape to the street roof, where I'd cling precariously, hoping to hang on long enough to get some sun. Instead I'd be covered with soot.

Winter was a different nightmare. The double window in the bedroom was minus several panes, which were never replaced. The snow filtered down between the buildings and piled up on the floor in patterns that matched the missing panes as I lay shivering in bed.

Jobs were unheard of, especially for dancers. I had been lucky in the summer, having gotten a job at a "summer theater in the round" in New Jersey, but for the fall season the competition was too severe. Every penny I owned went into dance lessons, which were essential if I was ever to get a job. Food was less important. I always ate at an Automat, where I learned to stretch a dime in a manner that might have won the approval of Horatio Alger himself—a manner that was standard among ballet dancers in New York. Lined up on the iced-tea counter were rows of glasses, each containing a wedge of lemon. I took several glasses, proceeded to the water fountain, filled them with water, carried them to a table, and poured in the sugar. At no cost I filled myself to the bloating point with delicious lemonade before spending the precious dime for a peanut-butter sandwich on raisin bread. This went on for nearly a year, and it took me another ten before I could face lemonade or peanut butter again.

Even though they couldn't really afford it, my parents were willing to help me, but I never asked. I didn't want them to. I had chosen this life and I would handle it in the best way I knew how.

My funds were completely gone and the landlord had posted an eviction notice on the door, when Fate led me to an audition for the Servel Ice Box trade show, which, though not in my fantasized life plan, would enable me to eat.

The show was auditioning for the road—the southern circuit—with one-night stands in every major city in the South, playing before conventions of traveling salesmen who worked for Servel. Normally only a deadbeat would take such a job, but at that time even solo dancers begged for chorus jobs.

I was standing in line with the other applicants, staring into the darkness of the theater and waiting for the audition to begin, when suddenly a harsh voice called from the back row, "Hey, you with the legs."

Everyone stood stock-still.

"You with the red hair and the legs that start at your shoulders—step forward."

I looked right and then left. There were short girls on either side of me.

"You mean me, sir?" I asked timidly.

"Yeah. What's your name?"

"Shirley Beaty, sir."

"Shirley Batty? That's a funny name."

"Not Batty. Beaty."

"Yeah, that's what I said: Beauty."

"Not Beauty, Bay-tee."

"Okay, so it's BAY-TEE. Don't you have a middle name or something?"

"Yes, sir—MacLaine."

"Okay, Shirley MacLaine, you're hired."

"But I haven't danced a step yet."

"Who asked you? You've got legs, haven't you?"

"Yes, sir."

"Well, go over and sign in with the stage manager if you want to be in this show."

"Yes, sir."

"Wait a minute. Can you do fouetté turns—you know —the ones where you keep going around on the same foot?"

"Yes, sir. Would you like to see them?"

"Why, do you lie?"

"Of course not, sir."

"Well, never mind then. Your job is to do those fouetté turns around the Servel ice-maker machine until the ice is made. And if the machine gets stuck you keep going—understand?"

"Yes, sir."

I walked across the stage, thinking of the small lifetime of hard work, the iron discipline of ballet, the money poured into the lessons, the grueling schedule I'd kept— and here all I'd had to do was put on a pair of mesh tights and stand up.

"Wait a minute, kid. How old are you?"

"Just twenty-one, sir."

"I thought you said you didn't lie."

"Well, I . . ."

"Forget it—you're the liar. I'm not."

In Raleigh, North Carolina, the ice maker got stuck. I fouettéed and fouettéed until I nearly turned into whipped cream, while the salesmen, turning dizzy at the sight, whistled and clapped for me to stop.

In most of the cities we played in defunct movie houses with stages to match, and dancing on them was like dancing on the Burma Road. A piano player and conductor traveled with the company, and to round out the band we used pickup musicians along the way.

The musicians had orders to stop playing as soon as the curtain closed, and the signal that we were ready to go on to the next number was when the curtain reopened. The musicians took their instructions very literally. Sometimes the men hired to close the curtain took a longer smoke than usual and missed a cue. Seeing the curtain still open, the musicians wouldn't stop, going right on into the next number. In order to catch up with the runaway music we changed our costumes in full view of the audience, dancing the next number as we dressed. Whenever that happened, the Servel salesmen brought us back for encores.

Swan Lake was the *pièce de résistance* of the show, and the fact that it was performed around a Servel washing machine added spice to the choreographer's conception. As Queen of the Swans, I decided to spice the spice.

Dressed in a beautiful white tutu, I adjusted my toe shoes and made ready for the rigorous workout ahead. The classical strains of *Swan Lake* rose to the rafters of the abandoned movie house that would soon be a bowling alley. Neatly sidestepping the rusty nails that protruded every few feet, I made my entrance.

I had blacked out my two front teeth and did the whole number with a saintly smile. After the show I was fired, and sent back to New York.

Three

My HUSBAND AND I met in a bar on West Forty-fifth Street in New York City. The year was 1952.

Securely trapped in the chorus line of *Me and Juliet*, my insubordinate spirit was rapidly becoming subordinate. The rut was unbearable. The security of the weekly paycheck, meager but constant, lulled me into a state of habitual nonproductivity. There seemed no challenge to anything.

I looked up. He was standing beside our table.

"Shirley," my girl friend from the chorus said, "this is Steve Parker."

He was of medium height, about five feet nine, and as I stood to make room for him, I quickly slipped off my high heels. He noticed and smiled. Our eyes met. They were the bluest truth I had ever seen. I nearly climbed into them. His nose and cheekbones were perfectly chiseled, and his jawline was so firm I thought he must know exactly where he was going. He was about twelve years older than I. My mouth must have dropped open.

"How do you do," he said. "Why don't you shut your mouth and sit down? Aren't you drinking?"

"No, I don't drink," I answered as I shoved the whole top of my ginger-ale glass into my mouth in an effort to be intriguing. I was nineteen.

"That's cute," he said, "What do you do for an encore?"

"I try to get it out," I mumbled, realizing that it was stuck. He reached over and pried the glass from my mouth before it cracked.

I fell in love with him immediately.

"You need taking care of," he said, laughing. "Don't do any more of those tricks, or I may fall in love with you."

Four hours later he asked me to marry him. Because I was a respectable lady from Virginia, I made him wait until morning for my answer.

He was not surprised. "Fine, then it's settled," he said. "It was only a question of time, anyway."

He was right then, and he has always been the only person in my life to be unfailingly right about me. He knows me better than I know myself. He knows what gives me life and what drives it from me. And when I met him my life began.

The world came alive. Frustration became courage, and hard work became inspired concentration. We read books together—books I had never known existed. He had traveled all over the world, and even though his own wanderlust had been partially satisfied, he recognized the same restlessness in me. If I was to know myself, he said, I must know others. He encouraged me to resurrect my collection of maps, and we pored over them, claiming the faraway lands for our own, and vowing to touch the soul of every one of them. We promised to devote ourselves to trying to understand people and ideas beyond our local experience.

He seemed to be an extension of what I wanted to be myself, and the more dependent I became on him, the more independent I seemed to become in my own life.

An enigmatic man with an air of sophistication, Steve was assertive, but he was shy among the profiteering rodents of theatrical society. An actor by trade, Shakespearean by choice, he often directed off-Broadway plays containing "some meaning," but his background propelled him in other directions, making it impossible for him to accept the competitive battleground of show business as a way of life.

His formative years had been spent aboard a cargo ship. When he was nine years old the Depression hit, putting his father, a ship's engineer, out of work. In the same year his mother contracted tuberculosis. The family was destitute. His mother was placed in a welfare hospital in New England, and his father, desperate for a job, finally found one on a cargo ship bound for the Orient—not as a ship's engineer, but as a stoker.

With no other living relatives to care for him, Steve shipped out with his father, and a small bunk in a cramped stateroom became his home. The world and its ports became his boyhood neighborhood and their inhabitants his playmates. Mr. Parker taught him everything there was to know about ships, including how to shovel coal, and at night they talked of the world and the places they would see together.

From childhood, Steve's favorite land was Japan. Sometimes his father allowed him to stay with old family friends, the Hasagawas. During those times he went to school in the port of Yokohama while the cargo ship continued its run to Kobe, Osaka, Nagasaki, Niigata, Shanghai, Hong Kong, Taipei, and finally back to Yokohama. Whenever the ship went back to the United States, Steve returned to New England to visit his mother.

The ruggedly good-looking blue-eyed boy with the securely independent nature became more Asian than Occidental. He learned his schoolwork in Japanese, and by the time he was twelve years old he could speak, read, and write several other Asian languages as well. Except for the separation from his mother, he enjoyed the wandering life, which lasted for five years, until he returned to America in 1936. Slowly the Depression came to an end, and the family enjoyed one year together before his mother died. Within a year, his despondent father died too, and Steve was left alone. After teenage years of odd jobs and a meager existence, he managed to complete his high-school education not long before his beloved boyhood land bombed Pearl Harbor.

He joined the paratroops and later found himself fighting in hand-to-hand combat with people he had actually gone to school with. He was invaluable to his outfit because of his knowledge of the Japanese—their language and customs. He continued to fight until he was separated from his outfit during a mission in the jungles of New Guinea, where he survived by making friends with head-hunters.

Steve was with the first troops that went to Hiroshima after the bomb. He surveyed the remains of the land he had once loved. Lost and numb, he cursed his partnership with both worlds.

He stayed in the army because he had no other path to follow. He was highly decorated and discharged with honors—a captain at twenty-two. He would return to his other world, of that he was certain. The question was when—and how.

Steve and I met in 1952, but so intense was our involvement, we forgot to get married until 1954. In fact, 1954 was a landmark for two reasons.

The Pajama Game was a musical based on Richard Bissell's novel *7½ Cents,* and it was all about life in an Iowa pajama factory. Early in 1954, when the show was forming, Steve encouraged me to audition for a place in the chorus. Director George Abbott said he hired me because whenever I opened my mouth on stage they could hear every breath in the peanut gallery.

Even while the show was still on the road, it was obvious that it would be a hit, and equally obvious that it would give Broadway a new star, the late Carol Haney. The out-of-town critics couldn't find words sufficient to express their delight in her sense of comedy and in her songs and dances.

The night before the New York opening, I was made Carol's understudy. I had never had a rehearsal, but as the producer, Hal Prince, said, "It doesn't really matter. Carol is one person who would go on with a broken neck."

On May 9, 1954, *The Pajama Game* opened in New York to rave reviews both for the show and for Carol. She had been a choreographer's assistant for years, but now the public thronged to the stage door, clamoring for a glimpse of the brilliant performer they had discovered "overnight." She was singled out as the musical-comedy find of the decade.

It looked very much as though I, on the other hand, would be chorus girl of the century. Four nights passed. I still hadn't had an understudy rehearsal, but whenever I wasn't onstage I watched Carol from the wings, trying to learn the part even though I doubted I would ever need to know it. Only four days after the opening and already I was deeply depressed. I was in another hit! More weekly paychecks, enervating security, and monotony.

After the first Wednesday matinee I went back to the apartment to fix dinner for Steve. While we were eating I had a phone call from one of the producers of *Can-Can,* which had been running about two years. He offered me a job as understudy to his lead dancer.

"We know you must realize," he said, "that nothing will ever keep Haney from going on in *Pajama Game,* and our girl is out every now and then."

I asked him to let me think it over.

While we finished eating, I discussed it with Steve, who felt that if being in another long run was more than I could take, then I should leave *Pajama Game* immediately. I agreed, and before leaving for the theater I wrote my notice, intending to turn it in that night. Running late, I rushed for the subway and would have done better walking. The train got stuck in its tunnel, and I arrived at the theater panting, late by half an hour.

Hal Prince and his co-producer, the late Bobby Griffith, were pacing the sidewalk at the stage-door entrance, wringing their hands.

"Where have you *been?*" they asked.

"Gee, I'm awfully sorry. The subway got stuck, but I'll hurry. Anyway I don't go on till the middle of the first act."

"That's what *you* think! HANEY BROKE HER ANKLE THIS AFTERNOON AND YOU'RE ON RIGHT NOW!"

I was carrying my notice in my hand. I stuffed it back into my purse. The world spun around four times—once for each time I had watched Carol do the part. A horrible thought jumped into my mind and kept running: *I know I'll drop the derby in "Steam Heat," I know I'll drop the derby in "Steam Heat."*

"Steam Heat" opened the second act and it was the show stopper—a song-and-dance number for a trio of two men and a girl. The routine called for a derby to be tumbled, thrown, spun, and juggled throughout the number.

They hustled me to Carol's dressing room. I asked someone to call Steve. I shook so hard that someone else had to put the makeup on my face. (I was sure to drop the derby.) A wardrobe woman zipped up my first-act costume and it fitted. Relief. Then came the shoes. *Disaster.* Her size four wasn't even big enough for my big toe. I rushed to the basement where I always dressed and found a pair of my own black tennis shoes. They didn't go with the costume, but if the audience was looking at my feet I was in big trouble anyway.

Above me I heard the audience stamping, impatient because the curtain hadn't gone up.

John Raitt, the leading man, was learning the words to my songs in case I forgot them, and Eddie Foy, Jr., one of the co-leads, was so nervous that he was throwing up in his dressing room.

I raced up and waited in the wings as the stage manager walked out before the curtain and gestured for attention.

"Ladies and gentlemen," he said. "The management regrets to anounce that Miss Carol Haney will not be performing tonight. Her role will be performed by a young lady named Shirley MacLaine. We hope you will enjoy the show."

His last words were drowned out as the audience set up a terrific boo. Many people rose and made straight for the box office to get their money back. *Chaos.* Hal Hastings, the conductor, stared up from the pit, a shaken man. He had no idea what key I sang in, or even if I sang at all, but resolutely he raised his baton. The musicians straightened in their chairs, and on cue they struck up the overture to try to drown out the hubbub that was still coming from the audience.

In the middle of the overture, Steve rushed in, and for a moment he just stood there, looking like a zombie.

He reached for my hand. "This should teach you patience," he said. "And remember—most people don't get this break in a whole lifetime, so, for everybody who waits, make the most of it."

Then, muttering the actors' good luck, *"Merde,"* he pat-patted me on the fanny and went out to join the audience. His napkin from dinner was trailing from the pocket of his jacket.

The overture ended. I had to go to the bathroom so badly I was afraid to walk.

The curtain went up.

Taking a deep breath, I made it safely to center stage. From the corner of my eye I could see the cast lined up in the wings, watching. A hush came over the audience.

They seemed to understand how I felt. The most important people in show business were out there. They had
come to see Carol Haney, but I was onstage instead. I
took another breath and spoke the first line. My high,
raucous voice blasted in the ears. The line was supposed
to get a laugh. It didn't. Just as I began the second speech,
they laughed at the first one. I hadn't waited long enough,
hadn't given them time. Just because I was ready didn't
mean they were. I slowed the tempo of my delivery and
soon we were on the same beat. I felt them relax, *en masse,*
and I did too. There is nothing worse than an audience
that's afraid for a performer. Suddenly the flow of communication that I had longed for all my life was there. It
wasn't the applause and laughter that fulfilled me; it was
the magnetism, the current, moving from one human being
to the others and back again, like a giant pendulum. I was
in time with the audience, no longer at odds with it.

John Raitt sang "Hernando's Hideaway" for me, and
I remember how strange Carol's song sounded in someone
else's voice. For weeks I had been hearing the lines and
songs in her voice, and now it took a combined effort to
accomplish what she had done alone.

Then came the opening of the second act and "Steam
Heat." Carol's black tuxedo fitted me and even the derby,
custom-made for her head, was fine.

The muted trumpet sounded in the orchestra pit as the
curtain opened on the number that had already become a
classic in musical comedy. The three of us held our opening positions until the applause of recognition had died
down. I held my breath, feeling the weight and texture of
the derby on my head, wanting to practice juggle the opening trick one more time.

In unison we danced our way to the footlights, threw
our derbies into the air, and caught them simultaneously.
The audience clapped again. Maybe I would get through

it after all. The trumpet led the orchestra to a crescendo in a swinging wail and the theater seemed to rock. Each trick went perfectly. Then the music stopped: time for the *pièce de résistance*. We would execute it in silence.

Our backs were to the audience. In unison, we rolled the derbies from our heads, spilled them down our arms, flipped them high into the air and caught them at the last moment before the audience could figure out how it was done. Then it happened. I dropped my derby. There was a gasp from the audience. The derby crashed to the stage and rolled to the edge of the orchestra pit, where it mercifully decided not to fall in. Because my back was to the audience and because I just didn't realize that I wasn't in the chorus any more, I didn't think about controlling my reaction.

"Shit!" I muttered to myself, thinking that only the other two dancers could hear it.

The first three rows gasped again, and the word spread through the theater. Well . . . I thought. I come all this way, wait all this time, and now . . . what a way to end!

I rushed to the footlights, picked up the derby, put it on, shrugged a sort of apology to the audience, and finished the number. I remember little else. I can't remember whether or not they clapped after the routine, and I barely remember the rest of the second act.

The curtain rang down on the show and then up again for the curtain calls.

The audience stood. They cheered—and threw kisses. I felt as though a giant caress had enveloped me. The cast backed off, formed a semicircle around me, and applauded.

I stood there alone, wearing the black-and-white convict-striped pajama jacket that matched Eddie Foy's convict pants. I reached out, beckoning the cast to close in around me and share the applause, but they only backed off more and left me in the center to bask. I was overwhelmed with loneliness. When you've trained as a ballet dancer you are trained to be part of a team. You devote your talent to being a link that makes up the chain. You don't think in terms of being different or special. The desire lurks underneath, but you continually suppress it. And so with the night I went on in *Pajama Game* everything changed. I was out in front of the chain and I felt lonely, and yet at the same time I felt so much that I belonged. The curtain rang up and down to prolonged applause. I knew I could step out of the line and be myself any time I wanted to now, I belonged to myself and from then on I would have to devote all of me to developing that self the best way I knew how. No more blacked-out front teeth and Servel ice makers. Everything had changed. A higher level of hard work, toil, and struggle was necessary now. Talent was nothing but sweat.

I returned to my dressing room to collapse. Steve was waiting. "We have a lot of work to do," he said. "Your drunk scene in the second act was phony, so the first thing is to take you out and get you drunk. Then you'll know what it's all about." Smiling, he wiped the perspiration from my face. "By the way—you were great."

"Was I really?"

"To them, yes. But you still have a long way to go."

"Thanks," I muttered, resenting him for not letting me rest on my laurels.

"By the way, that 'shit' shit was very quaint. I guess you can take the girl out of the chorus, but you can't take the chorus out of the girl. I've just talked to Hal Prince. Haney will be out for three weeks. Now let's go get drunk."

The second night I was on for Carol I met another man who helped change the course of my life. Although I didn't know it then, eventually I would have to fight him in court as well as in arenas that had nothing to do with the judiciary. The words he spoke were the words every young American female supposedly longs to hear.

"Miss MacLaine," he said, "my name is Hal Wallis, and I'm prepared to offer you a movie contract. In Hollywood."

He had come backstage after the show and was waiting for me when I emerged from the dressing room.

Hal Wallis . . .

What I saw was a well-dressed man of clearly more than average prosperity, slightly hunched, with cagy, calculating eyes, and a face like a suntanned pear. I knew the name; I knew he was a big producer. But I couldn't bring myself to swoon.

"Aren't you the one who makes all those movies with Dean Martin and Jerry Lewis?" I asked.

"Yes. I discovered them, too."

"Too?"

"Yes. I just discovered you. I was in the audience tonight."

"You mean you want me to be one of those girls who run up and down the stairs in a yellow sunsuit?"

"Does some other color sunsuit—ah—suit you better?"

It was only a first taste of what was to come.

At Wallis's suggestion, Steve and I met him later. I was wearing my blue jeans, which matched Steve's and we met him at the Oak Room of the Plaza Hotel to discuss his proposal.

The headwaiter, doubtless alerted for this or a similar breach, let us and our blue jeans in, and steered us toward a table in the corner, where Wallis, swallowing his concern for appearances and flashing a jaundiced grin, rose to greet us.

After drinks we had soup, salad, thick juicy steaks, baked potatoes, and Cherries Jubilee. But Wallis was content to nibble on Ry-Krisp, and as the conversation pro-

gressed, I understood why. He had a very special feeling
for his forty-odd million. He couldn't bear to part with a
dime of it.

What he was offering me was a seven-year contract
with loan-out privileges—most of the privileges being his.
After scooping up the last of the Cherries Jubilee, Steve
and I decided it would be best to let the offer hang until
we could find an agent to represent me. We also wanted
to see if there would be other offers.

We thanked Wallis for the dinner and went up to the
apartment to work on my drunk scene.

It doesn't take theatrical agents long to smell where the
new flesh is. Waiting on my doorstep were men from three
different agencies. If I'd tried to see the same men in their
offices a week earlier, I'd never have gotten beyond the elevator. Watching Steve handle them, I wondered how I, or
any young girl, could ever have coped with all this alone.
I relied on him for everything.

While continuing to stave off Wallis, with Steve's help
I concentrated on improving my performance in *The Pajama Game*. Every night after the show, Steve rehearsed
me, bringing in some of his director friends for their advice and criticism. He also found me a reliable agent, one
who was not part of an all-consuming corporation, and he
saw to it that representatives of every major Hollywood
studio came to watch my performance.

They came and they watched, and I wondered why
they even bothered. When they talked to me, I found they
were interested in only two things:

1. What were my measurements?
2. Would I pose for cheesecake?

Not one of them made me a concrete offer. That left
only Wallis, the man with the nose of a bloodhound.

I asked Hal Prince for his advice. "Don't go to Hollywood now," he said. "You don't have enough experience.

Stay on Broadway and do a few more shows first.'

"In the *chorus?*"

"It doesn't matter. Go to Hollywood now and you'll never be heard from again."

My new agent worked out a deal slightly different from the contract Wallis had offered, one that would bind me only five years instead of seven.

I signed with Wallis.

Hal Prince lamented: *"You'll be sorry."*

Carol Haney returned to the show; I went back to the chorus and waited for Hal Wallis to call me to Hollywood.

Two months later Carol came down with a terrible case of laryngitis and was unable to speak. Once again I went on for her, and once again there was someone special in the audience—this time a representative of Alfred Hitchcock.

He came to my dressing room after the show. "Mr. Hitchcock is looking for a suitably fey creature to play the lead in his next picture, *The Trouble with Harry*," he said. "I think you will do just fine."

"Me? But I already have a contract with Hal *Wallis*," I wailed.

"Mr. Hitchcock knows that. He would like you to meet him in his suite at the St. Regis tomorrow. If he likes you, he can work something out with Wallis."

The next day at the appointed time I rang the bell of Hitchcock's suite. "Come in, my dear." The accent was unmistakable. He swung open the door. "Sit down—and tell me what motion pictures you have acted in."

Well, I thought, this will be over in a hurry. "None, sir, I'm afraid."

Hitchcock looked at me and nodded. He began pacing. "Is there some television film I could see, then?"

"No, sir. I've never done a television show."

"Well—what Broadway plays have you had roles in?"

"None, sir. I'm a chorus girl."

He was still pacing. "You mean you've never acted in anything at all?"

"No, sir, I haven't—except as an understudy."

He came to an abrupt halt. Suddenly his leg shot up, his foot came down heavily on the seat of a chair, and his elbow came to rest on his knee, all in one lightning motion. "That makes you about the color of a shamrock, doesn't it?"

"Yes, sir, I suppose so." I stood up. "Should I go now?"

"Of course not. Sit down. All this simply means that I shall have fewer bad knots to untie. You're hired."

I fell back in my chair.

"I shall need you on location—in Vermont—in three days. Can you make it?"

I wanted to say, "Has a mule got an ass?" but I didn't know him well enough.

I left the St. Regis in a daze and floated back to the apartment, where Steve was waiting for me. I blurted out the news. Vermont—in three days! And I wouldn't have to run up and down the stairs in a yellow sunsuit after all.

Steve was happy. In addition to everything else, we were going on location in the area where he had spent part of his boyhood.

But when we told Hal Prince and Bobby Griffith, they thought I was making a big mistake.

"But will you let me out of my chorus contract?" I asked.

"Why not?" was the answer. "You'll be back."

The next day, between the matinee and evening performances, Steve and I were married, surprising nobody.

After the ceremony I went back to the theater, made my farewell appearance in *The Pajama Game,* thanked

Bobby and Hal for being so cooperative, told everyone goodbye—and went off to my wedding night, which was surely one of the craziest wedding nights in the annals of matrimony.

I once knew a couple who spent their wedding night stark naked playing parchesi. Ours wasn't quite that bad, but it was bad enough. And the reasons weren't even psychiatric. They were legal.

Before marriage, I was a minor under the laws of New York, and therefore my parents had signed my contracts with Wallis and with my agent. Now that I was married, even though I was still only twenty, legally I was no longer a minor, and I could, if I wished, declare both contracts invalid and renegotiate on my own.

At that time I had no desire to annul my contract with Wallis, but my agent—the one we had thought so reliable and independent—was another matter. Almost immediately he had sold a half interest in me to Famous Artists, a huge agency, and I felt I had a legitimate complaint against him.

Agents have a way of knowing when one of them has a falling-out with a "property." Once again I was fair prey, and the fact that I was making a picture for Hitchcock apparently gave me new luster.

I had sublet my apartment that morning; Steve had been living at the Lambs Club, where women were not allowed to cross the threshold. Since we didn't have enough money for anything better, we had taken a tiny room in the Piccadilly Hotel, just across the street from the theater.

After saying our farewells, we left the theater by the stage-door exit.

From then on, it was all Mack Sennett.

Blocking the way were six agents from Famous Artists. They were brandishing new contracts, flapping them in our faces, jockeying for position, jostling, stepping on each other's toes, screaming: "Re-sign! Re-sign! . . . Sign with us! . . . We'll make you a star. . . . We'll put your name in lights. . . . Get your new contract right here!"

We dodged back into the theater and slammed the door in their faces. Racing around to the lobby entrance, we found another mob scene—a swarming pack, bright-eyed and drooling. When we appeared, one very small man tried to climb through the bars of the box-office window to get at us. Again we fled, running back to the night watchman and asking for help. Through a secret passage-way so old it must have been used by Fanny Brice and Nicky Arnstein, we sneaked from the theater and made our way to the Piccadilly, thinking the worst was over.

When we stepped from the elevator and headed down the hall, we saw that the door to our room was wide open. Jammed into the room like stuffed olives in a slim bottle were more agents, oozing contracts, and jabbing at us with ballpoint pens.

The closet was empty. Our clothes were gone.

"For you I have reserved the honeymoon suite at the Sherry-Netherland Hotel—at the expense of Famous Artists Agency," said a swarthy man who happened to be president of Famous Artists. "And your clothes have been sent ahead to be pressed."

On the rickety coffee table was a huge bottle of champagne—a magnum—with iced caviar around it. A pudgy man with a crew cut gestured grandly toward the champagne. "With the compliments of the William Morris Agency," he said.

Perched precariously near the edge of our connubial bed was a three-foot-high wedding cake. On it was a note saying, "We'll be back later when the other bums have left!" It was signed MCA.

I burst out laughing.

Steve took over. "Now, gentlemen, what do you suggest we do? Obviously she can't sign with all of you."

The president of Famous Artists, who had moved us to the Sherry-Netherland, spoke up. "Shall we proceed to the honeymoon suite and talk this over in more pleasant surroundings?"

"Only if we can all come!" bellowed the others.

"A limousine is waiting, courtesy of William Morris," said the pudgy one. "Shall we go?"

Steve and I exchanged amused glances. "Shirley and I like to walk," he said. "We'll meet you there."

Their reaction was apoplectic. They thought we were trying to escape or that we were bent on a rendezvous with one of them at the expense of the others.

Eying us and each other suspiciously, they set to work. Like movers from a transfer-and-storage company, they gathered up the contents of the room and we all moved down to the sidewalk.

The strange caravan took off with Steve and me in the lead. Straggling behind us were agents and more agents, carrying champagne, caviar, and the huge wedding cake. The limousine and its mystified chauffeur cruised slowly along beside us.

On we went, eastward on Forty-fourth Street to Fifth Avenue, and then all the way up to Fifty-ninth to the Sherry-Netherland. The wedding cake was what did it; halfway there a passerby yelled, "Hey, lady, which one is the husband?"

We trouped into the lobby of the Sherry-Netherland and were borne to the lush upper regions. The honeymoon suite was a fairy tale—peopled with more wicked agents. A royal buffet banquet was set out on a serving table twelve feet long covered with snowy damask and flanked by what looked like the Cold Stream Guards.

Our newly pressed clothes had been hung neatly in

three closets in the bedroom, and a lady-in-waiting hovered nearby, should we decide to change.

The honeymoon bed was spread in crispy white Swiss lace, with bed lamps on either side that looked like fresh peach sundaes. The bathroom was all glass, with a sunken tub that looked like a swimming pool. The toilet rose like a white porcelain jewel from a sea of frothy pink carpet, and we could have held a polo match in the vast space between toilet and tub.

If a setting like this couldn't kill a marriage, nothing could.

"Hey, Steve . . ." I called, listening to the echo of my own voice, "should we ask them if they want to stay and watch?"

There was no need to ask. The long night watch began.

Settling back in an easy chair, Steve opened a tower of champagne and invited everyone present to drink with him. The agents, impressed with this gesture of camaraderie, were quick to comply, as were the Cold Stream Guards. What they didn't know was that the more Steve drinks, the more he talks. In a drinking-talking marathon, he would win hands down.

The telephone rang incessantly—calls from the Hollywood offices of the various agencies to see what progress was being made. Steve intercepted each call and parried each question with a running commentary on the Brooklyn Dodgers and the prospects of abolishing nuclear testing.

The agents were perched on the window sill, the arms of chairs, the edge of the writing desk. Their eyes grew bleary and gradually Steve began to pick them off. Some time after midnight the Cold Stream Guards floated out on their hats.

I fell asleep on the sofa, and when I awoke at seven the next morning the agents were still there, passed out in all corners of the room. Steve was still talking.

Stealthily, we changed our clothes and packed. Before we left we jumped up and down on the luscious bed—just to be able to say we had used it. Then we went to the airport and headed for Vermont and the world of moviemaking. It seemed a long time since I had stood in the kitchen and smothered saltines with Tabasco sauce.

Four

THE CREW ON THE SET was in full cry.

"Tilt the broad down a little."

"And make her two points hotter."

"Okay. Now screw her."

"Hit your mark, schmuck, whaddaya think this is, a ball park?"

"The light's gettin' yella—you want I should eighty-six the store and call it lunch for keeps?"

Alfred Hitchcock came waddling toward me, eyes twinkling, his roly-poly stomach well out in the lead.

"Pleasant period following death," he said.

"I beg your pardon?"

"Genuine chopper, old girl, genuine chopper."

"Excuse me?"

"And after your first line—dog's feet."

Okay, so I was the color of a shamrock.

When I finally had it all translated, it turned out that the lighting crew had said:

Tilt the big light down a little.

And make it brighter by two points on the light meter.

Okay. Now secure it.

Get in your light, you silly actor, we've only got so much equipment.

You're taking too long, going too slow. You want me to fire all of you so you'll be out of work for good?

And then Hitchcock had told me in his own version of cockney rhyming slang:

Good mourning. (Pleasant period following death.)

Real-axe. (Genuine chopper.)

And after your first line, paws. (Dog's feet.)
I was staring.
"Relax," Hitchcock said.
Real-Axe—genuine chopper.

We were in Vermont—and yet we weren't. Vermont was the real world. We were in a new and curiously mythical kingdom, one with its own laws and values—a Hollywood movie company on location. Its citizens, of whom I was now one, acted as if the surrounding territories (Rutland and Stowe) did not exist. The banners in our land were of tinsel and greenbacks, and the national motto was Work, Enjoy, and Forget, or, sometimes, Listen and Learn. The social structure was as rigid and well-defined as any military hierarchy: name, rank, and salary number.

The assistant director was approaching me, bent on keeping the hierarchy tidy.
"Why are you eating under this tree—with them?"
"Because she does my hair, and he puts on my makeup, and they're the only people I know on the picture—and they are my friends."
"You will eat at the table with the red-checked tablecloth and the silverware that was laid out especially for you. You are the star."
"Someday, maybe," I said, "but right now I'm a chorus girl."
Sighing, he reached down to help me up. "If you want it, you must act it. Now please come with me."
Sadly, I noticed that my two friends, the underlings, were already hurrying off, still sipping milk from their paper cartons. You don't embarrass the star with camaraderie.
I shoved my feet into the high heels. You don't take French wine and the upper echelon with your shoes off, either.

On location with a movie company all expenses are
paid. I couldn't get over the fact that I could eat as much
as I wanted and wouldn't have to pay for it myself. I
had pancakes, sausages, and eggs, four pieces of toast and
marmalade, and fresh orange juice for breakfast every
morning and, for a breakfast dessert, a fluffy waffle with
Vermont maple syrup, made on the premises of the lodge
where we stayed. At about eleven in the morning I raided
the catered company dining room for home-made apple
pie with coffee. When lunchtime rolled around I put away
two or three helpings of everything, including more apple
pie with ice cream. At teatime the Hollywood company
catered exquisitely concocted French pastries with whipped
cream and little chunks of chocolate. And by dinnertime
I was starved again. After a big steak with baked potatoes
and sour cream and chives and hot buttered bread I'd have
a Maine lobster, flown in expressly for the company, and
whatever the chef's special dessert of the day was I'd have
two of before going to bed.

At the end of the first three weeks I'd gained twenty-
five pounds. When I began the picture I was svelte and
lithe. By the time I had buried Harry for the last time I
was a blimp.

. . . And on location people really cared about you. I
felt the piece of dust creep up my nose. Fighting hard,
I managed a muffled snort into the Kleenex, but the dust
had lodged and it was just a question of time now. From
my position on the sidelines, I fervently studied the technique of the other actors doing a scene, trying to learn for
myself how to act in a $30,000-a-day production. But the
speck of dust was halfway to my brain, and I couldn't
stand it any longer.

"Achewwwww!" I sneezed loud and clear—ruining a

good take. "I'm terribly sorry," I apologized, mortified to the core.

"Sorry, hell," yelled the assistant director. "For God's sake, fellas, I don't give a damn how hot it is in here, shut all the doors! This kid might get sick!" . . . It made you feel wanted.

. . . And the fact that I was also on my honeymoon was so romantic that it captured the love-starved imagination of the company.

"Why the hell did she have to get married at this point in her career? She shouldn't let anything hold her back!"

"Bad advice, I guess. Anyway, he's not allowed on the set."

Giving up the protection of the wall I'd been shrinking against, I rehearsed kissing my co-star long and passionately—ten times before it was convincing enough to shoot.

Every morning at four-thirty there was a thunderous pounding at the door: a courier . . . a herald, summoning me to re-enter the kingdom.

Leaving Steve behind, I would stumble forth into the chill Vermont air, and when the sun came up and the cameras were ready for action, I became the whimsical young widow for the script and traipsed about the Vermont hillside burying, digging up, and reburying my husband's body, until I was wielding the shovel and patting the dirt and smiling with just the offbeat shade of nonchalance Mr. Hitchcock wanted.

Leaving Steve behind—I retched at the thought. Was this what it meant? Had I worked all my life refining a dream of self-expression to find that at the moment of realization the very essence of my life was jeopardized? I looked back at the year I was twenty and in many respects it had been a good one. But our love story was just beginning. I was leaving Steve behind on these chill autumn mornings, and he seemed to understand. The real story began when the situation was reversed.

Steve and I arrived in Hollywood to finish *The Trouble with Harry* with a dollar thirty-five between us. It had taken all we had, including the advance on my picture salary, to pay our debts in New York and arrange for a new life in the land of make-believe.

Through smarting eyes half closed by the smog, we saw our first inhabitants of Hollywood. They were bronzed, had capped teeth, and wore huge dark glasses. They had faces but were minus eyes. Sunshine bled from every corner and the dazzling white buildings gave me a permanent squint.

The jerky, wire-tense atmosphere of New York was gone. People moved as if in slow motion.

The men in tennis shorts, juggling gin and tonics and loping along the airport corridors meeting incoming passengers, were not really underclad airline representatives. They were high-salaried Hollywood executives who had adapted to life. In California the most important deals in the movie industry are finalized on the sun-drenched turf of golf courses or around turquoise swimming pools, where the smell of barbecue sauce is borne on gentle breezes, and the sound of cool jazz wafts over the stereo systems of homes that people seldom leave.

Accompanied by an MCA representative who still retained the New York influence (you could tell by the black suit and long, thin black tie), we were taken on a Cadillac tour of Bel Air and Beverly Hills, which, with palm-lined boulevards and circular drives, Rolls-Royces, and Japanese gardeners, were lush, emerald duchies, shimmering reflections of the fabulous profits that gushed from the silver screen.

Expensive perambulators were propelled by white-uni-formed governesses, enabling the duchesses to languish in the pastel comfort of their patios, occasionally moving to trail a slender hand in the pool.

Dressed in Swiss lace and clutching toys from Uncle Bernie's Toy Shop, the children of the rich and famous were led by the hand through their days, skirting mud puddles they might have wished to play in. Or, with a governess standing by, they might drive one of Uncle Bernie's "real" toy automobiles or ride one of his battery-powered camels, which with a swaying motion carried them over the desert to nightfall.

To Steve and me, each home was a palace and a new jolt. They loomed on cultivated hilltops or nestled in L-shapes and U-shapes on shaded slopes, jewel-like habitations set in acres of jade carpet. We stared at the fairy-land until our eyes hurt and our sense of reality reminded us that we were flat broke.

It was a long while before we returned to Bel Air or Beverly Hills, even for a visit. By then we realized that what we had seen that first afternoon was only a superficial glimpse. Hollywood wasn't really like that—exactly.

We bought a tanklike, second-hand green Buick for forty-five dollars on credit, and headed for the beach at Malibu. There we leased a tiny one-room apartment in a building set high on pilings that shook with each wave that crashed beneath it. I was up every morning at four-thirty trying to be a housewife—ironing, washing, clean-ing, and experimenting with the cookbook. (Somehow everything came out tasting like the Automat.) At six Steve drove me to the studio, where we shot the final sequences of *The Trouble with Harry*.

Late one evening on our way home from the studio we pulled up at a red light. As we chatted quietly about the day's work, something suddenly kicked us in the rear and my feet went over my head. I reached out for Steve, screaming. I didn't know where down was, and my head wouldn't move on my neck. The car came to a halt. We had been knocked sixty feet to the opposite side of the highway into the path of oncoming traffic. Our trunk was in the front seat and Steve was pinned under it. "Are you all right?" he called to me. He was twisted out of shape on the floor, with one arm tangled in the steering wheel.

I went blind with rage when I saw what had happened to him. Untangling myself, I rushed to the car that had hit us. A peroxide blonde sat at the wheel, glassy-eyed, as though nothing had happened. I screamed at her. She smiled. I looked at her more closely, and, seeing that she was stoned out of her mind, gave up.

Steve was taken off in an ambulance, suffering severe lacerations and a slipped disc. I walked around in a neck brace for a month, taking it off only when the director yelled, "Action."

The blonde turned out to be our next-door neighbor, and the green Buick was soon replaced by a belated wedding present from Hal Wallis—an MG. Having no alternative, because Steve was in the hospital, I learned to drive.

With the completion of *The Trouble with Harry*, I was swiftly becoming known as "that fast-rising, kooky young star." Steve was the man whose last name nobody knew. The publicity department "suggested" that we should be seen at premières. I borrowed a Joan Crawford reject from the wardrobe department and we arrived unchauffeured in our MG—a car hardly designed for long dresses. As I struggled to get my legs overboard, stars past and present, and luminaries young and old, rising and fading, emerged from their chauffeured limousines and trod the thick maroon carpet that stretched from the curb to the foyer of the theater, while hordes of fans acclaimed them.

The stars, of course, never attended premières to see films. They went to be seen, and their entrances became applause contests. Hollywood kings and queens moved regally over the carpet, apparently untouched by the fanfare. But their senses were shout-o-meters, carefully recording each decibel. "Three minutes of applause tonight," say the shout-o-meters. "Last week it was four. Maybe it's the dress that's wrong, or maybe I should have waited that extra thirty seconds in the limousine, making certain the carpet was clear. What's the commotion behind me? Should I turn around and look? No, they'll see me show interest in another. I'll just sneak a look. Oh, it's that ingénue blonde dumbbell from television. Why are they screaming then? She's in their living room every Thursday evening, so why all the excitement? She's common coin."

On and on. Now an ethereal vision in white ermine, a snowflake topped with a mass of piled scarlet hair. Now a svelte panther painted with gold lamé, crowned with a gold turban. Now an apricot sundae with chocolate velvet bows in just the right spots, hanging adoringly on the arm of an escort arranged by the publicity department.

And the men—freshly starched penguins, flashing new teeth, unctuous, gracious, when they'd much rather be in a bar or in the back room playing poker. They show up for a glance, a nod of approval from the Big Man: *My boy, you're doing the right thing by us. . . .*

Fear is concealed in smiles and flashing teeth. "Please say you still love me," the kings and queens are really saying. And, when they fare badly, they return to their palaces and sleep fitfully.

When *The Trouble with Harry* was released it was a bomb, an artistic bomb, highly subtle in its humor, but nonetheless a bomb. I fared slightly better. I was hailed as a kooky young discovery, a kooky young star, a kooky comedienne possessed of a kooky ingénue quality, a fresh-faced kook, a kook from the Broadway stage, a kook from Arlington who now lives in a kooky shack in Malibu. "Kooky" was a word I would never escape, and one I seemed to have grown up with. The closest the dictionary cames to its derivation is: Kookaburra, *Australia*. It means the laughing jackass.

For the fan magazines and gossip columnists, I was fresh copy.

She lives in a one-room shack at the beach.

She's never even swum in a Hollywood swimming pool.

She doesn't own a formal dress or a piece of fur.

Sometimes the cop at the gate turns her away in the morning, saying the casting calls are filled for the day.

She's married to a nice, understanding man, and they seem to be very much in love. . . .

I had never thought in terms of being a star or a celebrity. To me stardom was not a goal; it was a by-product. I wanted to do what I was able to do with all my might. To do otherwise seemed not only wasteful, but dangerous. For if the talent or individuality is there, it should be expressed. If it doesn't find its way out into the air, it can turn inward and gnaw like the fox at the Spartan boy's belly.

There were things about stardom that I didn't know, that I now began to learn. One of my most cherished assets was the fact that I had started at the bottom. The slow climb had given me time to learn, to adjust, to adapt, and to think. With each step there had been time to adjust to the forces within myself and to be sure of who I was. Now, with impending stardom upon me, there was never enough time. My head began to whirl in an effort to catch up with what was happening to me. Frantic days followed frantic days. There was no time for reflection. There was only time to mold and produce an engaging, attractive commodity and show up.

I didn't like the feeling. Slowly, slowly, I was slipping away from myself. Chunks . . . chunks . . . chunks . . . sliced away, gone forever, used by others for their own purposes. I tried to be generous with those things I could contribute, but I didn't want to give away my*self*, and I was most reluctant and resentful to have it taken.

Mr. Hal Wallis was, and is, a formidable creature. He walks with a slight hunch and a kind of shuffle. He wears knitted golf sweaters and black loafers just like the other guys, but it's no use—he just isn't *like* the other guys. He's a race unto himself. With his keen nose for talent and his infallible sense of commerce, he has produced some of the most brilliant films ever made. Unfortunately I was never in any of them.

To Hal Wallis I was always "that kid I found in the chorus." He owned me. No question about it. And I understood that a contract was a contract, and I understood that he was my boss, and at first I didn't resent the economic limitations of my contract. I had been, after all, lifted from a seventy-five-dollar-a-week chorus job to the relative utopia of a few hundred more. But I was not prepared to be regarded as a can of peas.

I had been trained to work hard and I enjoyed it. I thrived on trying to make things better, and was willing to put all my energy into doing so. But a can of peas doesn't have to try. It's moved from shelf to shelf and bought and sold according to the market. Its label is freshened and designed to appeal to the public. The stamp is applied and if the branding iron hurts—well, cans of peas don't feel. They relinquish their nerve endings to the manufacturer because the manufacturer always knows best. However, should one small pea think for itself there's an uproar in the pea factory. My small, round, green rebellion would come, but it would take a few more years for me to muster sufficient ammunition.

Wallis took me from the shelf to garnish a Dean Martin and Jerry Lewis product. The picture was *Artists and Models,* and just as I had always suspected, the yellow sunsuit was for me. I was the one who ran in and out of scenes yelling, *"Which way did they go?"* And, when I finally did find Jerry (I got Jerry; the other actress got Dean), I was supposed to jump on him and hold him down. I represented all the plain broads in the audience who could never get a man unless they pinned him to the floor. I guess that's when I first realized it was possible to make people laugh and cry at the same time.

She's STILL living in a one-room shack at the beach.

She's STILL married to that man, what's his name? and they seem to be very much in love.

But how long can it last?

The handwriting is on the wall.

Mister MacLaine . . .

Steve never came to the set while I was making a movie. He was spending a lot of time alone. He went through the paces of our Hollywood existence, helping me with emotional bolstering as I struggled to hang on to reality. I knew his life and developing reputation as "her manager" displeased him, even though we never discussed it openly. He was proud of the progress I was making and pleased that I was learning to function on my own. But the idea of becoming a Hollywood husband was anathema.

He picked me up at the studio each night, happy and interested in the events of the day, eagerly asking about the technical processes of film and camera, and telling me of his day of research in color laboratories and conferences with businessmen who were interested in international production. He seemed to be developing a plan of his own.

We drove to our shack high on the beach pilings to welcome the evening waves that crashed on the shore and under the bulkhead. We loved the sea. The waves returned with messages from other lands and talked to us in a language we understood. Often I found Steve staring at the breakers, silent and brooding, as the dormant seeds of wanderlust stirred in him again. He felt stagnant and unproductive, restless in the knowledge that his own potential was going unrealized. Our life together was the only home he had ever had, but a man's real home is himself.

One evening, we walked a long way on the beach, dug a pit in the sand, and cooked steaks over an open fire. We laughed and talked, speaking of how lucky we were to have found love and joy in each other, but I knew something was wrong. I lay back in the sand, looking at the starless sky, waiting, knowing that something was coming. But he had to be the one to say it. I couldn't. Finally he spoke. "I'm going to tell you something, Shirl, and I want you to try to understand."

The moment had come, perhaps the most important of our lives, and certainly the most important of his.

"When we first got married," he went on quietly, "I wasn't sure whether you had the stuff to make it or not. Now I know you have, and that's good, it's fine. I'm proud of you, prouder than you'll ever know. But I also want to be proud of myself. I've *got* to be. I've got to be my own man. I don't want to be your manager, and I know you don't want me to be."

I waited. He poked the dead fire.

"If I stay in Hollywood, I'll always be Mr. MacLaine. It's impossible to lose the stigma. I've been in this town long enough to know, and I see it happening to all those

other poor bastards who are in the same position. But it's
not going to happen to me, or to us, and I need your help
and understanding to protect what we have."

I still waited.

"I want to go back to Japan," he said.

I was stunned. I knew we had a problem, but I wasn't
prepared for such a drastic solution. He went on. "I'm not
at home here. I've renewed my contacts and I'd like to go
into theatrical production in Japan. It's a country I know
and understand and I think I can make a contribution.
There's nothing I can contribute here, especially if I don't
want to. You are well on your way and you don't need the
same things you once did from me. You're growing up now
and you need to respect me. You never will if I don't
respect myself. Please try to understand that I'm saying
this to hold our marriage together, not to bust it."

I felt drained and empty. I had never thought of even
a day without Steve. Since we met and married we had
never been separated for more than eight hours. My life,
thoughts and breath revolved around this man who had
seemed to bring the world to my doorstep. And now he
wanted to leave, wanted to be himself, wanted to do something to make me as proud of him as he was of me. I
wanted to shriek at the sea. I wanted to shriek at him:
Don't leave me. Don't leave me.

But I stood up and smiled, hardly daring to understand
what I was going to say. "Why not?" I said finally with
forced brightness. "Let's try it."

Not long after the night on the beach, I sat across a
huge mahogany desk from a loud-mouthed, adorable man.
His cigar was longer than he was, and he spoke on five
phones at once. He was a five-foot-five concentration of
human spark, and his name was Mike Todd.

With the cigar clamped between his teeth, zipping up

the fly of his custom-made blue jeans, he blew into his discombobulated office like hurricane Zelda, one hour late for the appointment he had made with me. Like a rehearsed stage cue, all the phones rang at once as he entered. Dressing and answering the phones as he went, he simultaneously carried on a conversation with me.

"Listen, kid, I'm makin' this picture, and I want you in it, okay?"

"What's the name of it?" I asked.

"Around the World in Eighty Days, kid, and I want you to play a campy Hindu princess, okay?"

"A Hindu princess with red hair and freckles?"

"I said campy, didn't I?"

"But, Mike, don't you think . . . ?"

"Listen, kid," he broke in, "I hear you and your husband are interested in Japan, true?"

"Yes, but what's that got to do with it?"

"Only that there happens to be a location trip to Japan in the flick. You leave immediately. Well?"

That was it. "What time is the plane?"

"Tomorrow morning at ten. Go over to Makeup and have your hair dyed black. We'll take care of the freckles when you get to Tokyo."

I gathered up the script and rushed out to tell Steve. It was a miracle in timing, and the trip would be paid for!

On the way out I asked Mike Todd one more time if he was certain he wanted a Scotch-Irish Hindu.

"What the hell," he said, "everybody's just people. You're married to a Scotch-Irish Jap aren't ya? And if I come over I'll be a Joop—that's Japanese for Jew."

I was sure that somewhere back in the Stone Age Steve Parker and Mike Todd were brothers.

Five

CHRISTMAS 1955, a year and a half after the night I went on for Carol Haney, we were in Tokyo. I had never been outside of the United States, except for a quick trip to Canada when Warren and I were very young. Foreign cultures and strange-sounding names had only been images to me. My imagination and fantasies of other places had worked overtime. So much, in fact, that when I finally found myself actually in a foreign milieu I felt a little like I was dream walking. I had had no preparation for the reality of foreigness. Particularly Japan.

White-aproned storekeepers scurried through a fairyland of small-sized things. Shadows of families at dinner played on *shoji* screens. Heads bowed as the shadows moved in ceremonial bows. Tiny, doll-like, black-haired children with bowl haircuts played with tiny cricket cages housing live crickets that would bring the family luck during the following year. The Western custom of Christmas brought profits on hand-painted tea sets, ancient woodblocks, and toys of all descriptions. Toys that moved on batteries with remote controls, other toys twice as large as the children, and all garlanded with gay bells and streamers of fuchsia, red, and orange.

Japan was a children's paradise, or so it seemed to me. It was clear from the first moment. Children roamed free and unattended in the crowded maze of shoppers, without fear, without harm. Kidnaping was unheard of. Hundreds of breathless, runny-nosed little ones were collected at the end of the shopping excursions. They bid goodnight to small Oriental Santa Clauses, and were whisked home and tucked into their *futons* on the floor after having said a quiet prayer to Buddha.

How influenced the world of the East was by our world, and yet how different. Most Japanese women wore kimonos and were sheltered from the chill December air by thick, fluffy wool or fur stoles drawn about their shoulders. How soft and vulnerably feminine they looked. But others, in contrast, had the chic feline look that seems to result when a lovely Oriental woman wears Western dress. They were invariably in the company of a Western man.

The traditional Japanese men watched in silent confusion, seeming unable to cope with the transition. His customary robes seemed pompous and out of place when he saw himself reflected in shop windows, and yet the Western suit he had made didn't fit him properly. The ancient, arrogant samurai walk he still imitated caused the English worsted to cling in the wrong places, and its fitted shoulders restricted the movement of a man still linked to a warrior past.

Too fast, he seemed to be thinking. It was all too fast, this meeting with the West, this swift leap into another culture's idea of modernity. His women were speaking up and his girl child was demanding equality with her brother. On the face of Japan there was confusion, and I was a witness—a witness to my own confusion, too, as to what was real and what wasn't—a witness led by a man who understood their changes perhaps better than they did themselves. And a man who understood that my first time in a foreign place would change my life for always.

Steve Parker was glad to be home. He had waited for the right opportunity, and it had come very quickly for us both.

There were tears of reunion—Oriental bowing, American backslapping. Tea in delicate cups made the rounds, followed by hard liquor. Cigarettes were passed out bear-

ing the trade names Peace and Hope and Dove. There
were jokes about the occupation, about General Mac-
Arthur, about kamikaze pilots. The war seemed a thing
of the past—except when the conversation touched Sachiko. Wherever we went, they all wanted to hear about
Steve's Sachiko.

Steve had told me how his paratroop unit was the first
into Hiroshima after the bomb fell. The devastation was
indescribable. Few families remained intact and thousands
of small children roamed through rubble, whimpering with
shock so great, so profound, that they seemed unable to cry
out. Among them was a two-year-old with saucer eyes and
a perpetual smile. So far as Steve could tell she was un-
hurt, and although her entire family had been wiped out,
she was too young to realize the meaning of the loss. He
asked her her name. She didn't know it.

Everywhere he went she followed him. Disregarding
regulations, Steve fed and clothed her and found her a
little room to live in. He named her Sachiko, which in
Japanese means "happy child," and gave her nourishment
and love. She began to learn English and delighted in the
games she played with Papa-san. Unofficially, Steve had
adopted a daughter. Realizing it would be impossible to
part with her, he applied for formal adoption. When the
papers were approved he told her that he was going to
take her back to the United States and take care of her for
the rest of her life. Sachie was overjoyed. She smiled and
smiled.

Two weeks later she was rushed to the hospital, where
she died of radiation sickness.

I began to understand how deeply Steve's roots were
buried in Japan. It was as though he had lived an entire
lifetime before I had ever met him. With obvious satisfaction and a sense of familiarity, he took me on a tour
of his other world. Through a series of tiny windows I

had first one glimpse and then another of the past life that had made him what he was.

One of his favorite haunts had been a "bird's nest" in an out-of-the-way section of Tokyo. It was strictly for the "in" group, an after-hours spot, owing some of its popularity to Tokyo's early liquor curfew. Even God wouldn't have known it was there, and for sure no Americans did.

The manager stood outside the sinister blue-black building shrouded in darkness, holding a flashlight to direct people down a rickety staircase. He recognized Steve the instant we stepped from the taxi, and in low voices they renewed an old friendship before we followed the beam of the flashlight down the steps.

A few small tables with candles were scattered before the bar. People were laughing and joking in the language I was gradually becoming accustomed to. The surface of the bar was scarred, and behind it was a mirror mellowed and broken by time and war. Some of the people looked up in surprise as we walked in. Clearly they had not expected foreigners to invade their private spot, but with typical Japanese politeness they merely shifted positions and dropped their eyes slightly instead of staring.

We sat at the bar and ordered "Scotch soda." I pulled out a Peace cigarette, put it to my mouth and sat waiting for Steve to light it. Nothing. He went right on talking, looking straight at the cigarette. Then he pulled out one of his own and handed me the matches! Silently I performed the ritual that prevails in two places in the world—Japan and our household. I had much to learn in this marriage of two worlds.

As we chatted, I noticed Steve stare at the reflection of a man who was sitting at the bar to our left. He was a Japanese of about thirty-six, dressed in a double-breasted, pin-striped suit, and he had a lovely gold tooth squarely in the front of his mouth.

"Who is he?" I asked Steve.

He shook his head. "I'm not sure, but I know I remember him from somewhere."

The man seemed just as mesmerized by Steve, staring and then embarrassedly looking away. Then they found themselves looking at each other. As a Westerner, Steve made the first move. "How do you do, my name is Steve Parker," he said in Japanese. The man introduced himself.

"I like this place a great deal, and am always happy when I return," said Steve inanely.

"I agree," said the man just as inanely, "and the weather has been nice today also."

I had already learned that coming right to the point was not the way things are done in Japan. There, the shortest distance between two points is always a circle.

They talked of their families, their places of birth, on and on. I was never introduced because I was merely an *okusan* (wife) and it was just as well because I would have shattered social protocol by coming right out and asking the man if he remembered Steve from somewhere. Their talk seemed to be revolving around the war, when suddenly their arms flew around each other and tears came to their eyes. *"Leyte!"* they shouted.

Leyte—1944. Assigned to secure a vital stretch of rice paddy on Leyte in the Philippines, Steve and his paratroop unit were advancing at night, searching out the enemy. A full moon played tricks with their vision, lacing the rice paddy with shadows. Steve was far enough from the nearest trooper to be out of easy sight.

Then from nowhere a Japanese soldier stood squarely in his path. They stood motionless, not more than a few inches apart, each staring, each unable to make the first move to kill. Then, at the same moment, they turned and fled from each other.

Steve fell over a rice-paddy wall and nicked his nose

on his own bayonet. It got him a purple heart.

The face of the Japanese soldier had been indelibly imprinted in Steve's mind and vice versa, and now in the moonless dark of a Tokyo bar they became friends for life, each convinced he was alive because of the other.

Steve had told me many stories of his childhood in Japan, of his identification with the Japanese people and of his horror at having to kill during the war. Now I knew of his pride in their growing recovery from disgrace and ruin. I knew of his Sachiko and his feeling of peace whenever he returned.

But there was more to it than that. A Scotch-Irish Jap, Mike Todd had called him, and Mike was not far wrong. For what I was beginning to realize was that the man I had married was not simply an American who had lived in the East. Steve was clearly Oriental in thought, philosophy, feeling, temperament, artistry, and appreciation of love and beauty—in all the areas where a human being is an individual. Most important, he was alive and vital here in Japan as he never had been in Hollywood. If his plans and negotiations worked out, he would stay here to run a business and make it his home. Whether I liked it or not, Japan was destined to play a very big part in my life. I would try to understand the land where patience and courtesy were a way of life, where it was not considered odd to spend an entire Sunday studying the veins in the petal of a flower, where I saw two Japanese gentlemen bow low, and still lower, because the lower the bow, the more profound the courtesy, and yet on the way up they clunked heads.

A noodle vendor on a bicycle was struck by a taxi. Noodles and pieces of bicycle flew through the air, followed by the vendor, who landed in the narrow street. A crowd gathered. The taxi driver noted the dent in his fender and then, hissing with concern, hurried to the cyclist, who had gotten to his feet and was standing in a spread of soggy noodles. They bowed in apology. The taxi driver left. The vendor scooped the noodles into the gutter and walked away.

Two men strolled down the street. One told a faintly risqué joke. The other, embarrassed, laughed shyly and covered his mouth with his fist. Then, motioning his companion to slow down a second, he urinated in the gutter. A woman walking behind them pretended to see nothing, for the Japanese see only what they want to see.

A young Japanese decided to cross the street against heavy traffic. He had only one thing on his mind—to get to the other side. As far as he was concerned, the traffic didn't exist. He stepped from the curb with the directness of a well-shot arrow. Brakes screeched, horns blew. He escaped death by inches. He saw none of it. He had reached the other side.

One day a person fell in the street from illness or accident, and passersby ignored his plight. His fate had been predetermined. That's the Buddist way—*Shikataganai*—and no one would interfere with that fate, to do so would place the victim in a position of obligation for the rest of his life. The victim always understands and deals with his plight in isolation.

A person will not answer an obviously direct question unless protocol is observed in his native language, and he is assured that the question is directed to him by the prefix *Ano-ne*.

We ordered gibsons in a restaurant catering to Westerners, and a doll-like waitress, dressed in gay kimono, looked puzzled until we explained that a gibson was a martini with an onion. Soon she returned proudly bearing a tray. On it was a bottle of sweet vermouth with the trade name Martini—along with a large raw onion, knife, and a chopping block.

We asked the waiter for a cup of coffee. Smiling, he headed for the kitchen, eager to comply, but on the way was asked by someone else for a napkin. Forgetting the coffee, he moved toward the napkin supply, until someone else asked for a check. At that point he walked into a wall.

You interrupt a Japanese engaged in telephone conversation. He sets aside the receiver and talks to you, endlessly, forgetting the person on the other end of the line.

My friend who owned a successful Japanese magazine invited me to his office for tea and a chat. In the middle of the visit he left and was gone for forty-five minutes. I looked for him and found him kneeling before an exquisite floral arrangement. He was meditating because it made him peaceful.

One day I asked if Mister So-and-So had called. The answer was No. A while later I found there were fifteen other messages, but those were not imparted because I didn't ask.

Steve asked if such and such details had been worked out regarding a business deal and the reassuring answer was Yes—which was not necessarily the case at all. But to say No would have been impolite when Yes is what he wanted to hear.

I sent someone I'd never met out on a small shopping errand. I gave him far more money than was necessary. In the meantime I had to leave for an appointment. Hours later the errand boy found me in another part of the city and returned my change.

Japan is a land where time has no urgency, where the important thing is human relations, where friction must be avoided at all costs, and where a highly ritualized sense of courtesy has developed to eliminate it. In Japan, courtesy has an esthetic value far greater than good manners in the

West. A negative truth is frequently subordinate to the virtue of courtesy. Courtesy, therefore, is more of a virtue than honesty.

I found one of the strongest motivating forces in Japan to be a harmony with nature. They never attempted to conquer it. It was said, "Be a bamboo, bend with the wind —before the wind—yield gracefully and you will never break." It is not submission; it is the only way to win. The land is not at odds with nature. Its people didn't harness water, tame the wilderness, and conquer space. They blended with the elements, and created a balance to nourish life by bowing to a greater force. It is the law of reversed effort: When drowning, relax—floating results.

In Japan there is no sharp delineation between right and wrong. Everything is approached from all sides at once. If disputes occur, a mediator is called in who does not necessarily allow the "right" to win, but rather arranges a compromise. No one must suffer the degradation of losing face, and to cause it is the most serious of all offenses, and *right* is sometimes sacrificed. *Right* is not necessarily relevant anyway, but people and their feelings are.

In business, speedy negotiations are distrusted. If something cannot be savored and nurtured and enjoyed, it is hardly worthwhile and probably better avoided. The *way* things are done is more important than the result.

I would try to understand Japan—try to be a part of it —not only because of the challenge of Japan itself, but because it was a large part of the man I married.

Steve was happier than I had ever seen him. He took long walks and long hot baths, and breathed long sighs of happiness. He delighted in the period of my adjustment and nudged me gently as I went about it.

My self-consciousnes in the communal baths (soaking among Japanese men who lounged around stark naked, discussing their day's business) made him chuckle. The adaptation of my long, angular, awkward body to the minuscule, dainty Japanese surroundings rendered him helpless with laughter as he watched me. My legs were too long to kneel on. They cramped in two minutes. If I stretched them in front, I collapsed in the middle, to say nothing of the fact that they jutted out from the other side of a table. I rarely walked upright. My head would crash into a door frame. There were no slippers or *tabi* (Japanese toed socks) big enough for my feet. I didn't know where to put my belongings and knickknacks; there were no dressers or closets. There was, however, a minute dressing table, two inches from the floor. If it had a mirror, all I could see were my feet. And my feet were always chilly because my shoes were at the front door.

The Japanese are taught that the Spartan way of life is the only path to happiness. A person can think and meditate better if he is always a little hungry, never quite warm enough, and never falling prey to the dangers of the soft life of self-gratification. Only discipline through deprivation can bring true enlightenment. It is the Buddhist way. A display of wealth is repugnant. Even a wealthy man never buys things just to have them. He gains status in other ways—by having the finest geisha and visiting the best teahouses and golf clubs. However, evidence of his prosperity in the form of material possessions is never found in his home or place of business.

The world beyond myself was becoming more and more real to me. Other customs and cultures made my eyes and ears bulge and flap with discovery. My curiosity of others and their ways of life was endless. The more I learned about others, the more I learned about myself. I was beginning to understand why I had become an actress. To wear and understand the cloak of another person had been a motivating force in me all my life. I loved being other people, and in doing so I was somehow more of me.

The world was so rich in characters, so rich in varying points of view, so rich in its differing approaches to life. I loved trying to understand anything different because I always found something different in myself in the process.

We had come to Japan to shoot location scenes for *Around the World in Eighty Days,* and early one morning we climbed aboard a fishing junk in the village of Numazu to shoot a scene that was supposed to have been in Yokohama harbor. My back was to the camera, because there was no way to cover the freckles without makeup. The wind came up, the water churned high, and the camera fell overboard. That was the end of location shooting.

Then I became ill. I thought it was seasickness and tried to forget about it, which was impossible after a while. One doesn't stay seasick for seven days after returning to land. Whenever I stirred myself to eat at all, it was always Italian spaghetti, and for some reason the color green made me nauseous. Steve called in a doctor, who diagnosed my trouble as the Asian flu and recommended a few days of rest. Sleep, which I had always regarded as a chore, was now something I couldn't get enough of. Listless and tired most of the time, I graduated from Italian spaghetti to giant-sized chocolate bars with nuts.

I developed a passion for the Japanese theater. It took me outside myself. It was a life and world all to itself, at once preserving the ancient traditions and outmoding every theater on earth in its modernity. Stages twice as large as the one in Radio City Music Hall were common. As many as two hundred scantily clad ladies of the chorus fanned out over the stage. Opulent costumes fashioned of brocades and silks of inconceivable hues were taken for granted by the audiences. Cost was no object, and with good reason, for the Japanese theater, to put it mildly, was healthy. The shows were continuous throughout the day, and there was never an empty seat. People jammed the aisles and the rear as though there were no fire laws. Many brought food and sat through several performances. Some nibbled at *osembe* and dried fish, and the sounds of crackling paper and crunching resounded through the theater. The Japanese never stopped eating. They didn't sit down and gorge themselves at a single meal, but they ate little meals all day long—rice balls with raw fish, pickled vegetables spiced with a hot mashed radish called *wasabe,* rice wrapped in *nori* (seaweed) and dipped in *shoyu* sauce, rice and pasty bean curds, all inevitably accompanied by tasteless green tea.

Onstage I saw the ancient Noh drama plays. The actors performed in overdrawn, larger-than-life masks. Their movements were labored, making one acutely conscious of the centuries inherent in one of the oldest art forms on earth. The actors didn't merely perform; they preserved the past and its formal, rigid, pompous, splendid ways. The audience was there not merely for entertainment, but also in a spirit of duty and reverence. Perhaps they found security and relief from the present in the rituals of their past.

The Kabuki theater, a uniquely Japanese art form, was like a giant, tragic fairy tale. Life was interpreted with vast brushstrokes on a magnificent stage, yet in exquisite detail. Vivid splashes of iridescent color caressed my eyes. I was almost afraid to look too closely, too directly, for fear the illusion would disappear. Suddenly the opulently dressed actors were above me, gliding from the stage on a ramp that stretched out into the audience. Their raven hair was piled into mountains through which rainbows of flowers were intertwined. The white geisha faces were painted in pinched, startled, slightly cowed feminine expressions. The geishas swayed with liquid movements, defying the weight of the lavish kimonos girdled with stiff, taut *obis* that restricted their very breathing. The *obis* were gathered in back in superb looping bows that spilled streamers of color. Full, sweeping sleeves swished softly above the heads of the audience, and tiny graceful hands protruded from the sleeves, gently cutting the air in understated movements.

From offstage came the clatter of woodblocks and the sound of flutes broken by the beat of drums. Thundering onstage with one great bounding leap came the Shogun. Fierce strokes of crimson outlined his eyes, sloping upward in a slant. His mouth was painted black, slashing downward. He stood with feet apart. His fiery-hued kimono was drawn tight about his hips, accentuating his arrogance as he began to swagger. Brandishing his samurai sword and emitting deep guttural sounds, he moved toward one of the transfixed geishas with lordly mien. Reaching her, he fell to one knee, wailing with fear and disbelief.

The play is called *Chushingura*. It is a true account from the past and the most popular of all Kabuki presentations. Steve particularly wanted me to see it as an example of the code of honor most revered by the Japanese people. It is a tale of revenge. Forty-nine samurai warriors commit mass murder to avenge the assassination of their master, after which, their debt to honor paid, they commit hara-kiri. Snowflakes fell over the dead company as the curtain was closed by black-clad figures. Tears filled the eyes of the audience and fierce pride shone in their rapt faces. Honor meant more than life.

After the performance an old, stooped stage manager directed us to the dressing room of the *sensei*—the teacher. Actors removing their makeup bowed to us as we passed. Massive modern turntables of thick steel, capable of making the stage revolve at any elevation and any speed, were being greased by mechanics.

A *shoji* door slid aside. The fierce Shogun was kneeling in front of a small mirrored dressing table. From the audience he had looked like a great hulk of a man, but as he rose to greet Steve we saw that he was only a few inches over five feet tall. He bowed with great dignity and invited us to take tea. Steve chatted with him in Japanese, pausing now and then to lean toward me with a translation. The *sensei* regarded me with disapproval because I did not speak the language of my husband. His own life was rooted in his nation's classical past, and he made it clear that any concession to modernity, such as learning English, was merely humorous to him.

The *shoji* parted again, and a flower-scented geisha glided into the room, kneeling like a fragile flower before us, giving us welcome and expressing the hope that we had enjoyed the performance. When the geisha left, I expressed my admiration for such grace and beauty, rare even in the theater.

"My humble thanks," said the *sensei* in Japanese. "This person is a true artist whom I have trained well. You see, he is my son."

I learned then that only men act in the Kabuki theater. The *sensei's* son had been trained to play the part of a geisha from the time he was seven, while a brother had been trained for the role of a samurai. Neither would ever play another part. All the members of the Kabuki company were descendants of the original theatrical families, thus creating a closed shop of theatrical royal blood.

The impact of the Japanese theater is enormous. It is both ancient and modern. Its achievements in production techniques are remarkable—false rainfall as real as an April shower, snowbanks and blizzards to rival reality, structures burning in the wake of Japan's chronic disasters, earthquakes. Beams and rooftops of ancient temples, stairways of monstrous palaces crash before the eyes of spellbound audiences, as real smoke rises from the ashes, and samurai and their geishas struggle in the debris only to be annihilated by the cruel sword of the neighboring feudal warlord. It is tremendously exciting entertainment, and could be for Western audiences. Steve's plan was to bring it to them. His future lay in the theater of Asia, and I would not be unhappy at all to claim Japan as a second home.

As for my sickness and listlessnes, by the time we left the land of the *mushi mushi's* (hello-hello), we were being congratulated at every turn by people who seemed to know more than the doctors. Although we wouldn't be certain for a while longer, we thought we had something that was Made in Japan. If it was a girl, we would name her Sachiko. We hoped she would be a happy child.

Six

IF I HAD HARBORED any thought that impending fatherhood would cause Steve to delay his return to Japan, it was quickly and absolutely dispelled. The thought of a new family only made him more determined to prove himself, and he left for Japan again almost immediately.

In California I faced the days of my pregnancy with melancholy, unable to fill them with work because of my condition. *The Trouble with Harry* had laid its artistic, Technicolored egg, and in *Artists and Models* I was an also-ran. *Around the World in Eighty Days* was in the final stages of editing when a close friend connected with the production called and cheered me with "You'd better have that baby fast and go to work before this picture is released, or you may never work again."

Right in the teeth. And he was right. It was all well and good for Todd to chew happily on a dollar cigar and get a big charge out of hiring a campy Hindu princess. I only hoped the critics would be looking the other way; whenever I came on the screen it was as though somebody just left. It appeared that my acting career, such as it was, had fizzled out in a master stroke of miscasting, complicated by the fact that I didn't know how to act.

I had nothing to do but sit in impatient agony and *wait*. The days got longer, the nights lonelier, the stomach larger, and the heartburn unbearable.

A direct intercom was hooked up from the delivery room to the maternity wing's waiting room, where Steve sat exhausted from the trans-Pacific flight.

"Tell your husband and say it loud enough. You will

be the first people in the world to know whether you have a boy or a girl," said the kind doctor as the baby was born.

I was dizzy from sedation, and my eye went directly to the cord, still unsevered. "Well, it's awfully long," I said, "but I guess it's a boy."

"Baby Parker—a boy," confirmed the attendant because I hadn't spoken loudly enough.

"Good," I heard Steve say, "as long as it's healthy."

The doctor shook his head gently. "I think you'd better look again, Shirley."

"Oh," I said. "It's a *girl.*"

"Parker babies—a boy and a girl," boomed the attendant.

Steve shouted, "Twins? Great."

"Parker baby only one—a girl."

"What happened?" Steve asked. "Where's the boy?"

The nurse took over the intercom. "There's absolutely no problem, Mr. Parker. Your wife simply made a mistake. I might suggest some glasses for her when she gets home, though. She wants you to know the baby is healthy. It's a girl—definitely a girl—nineteen and a half inches long and weighs exactly six pounds. She has bright red hair."

"And looks," I thought wearily, "like a cross between Pablo Casals and Winston Churchill."

The baby was taken off to the nursery, and I was wheeled to my room. Me—a mother. It was a feeling of responsibility I could barely fathom. How would I care for her, how would I know how? I'd never be able to handle the job.

What had I done, bringing a helpless child into my discombobulated world, a world of experiment, uncertainty? Had I brought a child into a world of two worlds? And to which world would she belong?

During pregnancy she was only a big stomach, something that moved and kicked intermittently, without a face, a future, or a self. But now the stomach was gone, and she was out. She was among us. I had *seen* her move, *heard* her cry, and soon I would *hold* the small, hopeful, demanding person who one day would stand up and walk, looking to me for guidance and assurance. Who really was the child anyway? In one afternoon her raw entrance of arms and legs and head had propelled me through a lifetime course of realization. It was I who was learning, I who felt inadequate with what I had to give.

And Steve—would the baby understand what he was, what he meant to do, what he had to do? Would the separations make her suffer? Would she see me suffer, and wonder why? And when it came her turn, would she be a woman? A real woman who understood that being a woman was the only thing that would ever really matter? Suddenly I realized I had never thought that way about myself.

The nurse came into the room. "What are you doing out of bed? It's only been half an hour," she said.

I muttered something about her not understanding what it meant to be a mother, as she handed me the soft, warm bundle.

Steve walked in. "Thank you for our new Sachiko," he said. There were tears in his eyes.

I relaxed. Sachie stirred. Suddenly I had been a mother for forty years.

The one-room shack in Malibu wasn't enough any longer. We would have to have a house with real bed-rooms, a real kitchen, a real heater, and rooms that would be occupied by household help. It was time to come out of the cocoon.

And so, proposing to rejoin the human race, we rented a big house. It was green on the outside and shell-pink on the inside, with white floors and a master bedroom of sweeping elegance, overlooking the Pacific. We were in Malibu Colony, home of the most exclusive movie stars, where your next-door neighbor might be Marion Davies, but you'd never know it; where the children of the famous romped together on the open beach while their famous parents remained behind high, sand-garden walls.

We were able to afford the house because we took a two-year lease on a deal made through friends. It would cost us three hundred dollars a month, and the owner knew we wouldn't abuse the premises because we were to be there for two years. Summer tenants were notoriously destructive in Malibu. I always secretly suspected someone had told him that the Parkers never gave parties.

The house swallowed us. Our meager belongings from the shack disappeared in rooms with sliding glass doors and high ceilings. The world of affluence was foreign to us. The house seemed to control us instead of vice versa. I felt that I was wearing someone else's dress.

Steve loved it, however, and later on Sachie crawled happily across its spacious floors. Caesar, our one-year-old boxer, and Bolo, our cat who thought he was a dog, adopted it at once.

Shortly after we moved in, Steve went back to Japan. He was needed in Tokyo in the initial stages of setting up his theater company.

Work—that was the answer. Sachie was happy, healthy, and well taken care of. She accompanied me on all my routine errands, gurgling delightedly at the sounds and sights of her new world. And, should I find employment, there was a nurse to care for her during the working hours.

But the telephone's silence was appalling. Wallis was making pictures with people he *didn't* have under contract. The other producers must have seen me in *Around the World in Eighty Days.* I began to panic.

Then I discovered television. My sanity returned for a few months as I danced and sang my way through several guest shots on musical shows. My muscle tone returned to normal and it was good to be among the working people of the industry again. Still no films, however.

In desperation I joined the road company of a Broadway show. It had been nearly three years since I had faced a live audience, and three years since that last chaotic performance of *Pajama Game*. It was beginning to look as though the light had gone out.

The cast of *The Sleeping Prince* included Hermione Gingold and Francis Lederer. It was produced on half a shoestring, which was just as well because nobody came to see it. Two weeks after it opened the producer asked if the members of the cast would take a fifty-percent cut in salary. We agreed. We would have made more money car-hopping at a hamburger stand, but the reviews weren't bad in Los Angeles, where we hung on for two months, and in San Francisco and Santa Barbara, where we toured for three weeks. The critics were especially kind to me. Perhaps I was learning how to act after all. Hal Wallis paid me the honor of coming to the play the night we closed in San Francisco.

"The critics said you were good, and I guess they were right," he said to me. "Come to my office when you return to Los Angeles, and we'll have a talk."

A talk? Did he have something for me?

Yes—and much more than I expected.

He greeted me with open arms at the doorway of his inner sanctum, and then proceeded to devour me with a kiss I found highly embarrassing. It wasn't a business kiss. It was more like something from one of his pictures. It was the first time something like that had ever happened to me. I edged away.

"You were excellent in your play," he said. "I didn't expect it."

That was his idea of flattery. He still had a grip on me. My mother had always said, "Regardless of the situation in which you find yourself, act like a lady." Would slapping him in the chops be acting like a lady? No. I sneezed. And then I sneezed again.

"Gesundheit," he said sourly.

We were both covered with spray. Apologizing, I offered him a handkerchief. "Well, sit down," he said.

I sat facing his desk. He sat behind it, surrounded by Academy Award plaques and statuettes, expensive tape recorders, pictures of giant fish he had caught, and a towering pile of scripts. He pulled out one from the top.

"Would you like to make a drama, with Danny Mann?"

Danny Mann had directed my screen test. "I'd love to," I said.

"Okay. The picture is *Hot Spell*. Report March sixth."

"Which part do I have?"

"I'll tell you the day you report."

That was it. That was our little talk. I felt sick. I left his office in a daze.

Morosely I made the lonely trek to the beach. The nurse was watching Sachie while I was in town. Apparently I had returned earlier than she expected. The front door was ajar. My shoes had soft soles and made no sound.

I was stunned at what I saw and heard. Sachie was trying to crawl on the rug toward the heavy-set woman. Leona knelt on the floor beckoning to her, saying: "Thatta itsa bitsa baby, come to your mommy. I'm your real mommy. The other bad lady doesn't love you any more."

I stood transfixed. Leona hadn't noticed me. "Itsa bitsa." I rushed upstairs and threw her clothes into a suitcase and called a taxi. With a look of pure hatred, she lumbered to the cab and was gone.

I held Sachie on my lap and sat staring at the ocean for a long time.

Sachie and I lived on in the big beach house alone. *Hot Spell* was eight weeks away. Steve was traveling all over Japan, and my only contact with him was by letter. Every night I talked to him with pen and paper, Sachie on my lap, Caesar and Bolo at my feet. The heater worked poorly. Our chief sources of warmth were the fireplace and each other. After supper we huddled together, staying close to the fire, putting off as long as possible the chilly climb to the bedroom. Sachie was healthy and never even had a sniffle. Her life revolved around me—sitting on my hip as I shopped, and in her little car seat on our drives.

Then the gossip started.

Poor Shirley, left alone like this, with such an adorable child.

He must be shacking up with a geisha over there. They bathe together, you know.

Couldn't he be satisfied to stay home and be her manager? What does he do anyway?

He should know that she's the talent in the family. Not him. By the way, what pictures has she been in?

An incessant whine of gossip. And the gossipmongers were not the only ones who zeroed in on the "poor lonely kid." The vultures began to hover. To the average male there is seemingly nothing so attractive or so challenging as a reasonably good-looking young mother who is married and *alone*. There is no risk involved. They are safe. She is in no position to make demands. And she *must*, mustn't she? Just out of sheer frustration? But she didn't.

I learned a lot about life just by deciphering the filthy shades of meaning that filled their gossip. I was an enigma. I intrigued them. They didn't have a pigeonhole for me.

Tough. But they were right about one thing—I was desperately lonely.

I began to go to Hollywood dinner parties, a unique phenomenon of the Western world. Only if one is working is one invited. *Hot Spell* had started. That made me eligible, and as long as one continued to accept invitations, one continued to receive them. Soon I became part of the group—the dinner-party group.

By accepting invitations, I knew I betrayed the fact that I was lonely, that I was dependent, that I needed them. It was a form of surrender, and a source of satisfaction to those who had surrendered long ago and eagerly waited for others to succumb and join them. It happened to me, but not for long.

The dinner party was the same scene played over and over. The houses were at different addresses, but the sets were the same—emerald lawns, pristine parking areas, Rolls-Royces moving up graveled drives. Guests who arrived in Buicks parked down the street, out of sight.

You are greeted by a butler, resplendent in either tails or a white jacket. His bow bids you enter, but he never speaks. Sounds of famous voices filter through to the reception hall, where you catch your breath in a final attempt to pull yourself together to meet them. You wonder if they were as anxious as you when they entered. Your wrap off, you straighten up, suck in your stomach, and look down, checking yourself one last time.

Then you hear her coming toward the reception hall—your hostess, her Paris heels clicking across inlaid wooden floors, and her petticoats swishing under a skirt of exactly the correct length. A brilliant pair of diamond clusters spill from her ears just below her coifed hair. She is well aware of their blinding magnificence, never forgetting what she paid for them as she smiles a charming but empty smile and with a wave of patronizing grandeur compliments you on your costume jewelry. You wish she had said nothing. She leads you into the drawing room because she remembers that you said you'd be coming alone. You hope the famous faces won't look up all at once—the stars, directors, producers, agents, wives of famous men, and husbands of famous wives. You want to take the evening in small doses, but you, like everyone there, are "on." And you get sucked into the greetings, the sweeping, larger-than-life greetings, with "Dahhh-lingsss" and hugs and anticipated pecks on your cheeks. You feel the women draw back slightly for fear a smudge of lipstick will mar their carefully studied makeups. During the conversational exchanges, you know that no one is saying what they really think and you know that they all know it about each other. But the feigned is the accepted code of behavior. Only a fool with bad taste, or someone extremely naïve, would expose his honesty. If it happens, everyone titters embarrassedly and remarks on how charming it is to have someone among them who has yet to become disillusioned. Honesty is not generally attractive; it upsets the accepted level of communication, and it is dangerous to expose your truth for the record.

But subconsciously the fencers in this sort of match wait anxiously for someone to reveal a bit of truth, and then it is like rain on a thirsty garden. The truth begins to flourish. The vacant, blinking expressions relax. Everyone perceives that the gears of communication have shifted. Now it is possible to get down to brass tacks. But a strange thing happens: malice takes over and everyone goes in for the kill. There is wit, caustic and hurtful wit. The person (the subject of conversation) is annihilated. And annihilation never comes cloaked in more entertaining attire.

You find yourself a bystander, a witness to annihilation, at first guilty and shocked. You had wanted reality, but

not this. Then you are stunned to hear yourself also reacting with sadistic glee. You analyze why you laugh and
realize only that it "sounds" funny. Your heart knows
how cruel it is.

Just as your stomach turns over they announce that
dinner is served.

Like opulent puppets the famous profiles are directed
toward the dining room, wondering whom they will be
cast next to for the remainder of the evening.

Nervous fidgeting, shifting frozen smiles, and exclama-
tions of sheer delight at being seated next to someone they
can't bear. Then come the lavishly served Rock Cornish
game hens, wild rice, artichoke hearts buried in mounds
of fresh peas and petite onions, followed by jokes dis-
couraging potato eating. The waiters, waitresses, and wine
bearers are always distracted by the congregation of so
many famous and adored faces, and their arms and hands
tremble just a bit under the weight of the elaborately presented food.

The conversation is always predictable: "But his picture was pseudorealistic. Life isn't really like that."

No. Life was like *this!*

Men and women feign interest in their dinner partners, and are sometimes curious enough to exchange private telephone numbers for a clandestine look at someone
else's boredom.

Pockets of animated conversation make attendance at
the long dinner table sound almost enjoyable.

"Let's talk about you. What did you think of my latest
picture?"

"But his last picture was a disaster. I don't care if he
is right for the part."

When a subject other than motion pictures is introduced, the nervous fidgeting increases. It is impossible to
discuss anything else. Change the subject quickly. Return

to familiar ground.

"We did fourteen thousand last week at Grauman's."

Then comes dessert, more often than not on fire—a spectacular, gala, nine-hundred calorie waitered production flaming from the darkness accompanied by coffee served in delicately wrought cups, and more nervous feet shuffle on Oriental carpets.

A world in itself, peopled by a shatteringly beautiful cast of characters. And nice people they were, too, when they were alone; together they were a depressing conglomeration of affluent lost identities.

But they were kind to me. It didn't matter *why* they invited me to be one of them; the important fact was that they did. Nevertheless, I found it empty and hollow and usually when work was finished for the day I retreated to the faraway beach house. I ate supper before the picture window, alone, listening to the pounding waves and watching the cold spray splash up against the window and trickle down in slow rivulets. I was never warm. Visitors were rare; Malibu was too far away, especially in winter. It was a cold, wet wilderness, brightened only intermittently by Steve's occasional trips home. These were often far from happy, for they were usually clouded by arguments.

After a year and a half I had begun to resent his absences. I even became suspicious, falling prey to the same nasty notions that contaminated the minds of the gossipmongers.

"Well, what's taking so long?" I screamed time and again. "Your company is set up and two pictures are finished already. Why don't you produce your live shows as you said you would, and bring them over here?"

Patiently he tried to explain the Orient to me again.

On one visit there was a tremendous explosion and clash of wills. There seemed nothing left to say. What he had told me was beyond my comprehension. I dragged myself to bed, leaving him sitting in silence in the living room.

On the pillow he had placed a poem by Rudyard Kipling:

> *Now it is not good for the Christian's health to
>   hustle the Aryan brown*
> *For the Christian riles, and the Aryan smiles and
>   he weareth the Christian down;*
> *And the end of the fight is tombstone white with
>   the name of the late deceased,*
> *And the epitaph drear, "A fool lies here who tried
>   to hustle the East."*

I would try to understand for a while longer.

Seven

I TRIED. I finished *Hot Spell* and went on from one insignificant picture to another. I was bound hand and foot by my contract with Wallis, and there was nothing I could do. I was grateful for the employment but the quality of the work was far below the price I was paying in loneliness.

The set became my salvation, my home, as it had been for countless performers before me. The pictures might be insignificant and utterly devoid of artistic value to the performers and to the world. Yet something of far more value happens to the performer. While he is making a picture he is part of a family.

The director becomes a father of dependent children. The crew become your brothers, and if you are *truly* kind to them they *truly* care about your well-being, your comfort, your anxieties. They are partners in your hopes and dreams, and they strain, often to the point of exhaustion, to help you squeeze the utmost from your abilities. Their smiles of appreciation and flashes of sometimes brilliant humor are a warm blanket. Should you occasionally become temperamental and unpleasant, they don't see it. They go about their jobs with a refined, diplomatic air, knowing that you are afraid and insecure inside and that the tempest will pass and friendship will prevail again. The crew members are the unrecognized people who give a picture spirit. They deal with the very essence of hypersensitivity in actors, writers, and directors. With solid constancy they try to give the set a pleasant atmosphere, often in the face of totally unwarranted rudeness, even cruelty, imposed by tyrants from the upper echelon who get their kicks from attacking the "little people." The crew is the backbone of the industry, and their contribution is infinitely more valuable than even they realize.

Making a film is an all-consuming process. Your home becomes a negligible place, where you take your evening meal and sleep. Your real home is a studio-constructed living room with removable walls and chandeliers that fly on ropes.

Your mornings don't begin until the men who spend their lives on the rafters flick the switches that will light your days. They wave down at you, and you are glad to be there. You try hard to remember each of your brothers by name, because you know it will delight him. Occasionally small tidbits float down from above—from something to eat with your coffee to a tune or a joke they heard the night before. Their lives are inexorably intertwined with yours because they rarely see their families either.

You begin a scene, and the character you play becomes your reality. You feel comfortable and safe with your crew-family protecting you. Their eyes never leave you. They are always prepared for an unflattering shadow, perfecting it with their lights and scrims, helping with subtle gestures to find the prettiest tilt for your head. You trust them implicitly because you know they don't have an angle. If you've had a sleepless night, they don't complain about the deep shadows; they quietly bring out more floodlights, hiding from the public what they've seen on the set.

And the level on which motion-picture work is conducted is so professional and yet so personal that it rivals the relationship between a doctor and patient. The director guides you, channeling your feelings and emotions in the right direction, helping and encouraging you to find the proper thread of communication. You learn quickly that to hide or suppress your private depths is cheating. Your co-workers need more than surface skin to work with and bounce from, and you only fool yourself by not having the courage to give everything you've got. At first, the nature of the work seems a colossal invasion of privacy, until you realize that no one betrays what you are revealing of your insides. They are grateful and appreciative and are comfortable in doing the same themselves.

And so, regardless of the mediocrity and seeming futility of many films, the chunk of one's lifetime spent in making them is important. It is a period of total dedication, and when the company disperses each night you are tired, but you know that you belong. And when you make your way to a dark, lonely house, you long for the morning when you can belong all over again.

I knew that my life was badly out of balance. I had my work and I had Sachie. As the months passed and the pictures ticked by, I adored her more than ever.

And then I no longer had Sachie. Steve had been ill with hepatitis and was alone in a hospital in Yokohama. I was in the middle of a film. I sent Sachie to visit him for Christmas. She traveled alone on the plane, strapped into the double seat, smiling and thrilled that she would see her Daddy again. The governess we had hired in Japan would meet her at the airport.

"Okay, that's a wrap," the assistant director yelled. "Thanks for your cooperation, and I think we have a fine film. Drinks on the next stage, compliments of the management, and I hope we work together again sometime."

That was it. Everyone shook hands, joked, exchanged small presents. The lights began to go out and the huge sound stage dwindled into darkness.

I was alone in my dressing room. The costumes were gone from the closet. The makeup table was cleared. The script's last page had been turned; it lay face down on a chair. There were no jovial voices to be heard above the arc lights, no wardrobe women seeking clues to "49-down" in the crossword puzzles they worked while waiting for the next setup. The chairs with our names stenciled across their backs had been folded, the names removed in readiness for the next company scheduled to use the stage. No extras done up as cowboys and Indians waited, making dates for the weekend. The incessantly ringing wall telephone was silent. No brass from the front office demanded to know what was taking so long and how many pages we shot that day.

All was quiet except for the sound of the janitor and the soft rustle of his broom.

"Are you getting about ready to leave, Miss Shirley?" he asked, looking at me with eyes accustomed to loneliness.

"Yes. I'm sorry. I was just sitting here thinking." I tried to sound casual, as though I were only tired.

"This was a nice picture to work on," he said, as they always did, "but I'll bet you're tired. So say hello to your family. You'll get to spend more time with them now, so that's good."

He said goodnight and I hurried through the heavy door. It was a clear, black night. It always surprised me to realize the world had kept on turning while we slaved inside, oblivious of time. The darkness blasted at me like an unfriendly greeting. The streets of the back lot were empty except for a few stragglers trudging toward the front gate. I wondered what they were going home to. Only people who moved slowly at the end of the day had nothing much waiting for them. A few late-shift carpenters waved as I passed. One or two whistled; I smiled.

I loaded my belongings into the MG—wash cloth, towels, toothpaste, toothbrush, instant coffee, and a picture of Steve and Sachie. In the morning, the home I had had for four months, the home I had had for yet another picture, would belong to someone else.

And then what for me? Another large family of brothers and sisters—a family to be wrenched away when the schedule was over and the director yelled, "That's a wrap."

I wanted to reach out and talk with someone about the terrible feeling of not belonging, of nowhere to go, of never being a part of anything permanent, and of how futile it seemed to have intimate contact with people when you'd never see them again.

I drove on toward my empty house by the sea, thinking of the bleak night I had put Sachie on the plane for Japan, the twinge I had felt when she proudly produced her own passport and handed it to the attendant at the gate.

> *Stephanie Sachiko Parker*
> AGE: two
> WEIGHT: 30 pounds
> HEIGHT: 2½ feet
> OCCUPATION: child

I hadn't been able to hold back the tears as I strapped her into the seat. The other passengers politely looked away and I wanted to melt into nothing. How could they possibly understand that I wasn't a "Hollywood mother," who moved a child around like a chess piece? But why was she going without me? Why couldn't I be with the two people in the world I loved most?

I had watched the plane take off. Sachie would travel eight thousand miles alone; it would make her a part of our dispersed unit. Why? Because there are things a man must do, and things a woman must understand?

It was a large question. And now as I drove toward the beach house I made a decision. The life I was leading was unbearable. It was true. I had wanted to work. That was part of me, and had been since childhood. The need to make a recognizable contribution motivated me not only professionally but also as a woman. But the contribution I was making seemed infinitesimal, and, what was worse, mediocre. It hardly seemed worth it. I belonged with Steve and Sachie. Surely he would see that. I was cut up into too many little pieces—actress, wife, mother. One would have to go.

I rushed into the dark house, my decision clear. To hell with my fond dream of "being somebody." It was far more important to be *with* somebody.

The next morning, the plane could not fly swiftly enough. I would learn to live on raw fish and rice balls.

Eight

STEVE WELCOMED ME WITH OPEN HEART. He had been lonely too and hadn't wanted to admit he needed me. Sachie had been his life saver. She had grown in the four months since I had seen her, and at two and a half seemed almost a young lady to me. Her stick-straight, blond hair and sprinkle of freckles were an amusing contrast to the formal kimono she wore. She was speaking Japanese sentences and had an air of maturity and independence. She and Steve adored each other. The three of us belonged together and I was home again.

Steve had taken a house in Tokyo in the residential district of Shibuya, not far from his newly rented offices. I busied myself with *ikebana* (Japanese floral arrangement), cooking, and reading. Sachie entered the International Nursery School of Nishi Machi. Children from all over the world came there for their education. She was too young for the first grade, but in Nishi Machi, kindergarten was an education in itself. Thai, Indian, Chinese, Burmese, German, French, English, Indonesian, and Japanese children learned to play side by side. Sachie and one little boy were the only two Americans represented. She began to pick up the languages of the world by osmosis, until very soon she could get along in five of them. The teachers had a rule at Nishi Machi. The language of the child who secured the ball during recess was the one the others would speak during playtime. Languages became an enjoyable form of communication instead of required study.

Steve's business flourished. He won two International Film Festival awards for his Japanese documentary films and was talking of bringing a Japanese spectacular to the United States. My career hung in limbo. The three of us were together for six months. Steve understood what I was doing, and why, and he appreciated it. It was the happiest time of our married life.

But it didn't last long.

After a while I became fidgety and restless. I needed to do more with myself. I had worked all my life, using my energies to the utmost, and now, even though I loved being with Steve and Sachi, it wasn't enough. It didn't even seem to be a question of unused potential talent. It was more that I was living at only twenty percent capacity.

Steve and Sachi picked up my frustrations. You can't hide those things from the people you love most. My dilemma seemed such a cliché; frustrated young housewife who has more to give than lovingly washing dishes, lovingly raising a family, and lovingly loving her husband. It was like a true confessions letter to *Ladies' Home Journal*. And all the women out there that I suddenly realized must be feeling the same way would get a letter back from Dear Abby that nothing was more important for a woman than her family. I wondered if that was indeed so when Sachi finally asked me one day why I didn't go back to work. I couldn't answer her by saying it was because she needed me with her. That just wasn't altogether true, particularly when it was her idea that I do it. She needed to know that I would always be there when she needed me, but not *whether* she did or not. As a matter of fact, *she* didn't like seeing me frustrated. It put a burden on *her*. And if I desired freedom and independence for her as a growing person, why shouldn't I desire the same thing for myself? How could I expect her to develop everything she could be as a person if I didn't? I realized I was confusing her by curtailing my own desires. I was encouraging her to do all the things

I was stifling in myself. And as children always do, she called me on it.

Steve didn't say anything for a while. He was waiting for me to make the decision myself, and when he realized I didn't have the guts, he finally spoke up.

"You've worked all your life to express yourself," he warned, "to communicate and to develop every potential in you. I think you're wrong to give it up just when the going gets rough. Nothing worth it was ever easy. I want you with me, but when I made the drastic decision to live here and pursue my work I didn't expect you to follow me, either out of emptiness or because you'd think you should. I expected you to have the strength to pursue your own course until you succeeded. It takes guts. Where are yours? You're more of a woman than a housewife, and after a year or so here you'd become miserable. You'd begin to hate yourself for your weakness, and you'd hate me because basically I was the reason for it. Keep trying a year or so more. If you're nowhere after really giving it that, then forget it, but not until then. Go back and work."

He knew me better than I knew myself.

I returned to Hollywood, gave up the beach house, and took one closer to the studios.

Sachie alternated between Nishi Machi and kindergarten in America, confused only about when to leave her shoes on and when to take them off. While the gossips of Hollywood looked on, I went from one picture to another in mediocre roles.

Then came the turning point—the break that Steve had anticipated—and Wallis nearly killed it.

The studio was Metro-Goldwyn-Mayer and the picture was *Some Came Running*. Frank Sinatra and Vincente Minnelli had seen me on a TV show and thought I'd be right for the part of Ginny: a part where "even *she* knows she's a pig."

They approached my agent, who began to negotiate a deal for more money than I ever dreamed I'd be paid—seventy-five thousand dollars—and Metro was willing to pay because Minnelli insisted. Then Wallis got into the act.

He told Metro they could have one of his commitments with me for half the price. When they asked what I'd get out of it, he told them he'd pay me what I was used to—my contract rate of $10,600. It didn't matter to Metro. It was cheaper all the way around for them and Wallis would make twenty-nine thousand dollars on the transaction. My agent refused to allow such a deal. Because he spoke with the voice of the powerful Music Corporation of America, all hell broke loose.

But the script was marvelous and I knew it was what I'd been waiting for. I called Steve.

"Do it," he said. "Do that damn picture even if it's for nothing. Money comes after recognition."

To spite Wallis I waited until the day the picture rolled before I reported for work. Minnelli and Sinatra agreed with me, and Metro's face was too red to object. The costumes fit me, and Ginny seemed part of my own character, so no preparation was necessary.

It was on location for *Some Came Running*, in Madison, Indiana, that my relationship with the so-called "clan" started. "Clan" was coined by a national magazine reporter assigned to write a story on the production of the picture and the characters involved. No one would see him, so he called us the "clan."

Frank Sinatra and Dean Martin, their friends, songwriters Jimmy Van Heusen and Sammy Cahn, and a raft of Italians who must have done something (one made great cannelloni) rented a house adjacent to the hotel that housed the cast of *Some Came Running*.

For some reason I was the only woman allowed in their house. I spent a lot of time there, tidying up for them, arranging flowers, and putting candy on the tables. All they did was play gin, but they were more fun to be around than anyone I had met in the business. Sometimes they would smoke, drink, joke, and play gin for fifteen hours straight. Minnelli, the director, was meticulous about dressing the sets and scenery and never used the actors until the last minute. That left all of us with plenty of spare time.

The people of Madison, Indiana, ringed the house we stayed in twenty-four hours a day. We couldn't come in or go out without causing a riot. The management of the hotel finally erected a rope barrier, which only made the people feel that something was going to happen.

In public, Frank and Dean attracted an inordinate amount of attention. It was something about the way they dressed. Not a crease was out of line. They were jaunty and absolutely self-confident. Women literally threw themselves at Frank and Dean; they would throw their hips up against the two famous men (who were looking for a good gin game somewhere more than anything else) and run their fingers through their hair while the men they were with looked on with red faces and apoplectic expressions. One night, a woman broke through the rope barrier outside the house, crashed into the hallway— knocking over two lamps in the process—and ran toward the living room where Frank and Dean and I were watching television. She pinned Frank to the couch, jumped on top of him and started to kiss him. Her husband came rushing after her, yelling "Helen, you don't even *know* him!" Helen, wearing a deep purple dress that matched her passion, was undeterred. She kept pressing matters, until Frank finally was able to turn her off. Quietly, gravely, he asked her to let him up, which she did, and he then escorted her out, giving her an autographed picture in lieu of himself.

I always wondered if the other guys hanging around with Frank and Dean got the leftover action. Probably a lot of the women who couldn't swing with the real swingers swung with the closest thing to it.

I, on the other hand, seemed to be kind of a mascot. No one in the group ever made an overture to me. They never questioned me about my personal life, and I never volunteered to discuss it. It was implicit to them that my life was complicated and I was trying something very difficult, so they let it alone. They respected whatever I chose to do, and they protected me from anyone on the outside who might be invading my privacy. *That* they were explicit about. If anyone approached me, one of them always stepped in front of me.

Eventually the clan expanded to include Sammy Davis, Jr., Peter Lawford, Joey Bishop, and a few others. I must have done six or eight pictures with one or another of them over a period of five or six years. And all during that time our friendships continued. They taught me comedy routines, cinema comedy techniques, and, most important, how to cheat at gin. As a matter of fact, Billy Wilder, while we were doing *The Apartment,* wrote in the famous gin game between Jack Lemmon and me because I was always playing gin on the set. Sometimes months would pass, while I was in Japan, or just traveling in general, when I wouldn't see any of the guys, but it never mattered, and when we were all together again no one even asked where I'd been. We'd take up just where we left off.

When *Some Came Running* was released I was nominated for an Academy Award. Suddenly I found that while once I could never find the right part, now I was right for every part. My presence in the business was acknowledged. No longer was I called in for a personal interview to see whether I was pretty enough. Good part after good part followed—*Can-Can, The Apartment, Children's Hour, Two for the Seesaw, Irma La Douce,* as did three more academy nominations, and lots of other awards, money, and finally a sense of contribution.

Steve's pride was wonderful and warm. And my soul still belonged to me. I felt I hadn't sold out. By juggling the logistics of both sides of the world, Steve and I had managed to be together most of the time. Sachie blossomed. I spent about half of every year in Japan when she was in school. And, when summer came she spent most of it in California, if I was working in a picture. The necessary separations only served to make our family unit stronger.

Steve's business prospered. He was the envy of every American businessman who tried to crack the code of dealing with the Japanese. His extravaganza, *Holiday in Japan,* had several companies touring the United States for three years while one played in Las Vegas. Many producers tried to copy the mixture of ancient and modern Japan, but they didn't have the patience or the time to understand the nature of the Asian mind.

Every year, at the request of the Emperor, Steve staged the Imperial Ball. He imported Asian talent from all over the Orient. From Japan he branched into the Philippines and exported the *Philippine Festival* to America. When the coup against Syngman Rhee took place in Korea, the newly formed government solicited his aid in developing their waning theatrical industry. His name became synonymous with theater in Asia. He was a fulfilled man. Our experiment had succeeded. With the help and understanding of each other, we had both made it.

Although my soul belonged to me, my *time* still

belonged to Hal Wallis. My contract had been for five years but with suspensions and extensions it now stretched to nine years. The longer it stretched, the more valuable I became to him. He could see my commitments on the outside.

During the ninth year, after I had made some really good pictures (none of them his), he notified me to report for a picture the script of which I found totally offensive. I asked him to substitute something else—anything palatable would have been all right. I wasn't fighting against the meager contract salary. In impolite terms he told me off, and ordered me to report for work. He was the producer, not I.

I decided to sue him under the California Labor Laws, which provide, in substance, that a contract to render personal services may not be enforced against the employee beyond seven years from the commencement of services under that contract. In effect the law protects employees *against themselves*. Wallis was furious. How dare the small-time chorus girl grow up and demand her rights?

I had made a deal with Metro to do *The Unsinkable Molly Brown*. Shooting was to begin immediately. But then Metro was afraid Wallis would secure a restraining order on my doing *Molly Brown* pending settlement of the dispute between us. And, should I lose the suit against him, he would pre-empt my services whether I was in the middle of production or not. Metro withdrew the commitment they had made with me and no other studio in town was willing to hire me under the circumstances. The can of peas had revolted, and the pea factories had shut down.

But the owner of the main pea factory got some pressure himself. If Wallis should lose the case the morality of long-term (often referred to as "white slave") contracts would be carefully scrutinized and probably be dealt a death blow. It was one of those points of law that "they" felt never should be brought to trial. If long-term contracts were dispensed with by court order, many up-and-coming actors would never have a chance to become stars. One of us would lose the battle, but who would lose the war? Two days before the trial Wallis offered to settle. I decided to go along with him. Nobody would win in litigation, regardless of the decision. For $150,000 from me, he released me from the contract. Nine years after he had seen me in *Pajama Game*, I belonged to myself. And during that time I had made nine pictures for Wallis, averaging $15,800 a picture. Finally I could make pictures when I chose to, and at my own price.

During my dispute with Wallis several things happened. The first concerned the late Mike Connelly, who used to write the Rambling Reporter gossip column for the *Hollywood Reporter* trade paper. It was commonly known that if he heard a rumor he would print it, rarely checking his facts. In fact, I suspect that half the time he made up the stuff himself. He was a very conservative man, politically; anyone who didn't wrap himself in the American flag was suspect. If Mike Connelly had a personal motto it must have been "my country and my rumors right or wrong."

Because I spent so much time out of the country, he called me a leader of "runaway production" even though at that time I had only made one film, *My Geisha*, outside America. My politics to him were "ding-a-ling." "She's crazy and has flipped her lid." When I campaigned for Adlai Stevenson and President Kennedy and when I went to Sacramento with Marlon Brando and Steve Allen to protest the execution of Caryl Chessman he printed I had lost my mind completely.

He wasn't crazy about me. Once when I went off to be by myself and just think, telling no one where I was going, he wrote that I had had my nose fixed and the operation was botched up and I was recuperating.

He said that I had tried to commit suicide over an unhappy affair and intimated strongly that on another of my trips I had had an abortion.

Over the years I read with growing rage the things he wrote about me. Each time something libelous appeared, I hesitated taking any kind of action because it would mean the newspapers would publicize even further the very lie I was suing him for.

The morning that Hal Wallis called my attorney to settle our battle out of court, Mike Connelly printed that I had lost the case. Committing suicide, having a botched-up nose job, and recuperating alone from an abortion were untruths I could bear, but when I read I had lost to Hal Wallis that was the limit.

I called my attorney and asked him how you could slug someone without being sued for assault and battery. He checked his files. "If you hit with the flat of the hand instead of a balled-up fist you don't commit assault and battery. Whoever you're going to hit, be prepared to get slugged back because maybe they won't know you're innocent."

I knew Mike Connelly wouldn't hit back. One thing was certain about him: he was 100 percent chicken.

I called my secretary Lori and asked her if she would be a witness to something for me. She asked if I had seen Connelly's item and I mumbled some answer.

We got in my car to drive to Connelly's office, although Lori didn't know where we were going. On Sunset Boulevard we parked in front of Connelly's office and walked in. The secretaries and typists at the *Hollywood Reporter* all worked on the first floor in a tiny open noisy room. I asked the receptionist if I could see Mr. Connelly please. I looked around the room and saw two press agents who were there to plant stories in Connelly's column, talking quietly together. I recognized one of them and nodded. At that moment Connelly came out of the elevator and walked toward me.

"Shirley," he said smiling. "This is really an unexpected pleasure."

"Yes, it is," I answered. "Especially for me."

"What can I do for you?" he asked.

"Well I've got to hear it from you, are you in the business of printing the truth or not?"

"Of course I am, you know that." He shuffled a little. I inched closer to him and removed his glasses.

"Then why the hell don't you print it?" And I wound up and hit him with all my might, slapppp across the face. I wanted to ball up my fist and belt him but I didn't.

"Shirley, what are you doing?" he shrieked.

"The same thing you've been doing to me for years— knocking you."

"But, Shirley!"

"But, Mike!" And I slapped again.

The two press agents scrambled for their dimes and put in calls to the Los Angeles *Times*. I only heard the beginning of one conversation. "You won't believe what I just saw . . ."

I said good afternoon to the secretaries, hoped I hadn't disturbed them, and left.

I went directly to my attorney's office, where he and Wallis's lawyers were discussing how we would settle the suit.

The telephone rang. The secretary said it was Hedda Hopper, another columnist who was just as lethal as Connelly, only she checked her stuff out more often.

"Shirley," she said "You should be absolutely ashamed of yourself—"

"O.K., I know," I said. She was a drag.

"No," she said. "Why didn't you knock him out cold at least? As far as I'm concerned you should be ashamed of yourself for not finishing him off completely."

That was a switch. I sent her a hat made of real orchids, which I'm told she wore till they wilted to death.

Holed up all day with attorneys, I wasn't aware of the furor on the outside. It was front-page news that I had sashayed into a gossip columnist's office and slugged him and was possibly going to be sued for assault and battery, depending on the damage done to Mr. Connelly's face. I certainly was glad Lori had been there to witness that I had only slapped him hard.

After the meeting I met a friend to attend a party in the back room at Chasens Restaurant. When we walked in everybody applauded, and waiting by my table was a huge pair of boxing gloves sent by Rocky Graziano.

Jim Bacon, then the A.P. stringer in Hollywood, walked up to me and said, "You'd better be careful now on dark streets—Connelly may come out of the shadows and hit you with his mesh bag."

Governor Brown sent me a wire saying he'd referee any fight I'd have in the future.

But the classic wire came from President Kennedy. It said:

DEAR SHIRLEY—CONGRATULATIONS ON YOUR FIGHT STOP NOW IF YOU HAD REAL GUTS YOU'D SLUG WALLACE—GOVERNOR NOT HAL

JFK

Nine

So MUCH OF an actor's life is played out in the newspapers. Many times actors are catalysts for people who don't speak directly to each other.

The visit of Nikita Khrushchev to the set of *Can-Can* was a case in point. We met and talked to each other, but the juicy stuff happened in and through the newspapers.

The 20th Century–Fox people asked Frank Sinatra and me if we'd act as host and hostess when Khrushchev was brought to see how a moving picture was made. Frank decided to sing "Live and Let Live" with Louis Jourdan, which seemed appropriate. And I learned a speech in Russian (phonetically) and led the can-can number, which was the big number of the picture.

The entire proceedings were televised, and because I had spoken in Russian and actually met, smiled at, and shaken the hand of the Premier, letters poured in protesting that I was making up to the butcher of Hungary. Khrushchev smiled his way through the afternoon, acted pleased with my speech, and was absolutely beaming through the flying risqué steps of the can-can. But I think Mrs. Khrushchev didn't dig it too much. She watched him beam even more when I introduced the girls to him. The newspapermen practically hiked my skirts over my head in order to get a picture with the stern Communist leader, loving every minute of it. He was pixyish, warm, and very real when we talked and crowded around him. But later something happened. Disneyland wasn't the only thing that upset him. When the press asked for his comment on me and the can-can he said, "The face of mankind is prettier than its backside." The press asked me what I thought of that and I said, "I think he's upset because we wore panties. Anyway if they wanted to show him something typically American they should have taken him to a ball game and given him a hot dog."

One day about a year and a half later I was sitting in Sardi's in New York City. The UN was in session and Khrushchev had come to bang his shoe on the desk. *The Apartment* had just been released and was well received. A man walked over to me and introduced himself as an interpreter for Mr. Khrushchev while he was in New York and said he had a message from him.

"The Premier sends his regards, wishes to be remembered to you, and says he's just seen your new picture, *The Apartment,* and you've improved."

One of the joys of being a successful actress was that I had the excuse and opportunity to explore so many levels of life. It seemed to me, sometimes, that I enjoyed the exploration more than the acting. I entered into the private lives of all kinds of people—and was welcomed because they wanted to be portrayed accurately.

When I researched Gittel Moska in *Two for the See-saw,* I spent a great deal of time in Greenwich Village in New York City, getting to know the life of a broken-down Jewish dancer who thinks of herself as a doormat. The Gittel I found wasn't William Gibson's Gittel, but she was enough like her and she was honest with me.

When Steve and I made *My Geisha* in Japan I lived in a Caburenjo (Geisha training school) for two weeks learning the intricacies of the tea ceremony, how to play the *samisen,* and the complexities of the Japanese dance, an art so subtle that at times the movements are barely discernible. No Westerner had ever been allowed into such a training school, much less lived there.

When I made *The Children's Hour,* I spent hours with doctors discussing latent homosexuality in women.

But the most unusual "excuse research" I ever did was after Billy Wilder asked me to play *Irma La Douce.* Even though I had cornered the screen market on loose women, Irma was different. She was a blatant hooker with a heart of gold, (as thay always are in the movies), but she was not simply a loose woman. Her body was her business, and she used it with pride and total lack of self-consciousness.

Irma was a hooker in Les Halles, one of the cheapest red-light districts in the world. Irma was the best hooker on the block, and she was proud of it. I had to find a girl, a real-life hooker, to match Irma and then get to know her.

Accompanying me for companionship, interpreting, and protection was the son of French friends of mine. I shall call him Christian, because that was his first name. He doesn't want his family name identified because he's married now and has two children, and he learned as much as I did downtown.

Les Halles is gone today, but when it flourished it was the wholesale market center of Paris, where produce brought in from the countryside was sold to restaurants and hotels and just plain people. We wandered through great banks of luscious red apples, pyramids of firm green cabbages, fruits of every description, and sides of mutton and pork and beef hanging slablike, row upon row, from heavy iron hooks.

Truck drivers arrived at Les Halles after midnight, and when they had unloaded their wares, many of them welcomed a little diversion before driving back to the farm again.

The side alleys adjacent to the market place were patrolled by prostitutes—young and old, fat and thin, statuesque and dumpy. The girls lined up on the narrow sidewalks, three or four feet apart, in front of rundown buildings several stories high. "A madam is in charge of each building," Christian explained. "There is a cashier's cage on the first floor, where the customers pay in advance as they enter. On the upper floor there are nothing but bedrooms, of course."

I could see that they wouldn't have much use for all-electric kitchens.

"Each girl turns over all the money she makes to her mec [a pimp and frequently the girl's only true lover], and in return the mec provides protection and takes care of her living expenses."

The girls seemed to be dressed according to what they thought were their best assets. If one had a good figure, she wore a tight dress and stood in a pose that accentuated her shape. If her face was her best feature, she played down her figure and concentrated on her makeup and facial expression. If she had neither, she just stood there. Everybody knew why she was there: she was for bargain hunters.

Christian and I stationed ourselves across the street from a stately, dark-haired girl, about my height, with a reasonably pretty face and figure. She stood with all her weight on one foot (heels at least four and one half inches high), her other leg bent, like someone posing for cheesecake. In fact, she never stopped posing. First a three-quarter angle, then full front, and every now and then she bent down to straighten a stocking seam, making a full circle on the way up—her derrière well defined in the white Chinese-style dress equipped with a long zipper that went from collar to hem. I learned later that there were couturiers who cater especially to the ladies of the night. Since time is money, and speed essential, there are no small buttons, snaps, or hooks. The answer: good sturdy, time-saving zippers.

We saw a customer approach the girl. There were a few words of negotiation and they disappeared into the building. The negotiations cover such matters as how much clothing the customer wants the girl to take off, determining the price. If she takes off nothing the price is about seventy-five cents. If the customer wants her to take off her dress and underclothing the price rises on a graduating scale. What bugs a prostitute most is to be asked to remove her stockings and garter belt. The sliding scale really isn't commensurate with the bother or the amount of time it takes the girl to put them on again. Those wasted precious minutes could be spent back down on the sidewalk providing for the future.

In five minutes the girl returned. Not a hair was out of place. Her coiffure was done in a beehive style, and somewhat resembled the Empire State Building.

Christian led me across the street. The surrounding hookers looked at me with concern. Perhaps they thought I was there to beat their time.

We introduced ourselves to the dark-haired girl and offered our credentials. She said her name was Danielle. Christian explained that I was going to do the film version of *Irma* and hoped she wouldn't mind if I observed her for a while.

Danielle smiled. I said I would be grateful if she would let me talk to her, if she could spare the time.

Her suspicion disappeared. She seemed flattered, almost ecstatic. "You will be one of us on the screen?" she asked with genuine delight.

I nodded.

"Good. I will be your technical adviser and show you how it is really done." Smiling broadly and speaking loudly enough to reassure the other girls, she said, "Yes, you will make a good hooker." It was like getting the *Good Housekeeping* Seal of Approval.

Danielle was working the early shift, from four-thirty in the afternoon until twelve-thirty A.M. It was August, a notoriously bad month for hookers because most Parisians are on vacation, and business was so slow she couldn't expect to average better than about thirty-five men a night.

Solicitation is illegal in France, so she was careful not to make any overt gestures to the men who walked by inspecting the merchandise. She simply stood in her tiny territory, swinging her bag, fixing her stockings, making her circle on the way up, and looking nonchalant. She didn't have to do much more anyway, since, like Irma, she was the best hooker on the block. She could size up a customer in a matter of seconds, talking price if he seemed acceptable, and ruling him out if he gave signs of being a drunkard, a cop, or a pervert.

For three hours we stood, out of sight, watching Danielle ply her trade. During that time she entered the building and came out seventeen times, which meant that her hourly average was slightly higher than the usual summer norm.

Most Les Halles customers were French—usually from the middle class, and of course the truck drivers. I did see one extremely well-dressed man arrive in a chauffeur-driven Cadillac. He was back downstairs so quickly that I thought the chauffeur should have left the motor running.

When it was time for Danielle's break, she motioned to us to follow her into the building.

"Now you will see where our business is conducted," she explained as she led us up four flights of winding stairs.

On the way up I did some arithmetic. Thirty-five customers a night meant that every night she climbed and descended the stairs seventy times in four-and-a-half-inch heels and a very tight skirt.

"Always *lead* the way up the stairs," she explained to me. "If a man panics or decides to change his mind, this will put him back on the track." She patted her fanny and swayed back and forth from side to side as she continued to climb.

We reached the top. Danielle threw open the door and motioned us into one of the bedrooms. The room was neither elaborate nor stark. There was a double bed covered with a red spread, a table, a lamp with a red shade, a sink, and a bidet. The walls were covered with mirrors. Some customers apparently prefer the grandstand to the playing field. A tiny hole in the door accommodates those who like to watch from the outside. And, thanks to the mirrors, they miss nothing. In a high-class house, the hole in the door would be déclassé; there would be a two-way mirror instead.

Very soon we had company. Other prostitutes began to drop in, and with them a number of mecs. Danielle had told them why I was there. They came to say hello and to express how eager they were for me to portray Irma accurately. One mec brought along a voluminous stack of pornographic snapshots that showed the girls in action. He suggested I buy some.

"They would be very valuable to you while you are making the movie. You could refer to them from time to time. Like a technical adviser."

I shook my head, trying to refuse politely. He bristled at my refusal.

Danielle took over. "First," she said, "you must have a demonstration of how fast I can get undressed." Before I could say a word, she had whipped off her dress, rolled down her stockings, and was ready to go to work. There was a generous burst of applause from the mecs and other prostitutes.

Beaming, Danielle motioned Christian toward her. Reluctantly he obeyed. Gently but purposefully she pushed him onto the bed and proceeded to pantomine her routine with a customer. Looking over her shoulder, she explained that each customer is given a wide choice of action, falling into two broad classifications. As she went on explaining various combinations and cross-combinations (with Christian giving a halting and red-faced translation) it sounded like "Choose one from Column A, two from Column B."

"One thing you must always remember," Danielle cautioned me as she zipped up her dress. "Regardless of how much clothing you are asked to take off, never *never, never* take off your shoes. It is very unflattering to see bare feet in this business."

I nodded gratefully, wondering how, with those heels, she managed to avoid putting out somebody's eye.

Christian scrambled up from the bed and tried to compose himself.

"*Alors!*" Danielle shouted gaily. "All of you wait here a minute. I will show you what real conservation of time is!"

She slipped from the room and we could hear her heels clattering swiftly downstairs. I asked where she was going. "Back to the street," someone said.

Soon we heard her coming upstairs again, a customer in tow. Stashing him in another bedroom, she stuck her head in. "Set your watches!" she said, and ducked out. We waited. In exactly four minutes she was back again. She had done what had to be done and sent her customer packing—all in four minutes. Eminently proud, she asked, "How was that?" There was another burst of applause.

"Maybe they'll include that in the Olympics next year," I said. Christian smiled wanly, still not quite himself.

One of Danielle's special customers was due in a very few minutes and she didn't want anyone to interfere with his time. She worked by appointment with him. "I have an appointment customer who pays me very highly and all he wants to do is talk," she went on. "And not the kind of talk you might think. He talks about his family and his business and what a failure he thinks he has been."

It seemed cheaper than going to a psychiatrist. "Is he coming now?" I asked.

"No," she replied. "This one is different. Much different. He does not talk. He hires me and three other girls, for one whole hour. Such a nice man." She glanced at her watch. "He will be here any minute. I wish you would observe me in my work with him so that you will have a better understanding."

I declined with thanks. To my surprise, she became indignant. "Well, Shir-lee," she pouted, "if you won't make an effort to understand what goes into my work, then how can you possibly play Irma on the screen?" Angrily she lit a cigarette. "And why should I spend any more of my time talking with you?"

The air was suddenly tense. The madam, the girls, and the mecs presented a solid front of sullen, righteous anger. I could feel their resentment. They all agreed with Danielle that I was making a stupid professional mistake in turning down such an opportunity for guidance. Furthermore, I was brushing off their prize hooker. My mind spun and I wondered if my director, Billy Wilder, might be playing a joke on me. There might even be a raid. I could see the news story: "Actress Shirley MacLaine was picked up in a Paris whorehouse, observing the action."

The room was quiet. You couldn't hear a bed squeak in the next room. It was the moment in the script that calls for the actor to walk to the window and stare out, undecided. But there were no windows—only mirrors reflecting sullen whores and mecs and me. I didn't like the looks of a couple of the mecs. I was a captive audience. I took a deep breath and murmured a few words of acceptance. Everybody relaxed.

The man arrived on the dot, and Danielle and three

other girls left the room with him. I sat there talking quietly with Christian. After a few minutes, the madam said, "Now."

She led me into the hall and turned to face me. "Now," she said gravely, "you will see why we are so proud of our girls and why we wish for you to portray them properly."

I followed her down the hall to a room three doors away. We stopped and she guided my eye to a hole in the door. I looked and couldn't believe my eyes. I hardly suppressed a giggle. The activity was frantic. It looked like something Jerome Robbins might have staged. By now the hallway was filled with the other girls and mecs, who had followed to watch me watching. I straightened up and thanked the madam for the lesson.

"No, no, it's no finished," she said as she brought a chair and gently nudged me into it. Seeing how casual everyone was made me relax a little. The activity inside continued.

It was time for the man to make his choice for the finish. He chose Danielle. The other three girls showed no resentment; they simply withdrew to the sidelines on the far side of the room and began filing their nails and talking quietly, completely devoid of emotion or curiosity, as businesslike as three stenographers.

At that point Danielle, hard at work and clearly bored, looked toward the hole in the door and gave me a little wave. That was just a bit too much. I stood up and thanked the madam and the others for their hospitality and went off to wait in one of the bedrooms until Danielle was finished for the night.

At one o'clock her work was over. With Christian translating, we sat on the bed and talked for almost three hours. I asked her to tell me how she got her start. Danielle was twenty-four when I met her and she had been in the business for seven years.

When she was sixteen she worked as a nurse's aide in a Paris hospital. One night a patient came in who changed the course of her life. He was there about two weeks, and during that time they got to know each other quite well. When it was time for him to be discharged, ne asked her how much money she made in the hospital. It was almost nothing.

"Do you like your job?" he asked.

"No," she said. "It is very depressing to be around the sick and the dying."

"I am in love with you, Danielle," he said. "Come and live with me and I will take care of you."

When he left the hospital, she quit her job and went with him. For a while things went well and she was happy. At the end of eight months or so, he said, "Look, we don't have enough money for both of us, and I think it's time you went to work." He was a professional mec, and always snagged his new prostitutes by first hooking them emotionally. He introduced her to another prostitute, and a madam subsequently arranged for her to become a part of the profession.

"Did you mind?" I asked.

"No." She looked surprised. Obviously she felt that sex was totally unimportant, and didn't regard it as a personal matter at all.

"Do you love your mec?" I asked.

"Of course."

"And he loves you, and doesn't mind that you are with thirty-five men a night?"

"No," she shrugged, "of course not. He got me this job and it is a good one. I get paid well and I like my job."

I asked if she enjoyed physical love with her mec.

"Oh, yes," she said, "but not the way I used to."

"What do you mean?" I asked.

She seemed pleased to explain, as though she were answering a question she knew intrigued everyone.

"It's a question of your private place," she said. "My private place isn't here any more." She patted herself and shrugged. "Now my private place is here." She reached up and behind her back, touching the space between her shoulder blades. "When my mec caresses me here, that is all I need. But if a customer accidentally touches this place I stop working immediately and give him his money back."

I was overwhelmed to discover that so necessary was it for a woman to have a private place between herself and the man she loved that she actually transformed nature.

"Most of us have different places," she went on. "My girl friend's place is her hair. No one is allowed to touch it but her mec."

I asked Danielle if she had ambitions to advance in her profession, to become, say, a prostitute on the Champs Élysées. Again she shrugged. "I would like to, of course. But it takes money to get started on the Champs Élysées. I would have to dress more expensively, and the girls there are not permitted to stand around on the sidewalk the way we do in Les Halles. The high-class ones drive around in cars and make their contacts that way."

She went on to tell me that she had a son who lived in the country with a nanny. She didn't know whether his father was her mec or one of her customers.

"Do you support him?" I asked. "Doesn't your mec take everything you earn?"

She nodded. "He does, of course. But whatever I can beg back from him goes toward the care of my son."

I began to probe, searching for something that might express a philosophy or give me some psychological insight into this woman. I suppose I was expecting a dissertation on the honesty and necessity of the oldest profession on earth, and how she was serving the human race in the only way she knew. But it was clear that she hadn't even thought about it. She was polite, even sweet, but after a certain point not very informative. I asked whether she felt she had more compassion for humanity because she accepted all people regardless of their level. She didn't understand what I was getting at and answered over and over again: "I like my job and it pays well."

The conversation dwindled. Her answers were fragmentary, and there were long pauses. She stuck a cigarette into her mouth and tried to light it, but her hand was trembling too violently. I asked what was wrong, although I thought I knew. She didn't answer. Her whole body trembled and her face seemed to come apart. It was like seeing the degeneration of Dorian Gray. She looked at me with a glassy, frantic stare, a look of panic, the look of a trapped animal. Then she bolted from the room. It was the last time I ever saw her.

From the madam we learned that Danielle was a heroin addict. After about two years, far from being happy in her job, she had begun to hate it, and had pleaded with her mec to release her. He refused and instead provided her with something that numbed her body and her mind, something that put her beyond caring what happened to her thirty-five times a night.

Once a mec has a good meal ticket, he allows nothing to take it away. He gets such a stranglehold on the girl that she dares not leave, and if she tries to he might kill her. There have been many murders of this sort.

While the girls work the streets they must depend on their mecs for protection. Girls come from other districts and try to set up shop on ground that already belongs to someone else. They arrive with their own mecs, who fight with switchblades, knives, razors, and even whips. Violent fights are commonplace and often to the death. The stakes are very high.

Once a prostitute becomes a drug addict, the circle is tightly drawn. The money must come from somewhere. The young ones and the old, the pretty and the ugly stand in line, night after night—in pouring rain, in bitter cold, in snow—always wearing the dresses with the long, fast zippers, swaying up a hundred flights of stairs a night, offering their numbed bodies and their deadened souls for their reward—a heroin fix.

A few months later, I put on my green stockings and began to play Irma La Douce. Danielle was never very far from my mind.

I won several awards for my performance of Irma. During a nationally televised awards ceremony I accepted my Golden Globe award by making a little speech. I told the people about my research in Les Halles and how important it had been to me. In fact, I said I enjoyed the research so much I nearly gave up acting. Before I knew it the network had cut my sound off the air and there I was moving my lips with nothing coming out. I wish they had let me finish. I wish they had let me tell it all.

Ten

THE BIGGEST SURPRISE brought by success was that suddenly people were interested in what I thought, not because I was older—I was still in my twenties—or because I knew what I was doing, but because I made $800,000 a picture. It was suddenly O.K. for me to call Samuel Goldwyn "Sam," and William Wyler "Willy." They had been people with a Mr. before their names when I was young-and-nobody, but now that stardom was mine I had become *somebody* and we could communicate as equals.

Success in Hollywood forced me to come face to face with certain things: young or not, ready or not, success forced me to evaluate myself.

Take money for instance. Before Hollywood, I had never had more than fifty dollars I could call "spendable." True, I had never lacked the money for necessities—food and a place to sleep—but luxury money was unknown to me. Now suddenly I had all the luxury money I wanted, but I still acted as though I had only the fifty dollars. I shopped in bargain basements and more often than not bought nothing. Several times I found myself haggling over something that had a fixed price, finally paying the money and leaving the purchase behind on the counter. I felt guilty because I could have what I wanted. I was reluctant to indulge myself, even though I had worked hard for it and economic security had become a reality.

I also found I wanted success and recognition without losing my anonymity. I was haunted by my psychological conditioning as a child to be inconspicuous. It was impossible. I had to adjust to shocking, baseless adulation and an enraging loss of privacy.

Unreasonably, I resented the attention I attracted even though I had fought for it. The most pleasant strangers provoked my fury because they simply looked at me, or watched how I picked up a fork, or stared while I spoke quietly with my daughter, or told me that they had seen the same facial expression on the screen. I felt that it was not their right to stare or to be interested in me. I was wrong, but regardless of how full of admiration their interest might be, I still resented it. I resented my enforced and constant awareness of self; I didn't want to live in a world of only "me."

At first, I reacted with stony hostility, hardly smiling when someone approached me with a compliment. For a while I denied that I was Shirley MacLaine—and I always felt ashamed afterward. After all, how could I call it an invasion of privacy when I had chosen to splash myself across the screen, seeking the applause and approval and attention of strangers?

But I did. I wanted to stand in a supermarket line again with people who were unaware of being observed. I wanted to hear the snatches of personal conversation, notice the way people dressed, the attitudes of their children, and observe the interplay between those who seemed happily married and between those who were miserable. It was all part of what had kept me alive, and it was gone.

I wanted to splash in the waves at Malibu again with Steve and Sachie without being stared at by passersby. Suddenly I felt exposed in a bathing suit, acutely conscious of my white skin that wouldn't tan, embarrassed by my masses of freckles, afraid that my figure might not be what people expected. "Is your mother Shirley MacLaine?" people would ask Sachie. And Sachie would say, "Yes, but she says she's really Shirley Parker." And then she would ask

me, "Why are you so special, Mom?" And I would try to
explain that I wasn't really special—it was my work that
was special. And she would say, "I wish they would leave
us alone so we could play again."

But the stardom I had fought for meant that "they"
would not leave me alone again. And of course I didn't
really want them to. I wanted to be wanted. I needed to
be appreciated. I did what I did to win their approval.
Behind all my resentment, I was terrified that I would
disappoint them.

Instinctively I knew that, if I wanted to maintain an
honest level in my work. I would have to remain vulnerable inside myself. If I built a shell and crawled into it, I
would fail. People want to see reflections of true human
feelings—their own. An actor can only hope to be a mirror
of humanity, a mirror to be looked into by audiences. My
problem was how to keep myself vulnerable and sensitive
while remaining resilient. How to be tough and tender.

As my new values emerged I began to realize that I
had *power*. Money was one thing, fame and recognition
another; both had to be dealt with. But to feel power was
devastating.

I found myself with the power to hire and fire people,
to impose my opinions on others—to be listened to. What
did I think of so-and-so? Did I like his story and the way
it was written? Would I accept so-and-so as my director?
So-and-so needs a job; would I accept him as co-star or
collaborator?

I found myself making decisions because they were
part of my new responsibility. Sometimes my decision
would wreck the life of someone I'd never met. Although
I didn't want to express my opinion—I had never really
learned to respect my own opinion because I always believed someone else knew better—I was forced to because

I was a *star*. And stars, for some reason, are supposed to
know. If they don't, they're supposed to act as though
they do.

The power of my position changed the people I had
known before. Some who had been direct and honest became wary—wary of offending in my presence, and anxious to be assured of my respect and high evaluation.
Others, reacting, became my harshest critics, afraid I might
think they were kowtowing to me. I tried to put my old
acquaintances at ease, to let them know that nothing basic
in me had changed. And I was distressed to discover that
often it was they whom I had changed. My success was
too much for them. They couldn't handle it. I wondered
what they would be like if success had happened to them
instead of to me.

In the years before success and for some time after, I
didn't hear much from or about my brother Warren. He
was busy finishing high school, playing football, and serving as president of his senior class. When he went to
Northwestern University on a football scholarship, I assumed that, like most college students, he would decide
what he wanted to do with his life after he graduated.
But he left Northwestern before he graduated and went
to live in New York. He worked as a sandhog in a tunnel-
digging project and later played the piano in a night club.

When Warren decided to become an actor, it did not
surprise me. Nor did the fact that when he came to Hollywood, chosen by Elia Kazan to play the lead in *Splendor
in the Grass*, he decided he wasn't going to be thought of
as Shirley MacLaine's brother. From the outset he announced that as far as he was concerned "she is Warren
Beatty's sister." I was amused, and thought he was right
to do so. The newspapers thought they smelled conflict.
They tried to create a sibling rivalry, à la Fontaine–De

Havilland or something like that. They would call Warren and tell him something I supposedly had said about him. If he said nothing they would call it a "pregnant pause fraught with meaning." If he said anything at all, usually out of embarrassment at the personal invasion, wham, the comment would appear in a newspaper story. So for a while there was a so-called feud going on that neither of us knew anything about.

It was true that we didn't see a great deal of each other. I was usually traveling or in Japan, and Hollywood was not one of my favorite places to spend free time, whether Warren was there or not. When I was working on a film I rarely saw anybody. So the rumors persisted.

Of course, the times we did spend together went unnoticed because we wanted it that way. We valued our privacy more than anything else. We would reminisce about Washington-Lee High School, the neighborhood pranks, and of course about what had happened to some of our old boy friends and girl friends.

One evening, Warren and Julie Christie had come to dinner at my home in California. We talked far into the evening about each other's childhood—ours in Virginia and hers in India. I heard a car pull up in front of the house. It was about one o'clock in the morning and I wasn't expecting anyone. Suddenly, without knocking or ringing the doorbell, a man opened the front door and walked straight across the living room to me. He put out his hand and said, "Hi, Shirley. Remember me? I'm Jim Hall from the Washington-Lee High School basketball team, and my friends bet me I wouldn't have the guts to drive clear across the country and do this."

I jumped out of the chair, glad my dogs were asleep—they would have chewed him up—and ran to hide behind Warren because I didn't recognize the intruder. When

Jim saw Warren he screamed, "My God, I've really hit the jackpot—Shirley MacLaine and Warren Beatty on the same bet!"

It was almost as though Warren and I were two celebrity freaks instead of a brother and sister who wished to be alone, hoping that whoever wanted to call on us would at least ring the bell.

But after we had both made it in the movies everyone reacted that way. They all seemed fascinated that two people they considered to be of opposing natures could come from the same family. Dad told everybody that was easy to answer. He'd say, "I've always done my best work in bed." Mother would smile, either confirming his statement or wishing that it were true.

Then the curious would say, "But did they both plan to be what they are?" or "Did you know they were that talented then?" or "Did show business run in your family?" Dad always said he had acted as inspiration. He had, in a reverse sort of way. Warren and I usually said it was "just life."

Eleven

AND SO, having adjusted reasonably well to fame, affluence, and power I reached for something more. I did it for survival, because I knew that to feed only on the rich food of my life would make me sick. I realized that it was mandatory for me to acquaint myself more with the outside world. Success is a world closed in on itself. I had to go look beyond it. I could never be anonymous; I knew I'd be carrying all my banners, but I had to go anyway. I had to achieve some sort of balance between myself and others because I was as passionately interested in them as they were in me.

I knew they would tell me their secrets because I was famous, and they would be flattered that I listened. I knew they would welcome me into their homes because they could tell their neighbors tomorrow that I had been there. But I would hold dear their confidences because I would want them to do the same with mine. If they questioned me about myself I would be honest, because if honesty about myself helped them, *I* would feel flattered. If I teased them that it was more difficult for me to be who I was than it was for them to be who they were, they would probably be pleased that I had time to be interested in them at all because I was *somebody*. But I also knew that after the initial newness wore off we would finally relate to each other equally. No one really was different from anyone else anyway. And that's just about how it was. My life expanded and opened up on all levels when I began to travel.

The money I made enabled me to go anywhere in the

world, and my fame opened the doors when I arrived. I was comfortable and taken care of everywhere because I was known. The American movie screen seemed to reach everyone. I felt that everyone was my family because they told me that in my pictures at some point I had entered their lives and hearts, portraying each of them. They said I didn't act like a celebrity, because I traveled alone. And soon they didn't treat me like a celebrity, because I ate and dressed and laughed and lived with them.

I found myself asking incessant questions about everything—sometimes bluntly, sometimes with finesse. English was fairly well spoken everywhere—enough to communicate, anyway—but the real communication, I found, was nonverbal. It didn't much matter what people said, it was the passion behind the words, or the lack of passion. Sometimes their silences were more revealing than their outbursts. Their laughter and intimacies with each other, which eventually included me, drew me into their worlds, their viewpoints, their concepts of life, death, happiness, their sense of honor, their systems of what was important and what wasn't . . . Asians, Indians, Russians, Arabs, Himalayan mountain people—even Japanese Indians made me realize how narrow and limited my horizons had been all my life. From a tree-lined suburb in Virginia, or a sprawling ranch house in sunny California, the world can seem a very different place from what it really is. One's version of the truth is so much clearer when one has only one view of it. As I traveled, I began to learn that truth is relative. I had always believed that what was right was right, period. That what I had been taught was wrong *was* simply wrong. That the truth was tidy and indeed easy to understand once you'd been *taught* to understand what the truth was.

But that, alas, is not what I found. Because not only was the truth relative, but it kept changing. One person's truth was not another person's—and none of them bore any relation to the truth back home. And what I thought were answers to my questions only seemed to be springboards for more questions. There are so many truths— one just as valid as another.

So in order to make even a stab at understanding what I learned and saw as I traveled, I had to reject nearly everything that had conditioned my moral ethics growing up in America. In fact, where understanding the relativity of truth was concerned, moral ethics, as I had been taught them, were a nuisance. What I had always considered morally wrong in a given circumstance was not necessarily so to others in the same circumstance. And the more I was a witness to the differences in morality, the more I realized that nothing was absolute. Nothing was absolutely right or absolutely wrong. My background had taught me the opposite. In the Western, Christian ethic there were lots of things that were absolutely wrong—no question about it—like stealing, lying, cheating, killing, and so on and so on. But that was only the world I had come from. There were lots of other worlds that made up the human race. And in some cases those actions were not only ignored but admired. They were often part of an ancient, ongoing culture. If they were encouraged and admired, they certainly weren't morally wrong to that particular society—so *my* point of view of *them* was irrelevant to *their* truth. It was difficult for me to suspend my ethics while trying to understand theirs, but in the process an amazing thing happened. I began to get more of a distant, objective view of *myself.* My own truth became better defined. I understood more of me while trying to understand them. And it made me more compassionate; not only for others but for myself as well.

Of course my traditional, American value system got knocked into a cocked hat as I traveled the worlds that made up the earth. Having addressed myself to success, getting money, getting property, getting things, and getting a chance to do more of the same most of my life, I felt fairly stupid fairly soon. What did so much of that have to do with living really? Okay, so you needed enough of it—but somehow from my world so few people understood when "enough" was theirs. Most always wanted more . . . and then more . . . so that living got lost and getting more became everything. I thought so many times as I wandered how fulfilling it would be for those people who had saved their money for a new car to buy a round-the-world plane ticket instead and go out and look at the world.

Some of what I saw was pleasant and some was incomprehensible. But all of it broadened my own understanding—not only of others but of myself as well.

At a Buddhist temple in Bangkok I met an old lama, dressed in his saffron robes, lying on a straw mat at the feet of the huge brass Buddha which presided inside the temple. The lama lived between the feet of the Buddha. Beside his mat was a low, delicately carved table. On the table were an alarm clock, sleeping pills, a box of Kleenex, and a few comic books. His begging bowl rested on the floor. When I entered the temple, the lama bowed and gestured for me to sit and be comfortable, and for an hour he spoke in broken English of the tranquillity of meditation and the reverence for all living things a Buddhist must make his religion. He spoke of the serenity and love of peace of the Thai people. The word Thailand itself means "land of peace."

I listened enraptured by his calm and gentle philosophy, then I said good-by and left the temple. The friendly lama retreated to his straw mat and wound his alarm clock.

The temple was beside a klong and I had come there

by canoe. Now, gliding back to Bangkok, I could see the day's activity of the klong dwellers in full progress. People sold vegetables and fruits and other wares from their canoes. Children played and splashed while their parents bargained.

Suddenly, not more than two hundred feet from me, a very young baby, an infant of perhaps three months, leaned over the side of the family canoe and toppled head first into the klong. I strained my eyes to find the child. Its parents heard the gurgle and turned around. Neither made a move to go after him. The child disappeared. With static expressions they watched their baby drown. I could see that their lack of reaction was genuine. I sat stunned. I had learned that many Buddhists will not interfere with what they believe is preordained fate. But to actually witness such a thing was staggering. This death was the will of God and, if the parents had jumped in after the child, they would have placed the child in a position of obligation for the rest of its life. The child's life would have belonged, from that day on, to its rescuer, and that was one fate a Buddhist would never inflict on another. I remembered how often I had heard that life was cheap in Asia. But that wasn't really it. To a Buddhist, death is only another form of life. Death is part of the cycle of life. Life and death are not regarded in terms of individual people—it covers a broader philosophic spectrum. Fate is their religion. The fate of the drowned child was not to be interfered with. It was accepted. By the same token killing is abhorred, because the act of killing interferes with the higher fate also. There was a profound philosophical difference between killing and allowing death to happen. However to have actually killed the child or even an animal was beyond a Buddhist's comprehension. Hence: Because death was accepted didn't necessarily mean life was cheap.

Some days later I went to a Thai boxing match. Boxing is to Thailand what baseball is to America. It is the national sport, and during the match anything is legal. What distinguishes Thai boxing from any other kind is that kicking, anywhere and any way, is legal. The boxers wear groin cups but are otherwise unprotected.

A ceremony begins the match. The two boxers enter the ring and perform reverences to Rama (the ancient Thai king) and Buddha. Each prays for the well-being of his opponent, not himself. With ritualistic dance movements and stylized religious pantomime the boxers seem concerned about carrying out the sport in benevolent fashion.

A group of musicians begin an accompaniment when the boxers say a last prayer for their opponent's well-being. The people are primed as the highly pitched music plays and the boxers leave their corners, meet in the center of the ring and proceed to smash, jab, pummel, and kick each other with both fists and feet. No holds are barred.

During the first Thai boxing match I saw I was sick. One boxer kicked the other in the head and snapped his neck and broke it. Of course he died in his tracks. The people went wild with enthusiasm, the peaceful Thai people. Two new boxers took their places, went through the ritualistic praying and dancing and miming, and began combat. One sliced the other across the forehead with his elbow. The skin on the forehead gaped open, blood poured down his face. The roar of the crowd at the sight of blood was deafening. They shouted their approval above the sound of the musicians, who could hardly contain themselves either. A doctor mediator was summoned from behind the ropes to survey the gaping forehead. The crowd shouted, "No, let him fight." The wounded boxer stamped his foot at the doctor to let him continue. The doctor looked up at the crowd and agreed.

Now, with renewed anger the wounded boxer attacked his opponent, his blood smearing his own face and the hands and feet of his adversary, who was kicking the head wound open further. The blood of the two men began to mix; each was badly wounded now, until finally the doctor rushed into the ring, to the fury of the crowd, and ordered two stretchers. Stretchers are always available and were kept close by. Attendants carried out the two boxers, whose heads looked more like blobs of protoplasm than faces.

How the placid, peaceful Thai people found entertainment in such violence was incongruous to me; their national sport was known to be the most bloodthirsty on earth. Then I began to speculate that perhaps one of the reasons the Thais lived and functioned comparatively peacefully with each other in their daily lives was that their incredibly popular national sport gave them an outlet for latent hostility and rage that surge in all of us. Perhaps violent sports were necessary and more preferable than the other things human beings could do to each other.

The paradox of Thailand made me realize once again the disparity between what I had conceived things to be like and what they were *really* like. Over and over I would discover how parochial were the values and axioms I had learned from my limited environment, my parents, the schools I had attended, the neighborhoods where I had spent my childhood, and the churches which, fortunately, I hadn't attended very often.

Of all my early misconceptions, those having to do with race must be ranked as the most jarring, and the most personally offensive to me, because the truth as I learned it was so directly in conflict with the "truth" I had been taught as a child, mainly by my father—my intelligent father, who adored philosophy, art, and music, who was a dedicated and highly respected school principal and teacher, and who referred to anyone with dark skin as a "nigger." His tone of disapproval varied in direct ratio to the blackness. His prejudice included African, Indian, or South American, and even crept into his opinion of suntans. "Those nigger natives would as soon eat you as look at you. They stay in the sun all day," he'd say, "because they don't know any better, but a civilized man builds himself a house and goes into it." Anyone who tanned quickly was suspect and extra-curly hair meant, "Nigger blood in 'em."

Although I was born below the Mason-Dixon Line, and was surrounded by black people, I never really knew any until years later. As a child, I saw them as a group, as a mass, never as individuals. I never imagined that they lived anywhere in particular, or had families or lives of their own—perhaps because they seemed to spend most of their time doing things for white people.

When I visited the Deep South years later, it was as strange to me as Thailand.

Mississippi was another planet—because I was living with black people and trying to see their world through their eyes—and it's true: you can't know unless you're black. It was in the early stages of the activities of the Student Non-Violent Coordinating Committee (SNCC) in the South that I began traveling through Mississippi to witness what went on during the voter registration drive and school desegregation.

It seemed that every white male there, no matter what his work was, was a member of the KKK. One evening in Rolling Fork, Mississippi, two white men seized a black man whose daughter had registered at a desegregated school, tied him to the back of a truck, and dragged him through the black ghetto as an example for anyone else who dared attempt such a thing. That same night I sat up with a man and his wife who had just gotten word that their seventeen-year-old son had been found, bound in heavy chains, at the bottom of a nearby swamp.

In Issaquena County about one and a half hours from Jackson, Mississippi, I stayed with a woman named Mrs. Unida Blackwell. Unida was blue-back and a stately, pliably dignified example of what black women can become if they believe in themselves. For hours we sat drinking beer and philosophizing about the suppression of women. She was speaking as a black woman, certainly, but more importantly she saw the plight of all women as a universal disaster. They put up with too much, she said—not only black women but all women, because they had bought the myth that they weren't equal to their male counterparts.

"I didn't want to be one of those women who sticks pretty shells on ashtrays for something to do," she said. "I wanted to get out and make contact and make some changes—changes that count—and that's what I'm doing."

Unida was the most celebrated civil-rights worker in the Mississippi back country. She had been arrested many times, her phone was tapped, and while I was there the KKK twice burned crosses in front of her house because there was a white woman inside.

Unida introduced me to several young women who had been arrested repeatedly during their civil-rights work. They described the wire-brush scrubbings they were given and the cells where the heat was turned on full blast in the summertime and off in the winter. They described the small doses of arsenic in the food—just enough to make them violently nauseated but not enough to kill; the humiliation of having their clothes taken away for days at a time and being left naked.

In Unida Blackwell's house there was only one bed. The SNCC workers and I slept in shifts, usually four in the bed. Unida's son, Joshua, slept in the living room in a chair. Unida's husband was working as a cook on a Mississippi river boat.

Her family seemed to understand that she was very special and tried hard to live up to her courage.

During those days with Unida, whenever we drove in daylight around the countryside to talk to people about registering, there were always a few of the guys along to keep an eye out for sheriff cars. And whenever one was spotted there was a yell and I was pushed to the floor. The law-enforcement officers of Issaquena County went ding-a-ling whenever they saw a white woman associating with black men. To avoid a lot of trouble it was better to keep me out of sight. For seven days and most of the seven nights all of us lived together. I'd purchase food at the neighborhood white-run market, so high-priced that I was out of money by the end of the week. We ate together, drank, talked, cried, and laughed together. It was a time of communication I'll remember always. I thought of my father often and wondered if a compassionate man like him wouldn't secretly be more attracted than repelled at hearing this experience. The people I met were warm and roughly humorous about themselves. They were kind and willing to be relatively patient with the rage of the white people surrounding them. They would plod through the summer of damp swelter, trying to keep their demands in check, hoping to convince the whites that they didn't want to hurt anybody, that they only wanted a piece of the action.

Unida is keeping the faith her way in Issaquena even today. I saw her again in Chicago at the 1968 Democratic Convention, where she was a delegate from Mississippi and I was a delegate from California. We teased each other about being militant women who wanted to change the world. Then we proceeded to be flattened by what we had come to Chicago believing was the prevailing democratic American process. We left understanding that what we got instead was the steamroller of American fascism.

After Mississippi, I went back to Virginia to visit with my parents for a few days. As soon as I got back home I began to tell my mother and father some of the things I'd seen in Mississippi. My father's response was "Don't you want to have a nice, long, hot shower before you tell us—we just had the upholstery cleaned."

I wondered if he knew—actually was aware of—what goes on. At first he didn't even seem to be listening as I talked. I didn't realize he was holding up his invisible protective shield—for the last time, as it turned out.

I told him about a girl named Thelma, and as I described her experience on her first day of school, his expression began to change. Thelma was twenty years old, and by then her "separate but equal" black school had prepared her for the eighth grade in the desegregated white school. I told Dad how the teacher made Thelma stand beside her chair until everyone in the class had been seated. As each youngster took his chair he walked by Thelma's chair and spit in it. By the time the classroom had assembled and seated itself there was a puddle of spit in Thelma's chair. The teacher told her she could be seated. Thelma was wearing a pink linen skirt that she and her mother had sacrificed a great deal for. But she was afraid and so she did as she was told. When class was over Thelma was ordered to stand beside her chair until the rest of the class had dispersed. As the youngsters came down Thelma's aisle, each gave her a jab in the ribs. Thelma said the jabs hurt but mostly she was ashamed that she had thought she could come to classes in a white school in the first place.

Dad listened to my story about Thelma with clenched teeth, and when it was over I could see tears streaming down his face. He slumped deeper into his favorite chair like an old man and said, "God, I want to change, but it's so hard—I think I'll die first."

I stood looking at him for a moment longer and then walked over to the windows. One by one I tried to open them. They wouldn't budge. "They won't open," my father said.

I turned around surprised. "What do you mean they won't open?" I asked.

"They just won't. They never have and they just won't."

"Have you ever tried to get them open?" I asked.

He looked at me vacantly. "I don't know—they've just never been open—so don't try to open them."

Mother came in from the kitchen, tall and thin, with a flowered apron around her waist and meat loaf on her hands. (Meat loaf had been my favorite dish when I was little.)

"Why aren't those windows open?" I asked. "It's hot this afternoon and there's a breeze outside that would help."

Her eyes stopped dancing and she quickly darted a look toward my father. "I don't know," she said. "Daddy says they've never been open."

Twelve

IN TRAVELING THROUGH the South I also had an opportunity to meet a leading black activist, a powerful man in SNCC. I shall call him Ralph Frazier. A friend had arranged for him to meet me. He was waiting for me behind a pillar in the public terminal of the Atlanta airport. He didn't come to the gate where the passengers disembarked. I didn't see any black people there, so I don't know if he wasn't permitted at the gate or if he didn't want to come.

I didn't know what Ralph would look like. I only knew he would meet me. I saw a massive, but not terribly tall, black man with bushy hair (long before it became fashionable) wearing a black-and-red-checkered lumberjacket. He didn't just stand behind the pillar; he seemed to lurk. He saw me but said nothing. I kept walking.

After a while my suitcase arrived at the baggage section. I picked it up, wondering what to do, when I felt a hand take it from me and lead me out the revolving door. It was the man in the red-and-black lumberjacket.

"I'm Frazier," he said. "I'm a friend of yours," and he led me to a broken-down station wagon where three other black men waited. Behind the station wagon was a green Dodge, which followed us as we took off.

"We always travel in two cars," he said. "You can't tell what the police will stop us for—especially if they see a white woman in the car with us. They arrested someone last night for having a faulty windshield wiper because they couldn't find anything else to bring him in on. Want to see a *nigger* party?" he asked me with a wink. He had borne down hard on the word, in a voice heavy with irony. I smiled.

"Sure," I said. We both relaxed.

With my suitcase jiggling around in the back I didn't know where I was going to sleep that night—and I didn't ask. It didn't really make any difference if I slept at all.

We drove through the heart of Atlanta and into the ghetto to a small house. I could hear laughter. I touched Ralph's arm and he said, "It's cool," and I relaxed again as the back door opened and a spray of beer spewed out at us and somebody handed me a can of Schlitz.

A record player was going with what would soon be called soul music, and everybody in the living room (furnished with one chair and four orange crates) was gyrating. Their bodies jerked and undulated in movements unlike any dancing I had ever seen. The dancing the black kids were doing was free-form. At times it was an ugly movement—on-purpose ugly, I think—as though they were in love with ugliness—as though they were dancing the distortions they felt. Their heads jerked up and down, seeming to say, "Uh, huh, enough, enough—tell it, tell it—tell it like it is"—and then they'd stop moving altogether on some accented beat and wait—wait until some spirit moved them again and they had something else to say. The kids were watching each other; every gesture meant something and if you couldn't be sure of what their hips and elbows and strutting shoulders were saying you could look in their eyes and find it. It was soul dancing laid out bare, and every movement was full of protest. Some of the kids had bloodshot eyes from too much beer (there was only beer, no hard booze). There was a poker game going on at a long, wooden picnic table.

Ralph pulled a folding chair over to the table and took over the poker game as we sat down and he said, "This here's Shirley." If anyone recognized me they didn't acknowledge it. Ralph didn't introduce anyone to me. He knew I was too off balance to remember their names, so he didn't bother.

The dancing kids kept dancing. They were grooving to the records.

Ralph picked up a hand of cards and began running soul commentary on bluffing. His voice took on a new timbre and he sounded as though he were preaching. At the end of his sermon on bluff he said, "A-men, brothers," and everybody A-mened him and nodded. I didn't know how to play poker so I watched. It was another world. A kind of tribal world where everyone understood each other without words. They seemed to live, eat, breathe, and groove on the same wave length, not resenting that I was in their midst but aware every moment that everything about me was different. I was an outsider.

Someone changed the record to a slower soul-grinding beat and I couldn't contain myself any longer. I didn't know what it would mean if I got up on my own and danced with whoever wanted to but I did it anyway. I could never resist dancing anywhere, any time.

The poker game continued as I moved away into the bare, hollow-sounding living room. One of the guys on the floor caught my eye and began to sway and bump his hips toward me. He had a rotund body with a great roly-poly fanny. He was John Lewis, the secretary of SNCC, and one day he would be castigated by his own people for not being militant enough. There was nothing militant about John; he was all love and soul and just to be with him made you smile inside, even though you knew he'd never make it because he was too sweet.

His dancing was laced with mischief. We grooved to the center of the floor and in two minutes were putting on a show. I had never met him before but felt I had known him all my life. Up and down, around and in and out we jerked and undulated and tripped out. I could see the others grin and nod as they watched us, lost in the movement. After an hour I was dripping with sweat and John was passed out cold on the one chair.

At four-thirty I still didn't know where I would sleep and I guessed Ralph didn't know either. A few of us got back in the station wagon and drove to John's apartment. The other guys said goodnight, "glad to have you with us," and Ralph carried my suitcase up the stairs of the brick building and ushered me inside.

It was then I learned that Ralph Frazier didn't live anywhere. As the head of SNCC he gave all the money he made to the black movement, and wherever he happened to be he was at home, sometimes sleeping in a different place every night. On this night it looked like John Lewis's apartment was the place. John, still stoned in the chair, was back at the party.

I looked around the small living room at the bookshelves. They were stacked with books on the Bolshevik Revolution, Marxist planning, and similar subjects. One picture of a pastoral countryside hung slightly crooked on the wall over a couch with broken legs.

There was an alcove kitchen with a small stove and a small refrigerator, inside which was a half pint of half-and-half and a lemon.

The bathroom shower dripped onto a pile of damp and smelly laundry. The tiny bedroom had a double bed, unmade, with sheets gray with dirt. In the corner were stacks of old magazines and newspapers. I thought, John certainly could use a woman around the house. Behind the newspapers was a folded-up cot. I breathed a sigh of relief. That was something Ralph could use.

As he pulled out the cot into the living room, Ralph said we should get a good night's sleep because he had lots to talk to me about in the morning. The morning was only two hours away when I closed my eyes, still reminding myself it was America outside.

When I woke up and came out of the bedroom, Ralph was gone. I moved the laundry out of the tub and took a shower. I got dressed and packed and closed my suitcases. I didn't know whether I'd be staying there or moving on. It didn't matter really, since everyone else was living that way too.

Ralph lumbered up the stairs with a bag of eggs, bacon, frozen orange juice, and half a loaf of bread. I cooked breakfast as he watched, and after we ate, he asked me to come with him to make a phone call at the corner market because John didn't have a phone.

We walked out into the sunshine, and the first thing I heard was a shout from a car cruising by. A young white girl was leaning out the window. "Hey, nigger lover, how was it?" she shouted. I couldn't believe what I heard and Ralph winced. "I'm sorry you had to hear that," he said, "but that's how it will be while you're here with us."

The manager of the store was white, and when we walked in together, his expression was pure hate. Ralph walked right up to him and asked for change but I was so intimidated I went outside to wait.

On the way back to the apartment someone else yelled "nigger lover," and Ralph suggested we sit on the brick wall in front of the building and talk.

"Do you know how much sex has to do with this thing we call racism?" he asked. "You wouldn't know because you've never been tempted by it—at least, not that you're aware of—but it's there. . . . Do you know," he said, "what it's like to be conditioned to love and desire everything that's pure and white? To believe from the time you're a small child that everything black is bad and everything white is good. It's basic, even with our language analogies. 'Blackmail,' 'a black day,' 'a black-and-white situation,' 'don't look on the black side of life.' And white always means purity and goodness and sunshine and honesty. The advertisements on television are always brought to us by beautiful, pure, lily-white, usually blonde women. From the time I was old enough to remember, I was in love with white women because they always brought me the message of a better life.

"Well, do you understand—can you realize—what that does to a young black man's mind when he's been teased by white women all his life and grows up and finds that the image he's been haunted by is the one thing he's not allowed to have? Stick to your own kind they tell us when our imaginations and fantasies long for soft pure white skins and everything they represent. Our girls seem rough and harsh to us, with skin like leather and hair like Brillo because we've been conditioned by the opposite. So you know what that does to our women—when they realize they're not as attractive to us as white women? They try to straighten their hair, lighten their skin, and be any way they can like the white woman—except it never works.

"And then double confusion sets in when they become aware that they are secretly fantasized by the white men. And they have a lot of evidence to prove it. So many of the bigoted white men here in the South with upstanding credentials and fine white southern families have black women for mistresses. Always being laid in secret, never openly, and producing clandestine second families with a bunch of little bastards running around. So it gets all mixed up. The open conditioning that society endorses, counterpointed with the forbidden pleasures that bigotry makes tempting. I guess you don't know what went through my mind last night with you all stretched out in your white loveliness in the next room, do you?"

I shook my head, which was a lie.

"You know the only way a black man can be accepted in your world?"

I shook my head again.

"It's if he has either brains and no balls—or balls and no brains. If he's got both he's too much of a threat. Ralph Bunche is O.K. because he lives from the neck up. Joe Louis or Rafer Johnson is O.K. because they live from the neck down. So we have acceptable scholars or acceptable athletes. An actor can make it if he plays a good nigger— but he's got to be perfect. Put a regular man up there, with all his faults and weaknesses and meannesses, and he's black and nobody buys it. Unless he is all 'black' or a slave; that they'll buy."

I thought of Sidney Poitier. He was always perfect, like the great black prince who rides into our lives telling us there's nothing to fear from the black man because he's all goodness and forgiveness and understanding, and it's O.K. to make him one of us now because he's forgiven us our transgressions and we'll all live happily ever after.

Another car drove by and someone shouted in a thick Southern drawl, "Kiss the nigger's ass and he'll get yours."

Ralph just shrugged. "Right now," he said, "I'm going through a divorce, and I'm involved with a white woman. I don't know what's real about my feelings for her or whether it's really conditioning that makes me want her. And I feel guilty that I'm leading SNCC here in the South while I'm hung up on a white woman. Looks like I'm going to have to make a choice because my own people won't understand me doing both. So you see the sex hangup is a big part of the problems whites and blacks have with each other."

He got up and led me to get my suitcase. "We'll be platonic friends," he said, "but I want you to know what I'm thinking."

I would have liked to tell my father about my talk with Ralph but I knew it would have made him sick. People like my Dad could barely countenance social intercourse between whites and blacks, much less sexual intercourse.

What was it about black people that frightened him? He would justify the prejudice all he wanted; it still meant *he* was *afraid*. Of what? Himself certainly. But why did he focus his own personal fear on the skin of another? Perhaps because he was afraid of the dark. Perhaps he could justify his bigotry because blacks were the color of the night. Somehow he felt safe in the daylight and with white people.

On the other hand, a black person would rise in his estimation if he had money. In fact anyone who had money received his praise regardless of how he got it. Why did that make so much difference? Dad knew what it took to get rich sometimes, and he used to talk so much about honor and trust. He would trust a man down to the buckles of his shoes if the man told him the truth, and if he was honorable in business he'd defend him against "hell fire and damnation." He had always demanded honor and trust. And if someone was black but rich and recognized Dad would call him a "colored man" instead of a "nigger." Why?

However, when he was deeply moved by honest emotion instead of what had conditioned him, he was his real self. I remember when our whole family went to see the all-Negro play *Raisin in the Sun.* I remember the male lead falling to his knees in front of his mother, wife, and sister, pleading for understanding for making their black lives more difficult because he had to be recognized as a man—a man who stood up for what he believed was right. And he felt that being the only Negro in the white neighborhood was right. My father understood him and everything in him cried out in agreement. I could see it. And when it was over I saw his shoulders shaking.

I think my father cried, even after the lights went up, because he wanted to believe what he honestly felt. He didn't like the feeling he had been taught, and his conflict was awful to watch. And I loved him very much then because he was trying to be what he really was. He didn't like feeling bigoted. He never used "nigger" when he referred to that play again—that is, until we left New York and he went back to his office in Virginia and someone said, "Yes, those niggers when they act, they really act."

But some years later when I told him the leading man, Sidney Poitier, was a friend of mine and asked if I could bring him home for dinner, Dad refused to have him. "It's not that *I* wouldn't be delighted," he said. "It's the neighbors. . . . I have to live here when dinner is over. You don't."

And so Sidney Poitier never came to dinner—and Dad never reached down and grabbed the real man inside himself, because he was afraid—afraid somehow of the dark—afraid of the darkness in himself.

Thirteen

THE MORE I TRAVELED the more I realized that fear makes strangers of people who should be friends.

Once for a period of one month I knew what it meant to be totally without fear. What I felt instead was harmony, honor, and complete trust of another people. They happened to be black people. They weren't civilized. They were primitive. And they themselves were the most nearly fearless humans I have ever known. Lying was beyond their comprehension and they believed in themselves. God didn't exist for them and the only thing they feared was nature. Their self-confidence was absolute and their arrogance was justified. They were the Masai tribe of East Africa.

I had been invited to join a safari. After a year of hard work in pictures, I longed for the outdoors and open skies, and the prospect of venturing really close to the wild animals of Africa thrilled me. Having lived in clustered cities most of my life, I dropped everything and accepted the invitation. I arrived in Nairobi with my camera and bush hat to find that the safari was already out and because of recent torrential rains had bogged down in mud. A rendezvous had been set up in what was then Tanganyika, in two weeks.

Uhuru (freedom) had been recent in East Africa; independence a reality. Jomo Kenyatta had reinstated the Mau Mau to respectable African society and the winds of change were blowing in the white man's face. White landowners who had claimed Africa as their own were leaving. Families split up and fortunes were forfeited. Bitter divisions split the ranks of the Africans themselves. The times were dark and confusing to an outsider.

I checked into the Farm Hotel in Limuru, two hours from Nairobi. It was run by an elderly French couple who thirty years before had come to Africa on safari, planning to spend only two weeks. They had stuck it out through the Mau Mau emergency and now nothing could wrest them away from the land that continued to spellbind them.

In the midst of the chaos of Uhuru stood the Masai. They are a warrior tribe, and their lands extend far to the north and south. Refusing to adapt to the white man's world, they prefer death to civilization. And dying they are—from the white man's disease. Syphilis is so rampant that it has been estimated the Masai will become extinct within fifty years. Fiercely independent, the Masai feel they are the élite among men. Their independence is directed not only at the world of the white man, but also at their neighboring tribesmen. And the justification for such independence is considerable.

My Land-Rover lurched over rutted gullies created by the recent downpour. I had learned to drive it because I wanted to be alone on my visit to the Masai village.

My safari hat, purchased in Nairobi, made a thick round ring of sweat against my head. But without a hat and the dark glasses I was lost—dizzy, irritable, blind from the glare of the merciless sun. My high leather boots would protect me from the cruel jaws of the huge safari ants, and I had insect spray to bombard the mosquitoes when I was out after sundown. How I hated to need all the paraphernalia because I couldn't cope with the natural elements. I wondered how I looked to the natural earth livers around me in all my protective clothing.

Africa sprawled before me. The undulating plains were alive with animals—antelope, dik-dik, zebra, wildebeest, warthog, and the inevitable vultures circling above waiting for a final heartbeat.

It was a circus without a tent; without brass bands and popcorn. The animals leaped with what looked like unfounded joy to me but to them was simply the way they always felt. A graceful little impala scampered after his lumpy warthog neighbor until the warthog turned around and snorted, and the chase was on in the opposite direction. Two zebra stallions fought for the affection of a mare. The winner was tacitly recognized. Baby baboons exchanged mothers until they were scolded in baboon language and told that it was time to play in their own backyards. The animals seemed to obey laws of their own society.

Africa seemed the harmonious voice of creation. Everything alive was inextricably intertwined until death. And even death was part of the life harmony.

Three lean Masai, each standing on one leg, like a stork, and supported by his spear, stood against the African horizon. Their orange cloths flapped in the breeze as they surveyed their cattle. The Masai believe their purpose in life is to herd the earth's cattle into their corrals; their entire existence centers around their precious beasts.

When they saw the dust rise from the tracks of my Land-Rover, they faced in my direction and without moving they watched quietly as I stopped and got out.

"*Jambo*," I said with forced brightness, and put out my hand. Layers of crusted blood covered their lips, serving up a tasty treat for the flies that swarmed in the corners of their mouths. They didn't blink when flies marched across their eyeballs. The Masai rarely eat solid food. They subsist on a mixture of milk and blood drawn from their cattle through a thin reed inserted in a hole pierced in the jugular vein.

Nestled against a rolling hill, the Masai *menyatta*

formed a circle of huts around the corral in the center. In the little Swahili I had learned I asked if I could please visit the *menyatta.*

They glanced at the Land-Rover and asked skeptically if I was alone. When I said Yes they welcomed me. Because I was defenseless they trusted me. If I had had the "protection" of companions, I suspect I would not have been welcomed at all.

Obviously enjoying the white man's ritual of shaking hands, they led me into the *menyatta.* The wind shifted, bringing a smell that would be identifiable to me for the rest of my time in Africa: dung—fresh, smoking dung—everywhere. Mixed with mud while still wet, then molded into cakes and dried, it forms the walls of the huts and provides perfect breeding grounds for the flies.

The huts are round. Each has a small opening covered with a flap of lion skin, which was obtained when the Masai male, in order to become a warrior (*moranee*), killed a lion single-handedly, demonstrating his skill and bravery in the struggle.

With graceful strides, the *moranee* led me to the hut of the chief. Other members of the tribe spilled from smoky huts as I passed. Evidently fires burn continuously inside the huts, and I wondered how the people could breathe. There are no windows and the ceilings are so low it is impossible to stand up inside. Only by doubling over at the waist can one enter the smoky openings. Perhaps the huts are constructed for warmth at the expense of fresh air.

Squalling babies and children at play rushed to the sides of their mothers and gawked in silence as I was led through the *menyatta.* For the most part the Masai children wear no clothing, but the women are clothed and laden with ornaments. Orange cloth is caught up at the left shoulder and bound at the waist with handmade belts

of beads. Their necks are laden with elaborate beaded
jewelry, the arrangement indicating each woman's marital
status. The promised brides wear less jewelry than those
who have already married and borne children. The beads
seemed to be painted plastic, probably purchased at one
of the Indian dukas sprinkled across the plains. Gay,
vibrant colors delight Africans of any tribe, and the Masai
are no exception. I longed to use my camera, but I had
read that the tribe has a deathly fear of it, believing that
the small box robs the subject of his soul and transfers
it to the glossy negative.

The chief—and absolute dictator—stepped from his
hut and offered me a gourd of blood and milk. For a
moment I panicked, not only because of the mixture, but
because I knew that the cattle were diseased. I stared at
the ground. "Don't think too long," I thought, "or the
damage will be done." I lifted the gourd and took a small
sip, holding it to my lips for a long time, hoping they
would believe it was a deep guzzle. I swallowed. The milk
was thin and low in butterfat from the scrawny, bloodlet
cattle. The blood tasted like blood, except for a little dash
of what I later discovered was urine, used to prevent the
milk from curdling in the hot sun.

Smiles broke out on the faces of the chief and his con-
stituents. The chief removed the gourd from my hand—
thank goodness. Evidently the sip was accepted as a gesture of friendly intent.

He put out his right hand and said in English, "Good."
I looked up in surprise.

His wizened face was firm but seemed kind. Grayish,
kinky hair played over his ears, which had been pierced
and stretched until loops of skin hung to his shoulders.
All members of the tribe sported gaping holes in their
lobes, which had been pierced at birth and enlarged

throughout childhood by larger and larger wooden plugs. The earrings worn by the adults varied from arrangements of beads and wire to pieces of cork and wood. The chief, however, had decided on a can opener. It hung from his left ear and I had the impression he was continually in search of its mate for his right ear.

"What you name?" he questioned me in stilted but clear English.

"Shirley," I answered, flabbergasted that he would be able to talk at all.

He hesitated, trying to form the word in his mouth. "Sss . . . Sss . . . Shuri?"

"Yes, sir, Shuri." It was fine with me.

"Shuri . . . Shuri . . . Shuri. . . ." Whispers of the strange name circulated through the *menyatta*.

The chief gestured toward one of the *moranee*. A warrior of about nineteen stepped forward. Pepsi-Cola bottle tops hung on wires from his ears. Placing his spear in the ground, he stood at attention, Masai style.

The chief spoke. "Name Kijimbele. English speak. Help you." Kijimbele's eyes darted in my direction. A grotesque scar ravaged one side of his head from his hairline to the bottom of his chin. I must have shown my horror.

"*Simba,*" said the chief, explaining that it was the result of Kijimbele's encounter with his lion-of-manhood. It proved to be one of many scars borne proudly by *moranee* of the tribe. On some, eyes had been totally gouged out and had healed without the aid of medicine. Some had useless limbs with severed tendons, while other limbs had been torn out by the sockets. And of course there were skeletons, picked clean by the vultures, of those who had lost the battle.

Honor is essential to a Masai—more revered than life.

The method of fair play during combat with the lion is as important as victory. The *moranee* has one opportunity as he rushes headlong toward the beast with his spear poised. If the plunge is a direct hit, his future and society's respect are assured. If he misses, the ensuing struggle is his alone, witnessed by his fellow warriors. They might beat the bushes to confuse the ferocious beast, but nothing more. When a *moranee* emerges the victor, his worth in courage having been evaluated, he lives as a proud and strong man, and example too. The primitive code of ethics seemed cruel to me but it was necessary to the Masai's sense of self.

Kijimbele smiled with perfectly shaped milk-white teeth.

"I have Mickey Mouse watch. One hand off. You fix?" He proudly removed the trinket that encircled his upper arm and with childish delight held it up.

"Yes, I'll take it to Nairobi."

"Most treasure," he warned. I guessed that he had picked it up from the remains of a safari, along with his bottle tops and the chief's can opener. He brandished it proudly as he escorted me through the *menyatta*.

Standing in silent lines, the warriors of the tribe watched as Kijimbele introduced me to the tribe. Black faces regarded me impassively. I had the feeling they held secrets I would never know. They knew the meaning of fear, and they knew the prevention of it. Fear is despised. Perhaps that is what they sense in the white man—fear. And perhaps that is what lies behind their refusal to accept any of the white man's ways. Perhaps they recognize that fear breeds dishonor, cheating, and lies, all of which are anathema to them. They approve of the tangible results of what is called civilization, but the methods by which they are attained are contemptible. I wondered if they would accept me or whether I would be condemned from the outset.

The women are tall, slim, and slightly swaybacked, possibly from many pregnancies. Their heads are shaven clean—a mark of beauty—and glisten with orange ochre.

Streams of spit flash every few seconds through an aperture each has in her upper teeth, straight and sure, never dripping, and always coming to rest on a small circle of dung. The Masai are mortally afraid of lockjaw, and during childhood one of the upper front cuspid teeth is wrenched loose, leaving a permanent gap through which the victim can be fed should lockjaw strike. And it often does.

I stopped to gaze unabashedly into the mouth of one of the women. She giggled and pointed to my hand. I didn't understand. She lifted one of my fingers and caressed one of the pink, polished nails. Her child saw her touch me and screamed in consternation. Clearly, few of the children had seen a white person so close before. With noses running, bellies protruding, and eyes wide in disbelief, they crowded around me to stare. Intrigued by freckles, one of them touched my arm, shrieking in delight at his courage. He looked down at his own finger—no damage. He tried again, this time touching the white skin between the freckles. He pulled away with a jerk—but still no damage. Then there was an invasion of small jabs and touches, all over me, accompanied by contagious giggles.

My long, painted fingernails, my passport to conversation, continued to be the object of attention. How was it possible to grow such long ones, and of such an unusual color? Ten children, one on each finger, studied the phenomenon. Freeing my hands gently, I peeled the polish from one nail. There was a communal intake of breath. Didn't such tearing hurt? Where was the blood underneath? Disbelief turned to compassion as one of the bravest boy children gently caressed my natural fingernail and began to spit and blow on it to ease the pain. I tried to gesture that it didn't matter, that it was all right, and I started to peel another nail. Again the blowing and spitting.

Kijimbele tried to reassure them, but they had found a new game. The Masai children closed around my hands, tearing the polish to shreds with cruel, delighted, childlike fervor, salving the pain of it with spits and blows as they worked.

The mothers asked if they could see my safari pouch, and inquisitively they rifled through its contents.

Then came the magic discovery—a mirror!

Straining to see above the heads of the children, I watched the women. At first, not comprehending their own faces, they moved to investigate the back of the reflection. No one lurked behind it. They had been right the first time. They looked over at me. Was I witnessing their embarrassment? People want privacy during times of self-discovery—I quickly looked away.

They began to chant into the mirror, their shoulders swaying, as they studied their profiles; their earrings batted back and forth like jeweled riders on ear-lobe swings. They opened their mouths and peered down their throats, making guttural animal sounds as though they were disappointed that they couldn't see their stomachs. Then finally there came the smiles back at themselves. Feigned smiles, enticing smiles, smiles of smug narcissism from the corners of their eyes.

Then the women began to dance. They undulated past me in a snakelike line, snapping their heads from the bases of their necks, their beaded necklaces rising and falling. Their thick ankles were weighted with heavy

iron anklets placed there when they were babies as symbols of their slavery to their men. Their ankles grew
around the bracelets. As they danced, they moved as one
body, one movement. They were a unity of women,
shared communally by the men of the tribe. One of them
wrestled my arm away from the children and drew me
into the line. The chant echoed over the plains.

The *moranee* formed a circle holding their spears in
one hand and their heavy wooden *pimbo* clubs in the
other. Then a contest began. From a standing position,
the first *moranee* jumped straight into the air, his legs
perfectly rigid and his arms holding his weapons at his
sides. He seemed to pause in midair before returning to
earth. He had jumped what looked to me to be the height
of a six-foot man.

The women broke ranks and sang accompaniment to
the jumping warriors. One after the other the men jumped,
paused, and thudded back to earth, over and over again,
until a winner was declared. The contest and the dancing
subsided. Dung fires sprang up throughout the *menyatta,*
and the cattle were rounded up for the long night.

I was invited to stay for the bloodletting and cocktails
afterward. Hastily, I realized that now was the time for
the box lunch I had brought: chicken, hard-boiled eggs,
and chocolate éclairs. Kijimbele asked for beer but settled
for a chicken leg.

Communal singing in smoky dung huts segued into
more dancing, this time under the moon. The songs had
meaning, usually about a warrior's desire for a particular
woman, perhaps one belonging to his own brother. If the
woman agreed, a spear was placed before the entrance to
her hut and off she went into the arms of another for the
night, leaving a husband delighted that his wife was desi-
rable to another. Wives had value. They were purchased
for a specific number of cattle, the price having been set

by the woman's father.

Kijimbele confided to me that his betrothal to "his darling" would occur in about three years when he would be able to afford her.

"Those rings mean you are bought?" he asked me as we walked to the edge of the *menyatta.*

"Yes," I answered, "the wedding band means I'm married."

"Where your darling?"

"In a place called Japan."

"That in Africa?"

We crouched on the ground. I sketched a rough map of the world with a stick.

"Japan is very far away," I told him as I pointed to the Orient.

"They have cattle there?"

"Oh, yes, very good cattle," I said, thinking of the delicious Kobe beef but not admitting that I had eaten it.

"Your husband pay many cattle for purchase you?"

"Oh, yes, many."

"It was worth it," he stated with flat sincerity. Kijimbele took my arm and helped me up. It was an unexpected gesture of chivalry. I wondered if he did that with his own women or only because I was white.

"You come again?" he asked.

"Yes, I think I will, if it's all right."

"And you take watch and fix?" He handed me his precious mouse watch, as the chief approached.

"You welcome, come again," said the chief. I thanked him for his people's hospitality and walked toward the Land-Rover. Looking back I saw the chief munching on a chocolate éclair and sipping a gourd of blood and milk as he ate.

I went back to the *menyatta* every day for two weeks, spending all waking hours with the Masai until news of the delayed safari arrived.

Time became irrelevant to me as it was to the Masai. For that short time, I lived as they did, by impulse and governed only by the needs of their cattle. Kijimbele taught me some of his language while he learned the corresponding words in English. When his magic mouse watch was repaired, he was astonished to learn the use of such a decorative trinket, and his time-telling prowess became a prime topic of conversation in the *menyatta*. My time belonged to the Masai.

Kijimbele and the *moranee* took me with them to graze the cattle, moving to new grass every week in a regular rotation. We would stand for hours, silently surveying the undulating plains. The plains animals trusted the Masai. With the familiar smell of smoked dung and dried blood they knew they were safe. They romped and scampered over hundreds of miles, their heads lifted to the wind. Every species integrated with every other as they ran wild and free. Zebra ran with dik-dik, wildebeest with impala, warthog with buffalo. It was a tapestry of harmony, with the Masai, their orange loincloths flapping against their spears, presiding over the windy plains.

The wind didn't fondle; it splashed itself against us. The animals and Masai seemed to talk to it, converse with it, understand what the windy splashes were saying. Sometimes it carried a warning; men and animals would abruptly change direction, the Masai turning completely around, plunging their spears into new earth, the animals making an instantaneous decision *en masse* to change course in the middle of a thunderous run. A blanket of birds, sometimes hundreds of them, darting and flowing in precise formation, never missed a beat when it was time to change direction. They turned and plummeted and climbed as though they were one. Did they have a squadron leader? Were they so finely tuned to one another that there were no leaders and no followers? Were there never any deviators? Did any birds ever decide they didn't want to fly with the squadron?

The discovery of a new water hole for both the animals and the tribesmen is to them a new lease on life. Water regulates all life in Africa. Most life is nomadic according to the water supply. The Masai and the animals are part of each other, linked by thirst. The two together are part of the wind. I was on the outside looking in. Or maybe I was looking out—out to what I saw as release, a different kind of freedom—a feeling of being part of everything that exists. I could never let anything rest as it was. I had to dissect everything—even a rose. I guess I really wanted to *be* the rose—to *be* the birds—to *be* the Masai. And all of that wanting was wanting to be me.

I was civilized, civilized into being profoundly aware of my own frustrations. The Masai were different. Their simplicity of purpose was so quieting, in a way so comfortable, so devoid of tension and anxiety, and soul pain.

Yet something is wrong. The Masai are dying. They are dying out from a simple disease the civilized world has long since conquered, and something that happened during the beginning of my third week in Africa brought all my conflict into focus. I would keep my memory of the Masai and theirs of me alive long after I left.

The day was blazing when I arrived at noon for my last visit. I was laden with hand mirrors, nail polish, and brightly colored cloths.

A group of women chattering exictedly by a hut on the edge of the *menyatta* swooped down on me and insisted that I go inside with them. As the lion-skin flap closed behind me I heard the hiss of hot, wet stones, and breathed smoke coming from a low fire. Squatting on a palm frond was a Masai woman in her mid-thirties, rocking gently to and fro. A thick blanket dotted with flies covered her. I turned to one of the elderly women and gave her a questioning look. She made a cradling gesture with her arms. Instantly, I panicked. A baby's birth was in progress, and they wanted me to take some part in it.

The hut was filled with women and squalling children who stood around the smoky fire, spitting and blowing their noses onto the dung-covered floor, wiping the excess with a finger and flicking it into the fire. Runny-eyed children, suffering from trachoma and syphilis, wallowed in the dung close to the laboring woman.

The oldest woman of the tribe pushed me toward the pregnant woman. "For you—for you," she seemed to be saying. "You deliver."

I lifted the blanket from the woman's leg. Blood bubbled on the palm frond beneath her. Suddenly I was aware of the horror of female circumcision. Her clitoris had simply been gouged away in order to suppress sexual desire. Both male and female Masai are circumcised during adolescence. The rite is witnessed by the entire tribe so that the physical endurance of the victim can be tested. Pits are dug and filled with cold water, and the adolescents sit in them until a measure of anesthesia is achieved. Usually the genitals are operated on with a crude piece of glass or stone. The witnesses watch for the slightest grimace of pain, which automatically makes the victim an outcast. I understood why this woman bore her child in silence. It was another point of honor; she was conquering pain.

Swarms of flies bombarded the fresh blood, contaminating the rapidly approaching baby. The mother gave one last convulsive movement. The baby came. The flies flew away. I knelt down, not knowing what to do. It was a little girl, all black and shiny and wet. I lifted the screaming, slippery creature in my arms. The umbilical cord wouldn't reach. I didn't kow how to cut it. The elderly midwife stepped forward. Reverently, she knelt down and chewed the cord in two with her teeth, and then reached across to the fire, picked up a sizzling rock, and cauterized the remainder of the cord.

The baby was so slippery I was afraid I would drop her. Her little arms and legs beat the air in protest against her new environment. I felt totally inadequate. I couldn't think. The filth was appalling. The midwife slipped the baby from my arms and wrapped her in a cloth to shield her from the flies. The mother convulsed once more, and the afterbirth came.

The palm frond was black with swarming flies. I couldn't bear it. Scooping dried dung and mud from the ground, I sopped up as much blood as possible and cleaned the suffering woman with a relatively dirt-free scarf from around my neck. I piled the afterbirth against the dung wall away from the palm frond. I was sure there would be a ritual attached to it later.

Held by its tiny spindly arms, the child was passed around the hut from woman to woman. Lifting the baby, each woman spat into its mouth. My mind whirled. What foul germs was the child contracting in the first hours of her life? How did any children survive? Some women blew their noses before the spitting ritual, and then held the mouth of the baby with the same fingers that had wiped away the excess.

Then they handed the child to me. I was supposed to follow suit. My stomach turned. How could I explain? It occurred to me that the spit of the Masai women was full of germs to which the baby was probably immune. But my spit might introduce foreign germs, which the child's system would never overcome. I held the child in one arm and pointed to my throat, making a bad face as though it were sore, and waved my hand in refusal for the baby's sake. They seemed to understand. I passed the child back to the midwife.

The mother moaned quietly, her face expressionless. The dung around her absorbed the blood as it spilled over the palm frond. Her eyes stared blankly. I smiled at her, hoping for a reaction. There was none. I realized she was blind. Later I learned that she was in the advanced stages of syphilis, and her "brain was sick." She was bleeding profusely now. I couldn't sop up the blood fast enough. Frantically I searched in my safari pouch for aspirin. Gently, I hoped, I forced her to swallow two of them. It was all I had, all I could do.

Another ritual was in progress. A tiny round bowl of salt was passed around. The women dipped their tongues directly into the salt, nodded their heads, and passed it on. Then the bowl was in my hands. Don't hesitate. I thought, either do it or don't do it. Lightly the tip of my tongue tasted the salt. I tried not to think of the rush of germs that must be entering my mouth. I was helpless before their ritual. Sanitation suddenly was meaningless. I nodded as they had and passed the bowl on. For the first time since I had entered the hut two hours before, everyone smiled. A crowd was gathering outside. I longed to breathe fresh air.

It is Masai custom for the father to ignore his child until it is two years old, but the circumstances of this birth must have been unusual, for the father entered the hut. He acknowledged neither his wife nor the child, but went straight to the midwife. He was told that I had received the baby and had administered aspirin to the suffering mother. He listened, nodded, and—never looking at me or his family—left the hut. Choked with the smoke and the smell, I staggered out after him.

The chief stood in the entrance. "You Masai blood sister now. Baby named Shuri."

In the blazing sunlight I tried to collect my thoughts.

I no longer wanted to melt into the milieu of what was primitive and basic or simple. I didn't want to be a missionary, but this new child needed medical help and care. I didn't want to change anyone's mind or belief or codes of behavior. I only wanted to help sustain something that lived and breathed. Life was an absolute, the thing I believed in.

I admired the Masai courage and endurance and conquest of pain, but I could help them with the knowledge I had gained from civilization. It was valuable—valuable— to them. If they considered this vulgar interference, I would have to take the chance. The sensitive, polite, social observances of ritual were over, and I became angry; angry at filth, at tradition, at dung huts, at the cows carrying syphilis, and at ignorance.

I turned to the chief. "I'm afraid," I said. "I'm afraid that child will die without proper care. Her mother is dying of syphilis this minute. Shuri was born with it, too. And even if she was free of that, the dung, flies, and filthy surroundings will get her. Let me take her to a hospital where they have penicillin and healthy food and doctors. Don't let her die. She has my name now. Don't I have a small right to protest?"

The children stopped crying. The women quit chattering in celebration, and the watchful *moranee* crowded around me in silence. They hadn't understood my words, but they seemed to sense that a confrontation was taking place.

The chief understood—not completely, but enough. He looked down at me with frightening penetration.

"Shuri not sick," he growled.

"You can't see it yet, but she is. Let's not wait until *you* can see it." I was asking him to violate the very principle by which the Masai are ruled.

There was a difference between conquering something

and simply being ignorant of it. The chief didn't move. Kijimbele looked back and forth at the two of us, caught between a little knowledge of my world and a thousand generations of his own.

The chief's eyes never left mine. Dependence on the white man's hospital? Subservience to the white man's cure? Possible future contamination by the white affluence?

He raised his hand. "We wait and see."

Here it was—the disease of tradition, the prevention of change, the one human quirk that continually leads to open conflict, which can be remedied only by doses of patience. Someday perhaps change will occur when times are ready for it instead of always when it is too late. Someday change will be accepted as life itself.

O.K., I would wait.

I nodded to the chief.

"Yes, sir," I said. "My safari has arrived in Tanganyika. They are waiting for me to join them this afternoon. So I must leave you and Shuri and take a plane. But I'll return soon."

His confusion vanished momentarily. "You go safari Tanganyika?"

"Yes, sir."

"Many Masai there."

"Yes."

"You now Masai blood sister. Whenever you go East Africa, Masai protect you."

I didn't know what he meant, but I thanked him.

The *menyatta* returned to its normal activities. The mother rocked herself gently, seemingly unaware that she had given birth. The elderly midwife held Shuri. The children returned to their play, and the fire continued to blaze in Shuri's hut, where she would await her fate.

I rushed to the airport in Nairobi with frayed nerves, hoping that the safari would bring me back to nature and

serenity. I would try not to think of Shuri for a while.
I would concentrate on taking movies and still pictures,
something I had wanted to do since my childhood days
of reading every book in the series called *Bomba the
Jungle Boy*.

I had taken the Masai chief with a grain of salt when
he promised to protect me throughout East Africa, but
when my small private plane landed in an isolated field
in Tanganyika, letting me out to sit on my luggage and
wait for the safari, I knew I wasn't alone. We had spotted
the safari from the air, and I knew it was at least an hour
from the field. The pilot had taken off again, headed back
to Nairobi.

I smelled the Masai before I saw them. Then in the
brush I spotted spears and ochered heads. I stood up and
smiled. Walking toward me were four *moranee* with their
spears in one hand and *pimbos* in another. One of them
said in English, "You white woman named Shuri?" It had
been approximately two hundred and seventy-five miles
and two and a half hours since I had informed the chief
in Kenya that I was going to Tanganyika. How had these
moranee known my name? How had the news traveled
so fast? I knew the Masai didn't use drums or smoke
signals.

When I explained the phenomena to the white hunter
on safari he was not amazed. He told me, first of all, that
to be a Masai blood sister was not to be taken lightly.
They meant it. And, secondly, the white men in East
Africa were seriously considering whether the Masai had
indeed achieved the seemingly impossible feat of thought
transference.

All I knew was that for the next few weeks on safari
there were Masai following me, with fresh relays every
few miles, as the safari photographed animals and traipsed
through the African countryside. And every evening, re-

gardless of where we pitched camp, a *moranee* stood posted outside my tent until daylight broke.

When I returned to the *menyatta* in Kenya the chief there knew of everything I had done on safari, including my refusal to shoot any animals and my arguments with the safari members every evening around the campfire. He even knew that I had knitted a tiny apple-green sweater for Shuri.

Kijimbele was waiting for me two weeks later when I returned to the *menyatta* in Kenya. Kijimbele and the midwife led me to an isolated hut. Smoke curled through the lion-skin opening. I took a deep breath and entered.

Shuri was covered with a cloth and lay in her mother's lap, sucking at her breast. The mother babbled incoherently. I lifted the baby up and uncovered her. Shuri lay inert in my arms. She was covered with running sores. Pus trickled from open breaks in her skin and left filthy trails across her tiny body. Her eyes were so infected she couldn't open them. Her mother was delirious. Syphilis had reached her brain.

The chief waited outside. "You take and fix," he said to me as I carried Shuri out of the hut. "Mother, too." Several Masai women led the mother out of the hut to the Land-Rover. The midwife held Shuri as I drove to the hospital.

Kijimbele ran after the Land-Rover. "They use long thing like this to make medicine?" he asked, describing the needle with his hands.

I nodded.

"It hurt?"

What a question to come from a young man who single-handedly had killed a ferocious lion and undergone circumcision without anesthetic.

I shoved the Land-Rover into fourth and yelled back,

"Not as much as being sick."

At the white hospital, staffed with Kikuyu interns and nurses, Shuri and her mother received penicillin every four hours for the first three days. Without it, the child would have died immediately. The mother's natural resistance would have enabled her to hold on a little longer. The penicillin and a stay in the hospital cured their syphilis, but the mother would be insane as long as she lived.

"We wish more of the Masai would come in for treatment," said the Kikuyu doctor. "We can't save them otherwise. Anyway, these two are cured, and the baby will be immune for life, unless she catches it from her husband by direct contact."

By the end of the week my nerves were raw. There was so much more I wanted to do. I knitted several tiny apple-green sweaters for other Masai children and conducted classes showing them how to use the knitting needles as I went along. What a miracle of productivity could be wrought with two smooth sticks and colored string.

I explained the miracle of penicillin to the chief and urged him to persuade more of his people to accept treatment. "We wait and see," he said, but I knew he abhorred the Kikuyu and their hospital as deeply as he did the white man. His people's survival was up to him; he was their chief. Perhaps some day he would be judicious enough to take only that which he needed from the civilized world. He wouldn't necessarily have to join the ranks. But, from what I knew of them, the arrogance of the Masai was uncompromising.

"My husband has called for me," I explained to the chief on my last day at the *menyatta*. "I was waiting for him to come here, but he can't, and so now I'm going back to him."

With his kind and wizened expression he looked

mischievously into my eyes. "You return someday?" he asked.

"I hope so. I want to very much," I answered.

"With husband?"

"Maybe, yes."

"Good. You tell husband I offer five hundred cattle for you. When he comes we do business."

I laughed in delight and he pumped my hand strongly and for a long time. He had always gotten such a kick out of the custom. This time he nearly drew blood.

I made my good-bys as hurriedly as possible. I always hate to say good-by. Sometimes I am even impolite. I am always afraid I won't be able to control myself. It is hard to accept the fact that the world is a transitory place and that, when we touch each other, the stinging fullness of those times is all we have, and that the likelihood of recapturing them is slim.

Kijimbele waved his Mickey Mouse watch, now attached to the top of his spear. His companions stood next to him proudly immobile, their arms waving mechanically. The women were clustered in flowering circles around a pyramid of mirrors, gaily colored materials, soap, wash basins, and apple-green yarn. Their children scampered about, a few of them in tiny apple-green sweaters, looking like misplaced flower centers.

The chief stood holding Shuri proudly in his arms, directing her blind mother to wave in my direction. His long ear lobes swung from side to side, but the can opener was gone. In its place through the holes were two magnificently twisted knitting needles.

The dust from the wheels closed in behind me as I drove away. The long grass waved ahead of me.

Fourteen

I'VE ALWAYS FELT THAT I would never develop into a really fine actress because I cared more about life beyond the camera than the life in front of it. Over the years my search became broader and broader. After two months on a picture my car seemed to veer toward the airport of its own accord. I still loved acting and enjoyed it. I was a professional, but basically I was more interested in the people I played than the movies I played them in.

However, it seemed the more I learned about people the more confused I became. It almost seemed that it was better to see things from the surface only, for a few days or a few weeks at the most. Then I could make a stab at understanding. Beyond that a lifetime wouldn't be enough. Often I contributed to my own confusion by staying long times in places soaking into whatever the "thing" was. As though by becoming someone else for a time I would understand something of how they lived, ate, thought, and died, as Mother had said, but I was still me when it was all over. And they were they. And it bothered me that we were still separate.

Steve understood what I was after. He was established in Japan and had no intention of returning to the United States, much less Hollywood. He had had his search and intended to function where he was happiest. He knew I hadn't finished mine and needed to go on and that to "settle into being a family in Tokyo" would frustrate me very quickly. Sachie had completely accepted the fact that for a great deal of the time her mother and father

didn't live together. She never questioned "our arrangement," for she understood how deep our love and friendship went—and that constant attendance wasn't necessary to keep it nourished. Steve had his friends, some of
whom I've never met to this day, and I had mine, a few
of whom derived mischievous pleasure from insisting that
Steve was an Asian myth. The important thing was that
Steve and I understood each other. But not many other
people understood.

I confused a great many people because they couldn't
fit me into an acceptable pigeonhole. Frequently there
would be a pattern to their reactions. At first they thought
I was divorcing, then that I was running away from some
problem, then that I was a promiscuous jet-set swinger.
After a while they gave up trying to define me and
settled for calling me a "free spirit." To them I suppose
I was, but in my opinion I had a long way to go.

A few of my close friends decided I was a bleeder—
I bled for everybody, they said, from Caryl Chessman to
the Chinese Communists, from the typhoon victims in
Nagoya, Japan, to mixed-blood orphans in Vietnam and
Korea; from anti-war protesters in America to the bene-
ficiaries of the Tom Dooley Foundation in Laos, Vietnam,
and Nepal. And it was true I did bleed, but mostly because
the more I traveled the more I saw other people bleeding.

I have been nearly everywhere in the world that
my passport allows—all through Southeast Asia, Russia,
Rumania, East Germany, Western Europe, North Africa,
black Africa, Australia, the South Pacific, Scandinavia,
the Caribbean, Mexico, Canada—but the land that influenced me the most was India.

On my way back to America, after six months with
Steve and Sachie in Japan, my plane stopped in Bombay
and I got off. I had only intended to stay overnight, but
I stayed three months.

To me India was life. She represented struggle. Her presence was something I could reach out and touch. Her life never hid, nor did it pass as something else. It was what it was there in its nakedness, struggling against impossible odds to be itself. It was stark and ruthless much of the time. I felt strangely comfortable, strangely familiar as I traveled from Bombay to Hyderabad, Madras, up to New Delhi, Jaipur, Udaipur, Aggra, Benares, and finally down through Bengal and Orissa. I stopped wearing Western dresses and wore a sari, draping it myself and feeling comfortable in clothes for the first time in my life. I could walk comfortably, sit in any way I wanted to in a sari, and never feel restricted. It went with the climate and made me feel graceful. I ate only Indian food—masalas, curries, tandoories—and most of the time I traveled alone, meeting people along the way who were engaged in their own search.

On and on I traveled through the villages of the Indian countryside, until I reached the Bay of Bengal, a bay of velvet summer water with soft warm waves. It was five o'clock in the morning when I arrived, and I began to walk south on the beach. Wiry brown men with coned hats turned out to be "swimming helpers," ready in case anyone wished to risk the treacherous footing beneath the waves; abrupt drops as deep as twenty feet were a peril to bathers.

The sun was just coming up when I saw at least five hundred white sails billowing out to sea, with erect, standing fishermen digging thick oars into the surf to propel the boats faster. A fleet of Orissan fishermen, leaving at sunup to finish their work before the heat of the day.

I ran toward the beach where the boats had been launched. Far out to sea sails billowed—the fishermen standing silhouetted against the sunrise. They were expert fishermen, migrants from Madras. The halved trunks of trees lashed together with ropes made their boats, which supposedly never capsize; no weather is too rough for them, and the villagers say they are in touch with the cold language of the fish beneath the waves.

I stopped running and lifted my head in the breeze. The odor was unmistakable; and as I advanced slowly, looking down as I walked, I saw, neatly spaced along the beach, hundreds of little piles of dung about half an hour old, heralding the dawn of a new day in typical Indian style. In another hour, the tide would be high, and the fishing-village bathroom would be spotless again until the next morning.

Ahead of me, thatched roofs loomed, until finally I walked into the village built in the sand. Fishing nets were spread on the dry sand, entangling children as they played. Pots smoked over wood fires. Mounds of prawns, all varieties of small fish, and one monstrous swordfish about ten feet long with the insides gutted out and the rest ready to be sold assured me that the fishing village was reasonably affluent. The women who gazed at me as I walked through their village, invading their privacy, were not as feminine as most Indian peasant women. They seemed more cynical, perhaps because of the harshness of the sea. They wore bright-colored saris with salt crusted in the folds, and an avalanche of gold jewelry spilled from their noses. I wondered how it was for them when they caught colds and sneezed. There were no men in the village— they were all at sea.

A woman with gold nose jewelry and a faded purple sari approached me. She tugged at my arm, and then, holding her infant son about two months old in front of her, she asked me in Hindi if I would please buy her baby.

The baby smiled at me and reached for his mother's

nose jewelry. His head bobbed back and forth and a dog that belonged to the village sat on his haunches beside the woman with his right front paw in a well-trained begging gesture.

The woman's expression was casual but underneath she looked dark and devious, as though she meant what she had said. Next to her sat an old woman naked from the waist up with two children nursing as she mended a sprawling fishing net. Squalling children romped everywhere. The women nearest to me stared in my face. One of them said it was understood that I could bargain for the child, that I wasn't expected to pay what the woman would ask for. They waited for me to answer.

"Thank you, I already have one," I said and walked on quickly. A small band of village children followed me with their palms turned upward in front of them. I walked faster and they walked faster. I turned and smiled. They smiled back. I broke into a run. They loved the game and ran after me, not even aware that their palms were still turned upward stretched out in front of them, laughing and begging as they ran.

India is a paradox, passionate, pulsating, even humorous in her poverty. And in her villages the subhuman drama plays itself out against a backdrop of such beauty that it seems a grotesque mockery. Outside of her cities, India seemed to have a unique color spectrum. An Indian blue isn't like a blue anywhere else in the world. An Indian sky, hung with clouds, seems iridescent. It envelops the green tops of the rain trees, while hundreds of green pigeons chatter in and out under the foliage. A vermilion Indian sunset screams so loudly it is indecent. Color, any color, seemed to spring at me in mid-air. A crimson sari undulated against the dazzling jade of a rice field. Ornately wrought, gaily colored pieces of native jewelry were beautiful accents against arms, shoulders, faces.

I was walking through a dream when I stopped beside a still lagoon, on whose serene surface floated ivory-colored lotus flowers. Overhead the pepul tree dropped red berries into the water, making circlets and rings that eddied outward against the skinny legs of a water buffalo. I watched the children brushing their teeth with twigs of the neem tree, and the uncertain dignity of the teenage girls as they mixed oil with the leaf of the kajal tree to make a cooling eye mascara, and I felt as though I were watching an unrehearsed band of exquisite actors.

The huts of Eastern Indian villages are thatch-roofed and mud-walled, scattered among the magical lagoons. Coconut palms bend gently under the weight of the men who climb them for the fruit. Below, the women wait to catch the coconuts, as someone nearby plays haunting sitar music.

Friendly and generous, the people of the countryside offered anything they had as I passed through. Inside their huts the walls were hung with colorful prints of Hindu gods. Teenage girls gossiped behind their hands at my gold earrings and gold wedding band, my white skin and blue eyes, calculating how to adopt some of my Western ways, while I wondered if I could pierce a nostril and insert an emerald stud into the side of my nose.

The men of the village were too proud to show open curiosity. One or two old men would give me sidelong glances of interest—the affection of aloofness not that important at their age. And the children—the friendly, open, trusting children—were aware that a foreigner was in their midst. Milling about the village in clumps, they never ran and hid behind their mothers' skirts as some city children might. They were too independent for that.

They giggled and teased, and squatted along the roadside. They stripped and tumbled into the lagoons to shriek and splash, their skins glistening in shades from dark cream to blue black.

An ox-drawn cart, piled high with coconuts, would lumber down the main dirt road, a parched-looking, withered old man perched on top, lazily dragging a long thin bamboo reed he would never use, or even think to use. His oxen would get him to market in plenty of time. One load a day was plenty. Who needed to rush—who needed more than enough?

When an Indian rain fell, it had clearly defined boundaries. I could stand still in dry sunshine—actual sunshine—while three feet ahead of me rain fell in sheets. No one ran for shelter—life went on as though a storm was a natural part of the day. The rain stopped as abruptly as it began, leaving only shining leaves and wet bird feathers to prove that it had really rained.

But when I arrived in Calcutta everything changed. The lilting backdrop of the countryside was gone. There was nothing to soften the poverty. In a city anywhere poverty can be bad enough but in Calcutta it is sheer dehumanization.

My room was on the third floor of the Grand Hotel, overlooking Chowringhi Boulevard, the main thoroughfare of Calcutta. Day after day I sat on the windowsill watching the human mass of street livers come to life at dawn.

The sidewalks were strewn with sleeping, sari-clad babies. Like Japanese kimonos, when saris are fresh and clean nothing is more graceful but when soiled and slept in they look more like bundles of rags. These saris had once been white, made of what appeared to be a kind of gauze which creased and wrinkled at the slightest pressure. They were the uniforms of the destitute.

Below me, multitudes would flow in changing patterns as they rose and made their ways to the gutters. People spitting betelnut juice made red shallow pools on the streets.

Up Chowringhi Boulevard a public bus would roar to a stop, belching oil smoke from its rear. I could smell it all the way up to the third floor. I never felt I could breathe in Calcutta. Fuel is scarce, so they burn anything and buses burn a particularly crude oil. Layers of human beings would ooze from the bus. Another bolt of humans would make for the bus, their disheveled saris and dhotis trailing. The packed mass inside the bus would contract and make room for more. I would suck in my stomach just watching them. One or two stragglers would be left out, running alongside the bus, grasping and gesticulating for help from their friends, but the limit was the limit. They would stop on spindly brown legs, shrug ever so slightly, and glide back to their homes on the sidewalk.

One early morning the swelling of thousands of voices woke me. The sound came from out of the distance through the industrial smog hanging in the air. The roar became a chant. Then through the smog I saw them— what were reported to have been 250,000 Indians walking slowly and chanting in Bengali, "We want food—we want food," came toward the hotel.

Bobbing along above the center of the mass of humanity were huge portraits on red backgrounds of Lenin, Khrushchev, Karl Marx, and even Joe Stalin.

. Street sleepers on the sidewalk below rose to their feet. One by one families of skeletons fell into line. "We want food—we want food." I had the impression that the faces on the banners meant nothing to the new marchers. They were protesting the only way they knew how. Women with thick, oily black braids gracefully swinging from side to side led docile children into the massed ranks of human beings. On and on they walked, irregularly, some laughing, some defiant, some bewildered, some hopeful—but all hungry.

These thousands and thousands of lifeless people with absolutely nothing—nothing but their common need— were capable of exploding in violent anger, and when they exploded it was terrifying.

A week before, a young girl of eleven had been babbling as she begged to passersby below my window. Her bandaged, outstretched hands bobbed in front of her, begging for pity. Suddenly a man everyone thought was her father issued the girl a sharp order. She shrieked at the top of her lungs and with her teeth she ripped off the bandages to hold up two bloody stumps. It turned out that she had been kidnaped by the man and he had cut off her hands to make her an effective beggar. Although his crime was common in the begging business, it took the gathering crowd only a few minutes to tear the man to pieces. They needed a reason to explode and had found one.

For two and a half hours I watched the masses of the hungry. This day was no different from any other day to the Indians below. Time doesn't seem to exist in India. It seems irrelevant. Darkness doesn't necessarily mean sleep and daytime doesn't mean activity. With so many people everywhere activity is constant, and sleep is constant. There isn't enough room, even on the streets, for everyone to sleep at the same time simply because day is over. Food doesn't come at mealtimes. It comes when it is found. An orange rind is hoarded. Never gobbled, it is to be nibbled furtively over a private dustbin, where if any of it falls accidentally it can be retrieved without a squabble.

Everywhere are outstretched upturned palms extended on spindly brown arms, begging. The upturned palms are

thrust under the nose of every tourist. The expression of
the Westerner usually reflects a pitying disgust, and often
guilt. A tourist would snap a picture of a loping, diseased
cow dumping dung in the street while being fed food taken
from a wailing hungry child; the child would then be reprimanded for showing disrespect for the sacred animal. The
tourist would move on to the backstreets, where prostitutes as young as twelve solicit from cages, painted and
dressed in shocking colors to divert the attention of their
customers from the bleak reality of their surroundings.
Thick and oily perfume hangs in the air.

With the first evidence of charity, armies of crippled,
pleading youngsters surround bewildered tourists demanding equality in charity. At first I gave the youngsters everything I had whenever they surrounded me, but the word
seemed to spread all the way to the Taj Mahal whenever I
came onto the street so I had to stop or I would have been
crushed to death.

My hotel wasn't far from the apartment of Martin
and Bhulu Sarkees. I had met them through friends in
Bombay. Bhulu was from a prominent Nepalese family
and Martin was a crafty Persian. He operated a cinema
in downtown Calcutta not far from their apartment and
took mischievous pride in cajoling the local passersby in
to witness recent imports of what he called "entertaining
American rubbish."

Martin was a thin, prematurely haggard-looking man
of forty who always wore pin-striped zoot suits and a long
watch chain. Somehow, these were in keeping with his
life in Calcutta, which revolved around the Blue Fox
Restaurant and the Calcutta race track. He loved a good
practical joke, good wine, and, of course, the races.

Bhulu was a dark-eyed, dark-haired beauty who wore
a perpetual expression of accusation. "Martinnn, where

have you been?" her voice would stab the air with precision. After receiving proof of his innocence, which he frequently invented, she carried on with life.

There were many sides to Martin. Probably because he was a Persian, he could zero in on the real meaning of any circumstance. He quickly understood my swift rapport with India. He shared my interest in Westerners who had converted to Eastern religions. He loved to describe them as "those materialistically inclined Yankees who sold their souls for greenbacks in the West and came to India to organize cartels and exploit labor but instead stayed to discover themselves."

One of the things Martin cared most about was an orphanage for boys outside Calcutta. He supported it in any way he could, and when he introduced me to it I was overwhelmed. It was an orphanage for the children of the street livers. The children were not necessarily orphans; most of them were discarded immediately after birth because their parents couldn't afford to keep them.

The orphanage was run by Father Aloysius Vani-gasooriyar. Father Van was Ceylonese, a descendant of royal Ceylonese blood, who had given up all claim to his inheritance to become a priest. A young and extremely handsome man, he said he had converted to Catholicism "because it was the only way to be organized in helping the poor."

Most of his boys had been placed in refuse bins at the end of alleys; some had survived to become orphans of the street. How they found food was hard to imagine— and what they ate was worse. Those who survived were immune to indescribable diseases by the time they could walk. And, when they did walk, for some it was on all fours because they lived with the street dogs.

A few of the scores of discarded children were brought to Father Van, and he began the work of restoring them to human society. Many of them died because it was too late. But the ones that did make it were so full of the thrust of life, so determined to triumph over death, that the secrets of evolution seemed to be locked in their spirits. Tenacious as crustaceans, they were living proof of the will to survive. Some of them *should* have died, mercifully, for their own good—but they didn't; they struck and fought and yelled and grabbed life in their balled-up fists and wouldn't let go.

The boys were housed in what the soft-spoken Ceylonese priest calls his Indian Boys Town. Father Flanagan, founder of the original Boys Town, was his idol, and Father Van wanted to do for his Indian boys what Father Flanagan had done for his boys in Nebraska.

By Western standards, the boys didn't have much, but in terms of Indian city life, they lived like princes. And the orphanage was an oasis of hope. The boys planted and harvested their own rice. They were hoping for a cow. Someone had given them seventeen baby chicks and soon they would have a rooster. Barefoot, dwelling mostly outdoors, and possessing hardly any belongings, the boys lived together with a communal spirit that rivals even the state-operated schools and nurseries I once saw in the Soviet Union.

The orphanage was two years old when I first saw it, set on twenty-three acres just off the main road between Calcutta and Diamond Harbor. I came laden with huge tins of cookies, baskets of fresh fruit from the "foreign market place" in Calcutta, and chocolate.

Father Van had told the boys that a foreign lady was coming, so in a howling happy mass they rushed to meet me. "Auntie's here—Auntie's here," they screamed, each jockeying for a finger or a little space of skin to hang on to and touch. They jumped up and down all around me, guiding me to the circular clearing under the banana trees where they played marbles. As if to entertain me and not themselves the began a game, eyeing the sumptuous goodies Father Van took from the car and deposited on the communal dining table.

Day after day I visited the orphanage and day after day the same scene was enacted as a hundred and more children would set up a clamor whenever it was time to distribute the things I had brought. Some of the boys would never leave my side, even though they were hungry for sweets. They seemed to be jealously measuring the amount of time each could spend close to me. They gripped and squeezed at my hands and arms; often a boy would cry because he didn't want to give up his turn touching me.

Father Van was gentle and understood. He never raised his voice to the boys. "Sometimes," he said, "if I talk sternly or in a loud voice it will send some of them into a depression for days. They have been so badly damaged emotionally that I must be kind and gentle in the extreme. They take advantage of my tenderness but I have no other choice."

He did always insist, however, that the boys be considerate of one another. They would line up according to age with their palms turned upward. I hated that cupped begging gesture as they took the food in their hands. Perhaps if they had had plates I might have felt differently. Each child would look up into my face and, with sincerity but still as if by rote, say, "Thank you." No one forgot to say "thank you"—ever.

These boys were the lucky ones, the ones who had been rescued in time. Not so lucky the "boy with no name" who seemed about eleven years old. He did not speak, but only made barking, snarling sounds. Three months before, Father had seen the boy's crouched figure with long, filthy matted hair crawl out of a refuse bin.

The child-creature had shuffled on all fours to a water pump, where he lapped up the water like a dog. Father put out his hand to touch him, and the boy tried to bite him. Father stepped back. The child waited, his eyes shifting in terror, because Father was standing between him and his refuse bin. Father Van, realizing the child felt trapped, turned and walked away. The child crawled back to the bin, too frightened to scrounge for food that night.

Every night for weeks Father returned to the bin. Gradually the child became more accustomed to his presence, until finally one night he let Father touch him. It was only a light, glancing touch, but the child didn't bite him, and seemed grateful to eat the food Father handed him. Soon he began to follow Father during his nightly visits to the streets and refuse bins until ultimately he followed Father home to Boys Town.

The creature began to know that he could feel safe with Father, but the other boys were beyond his comprehension. He sat on his haunches at the edge of the property, watching the boys go about their activities, associating with no one, and gobbling his food with snorting sounds at mealtime. At night, he slept behind a rock. He felt comfortable spending most of his time alone in the cow shed. I visited him there every day. Whenever he heard me coming he stirred and shuffled through the leaves to greet me. He would allow me to shake his hand, then he would shift his weight to one leg and cross his hands and rest them on top of his head and stare at me with a docile smile on his face. He loved to listen to Father and me when we talked about him. We never knew how much he understood but he must have perceived that we cared deeply about him. Completely dependent on Father, he wouldn't move without an order. Father said the boy would have remained in that position with his hands over his head for a week unless he was told to sit down. The strange truth was that the abandoned children went from living the completely independent lives of prowling wild animals to becoming creatures of pitiful dependence when they were found and cared for, evidencing no individuality or spirit. Their survival drive broke down completely and they became parasitic. This loss of fight was Father Van's most serious problem.

For a time, Father had another refuse-bin boy who was in much the same mental condition. He placed the two together, but neither recognized the existence of the other. In total isolation each watched the world of the healthier boys with non-comprehension. They didn't fight, but they never communicated either. They never played together, or roughhoused or even acknowledged the other's presence. They just sat on their haunches and stared— hour after hour, day after day—until one of them died. The other seemed not to realize he was gone. He trusted only Father Van, whom he allowed to wash and touch him. "It seems fruitless sometimes," Father Van told me, "because every time I wash him up and his hair is clean again and he looks presentable, he goes and rolls in the dirt until he smells the way he's used to smelling."

When I visited the Nursery for Dustbin Babies I cried. Many of the infants were blind, some deaf and dumb, and all were smaller than they should have been for their ages. The tiny ones, unable to walk, were lying on mats spread out on the floor. The rest were squalling, grasping, banging, nudging, and encircling Father and me as we walked among them. They had won their battle against death. They seemed old from the fight and too exhausted to be children. Twin girls, seven months old but looking no older than a week, had survived three abortion attempts by their mother, who then ironically died in bearing them. Their chins receded, and their bones hadn't completely formed. They were identical twins, and each looked like a miniature chicken monkey. They opened holes in their faces and pushed air out, but they hadn't enough strength to cry. They made pulsating movements, but no sound came. Their father, a rickshaw coolie, lived on the sidewalks and made about seven rupees (eighty cents) a week. Finally, unable to manage any longer, he had carried the babies to the doorstep of the nursery. The nuns said the twins would live.

One very jovial, smiling little girl had been throttled by her parents but had refused to die, so they tied her to the railroad tracks outside Calcutta, where she was discovered by the Calcutta police before the train came. She was a bit demented from repeated beatings. But there she was, another crustacean.

There were many Anglo-Indian babies, half white and blue-eyed, who had been discarded by their mothers because even the lowest caste of Hindu frowns on children of mixed blood.

The death toll in the Nursery for Dustbin Babies is enormous but that is life in Calcutta.

Seeing these children and working with the orphans, sinking down into the stench and destitution of the street livers, almost wallowing in the dehumanization of Calcutta, I felt myself becoming obsessed with the inhumanity of it all. Sometimes I wondered why I stayed—why I didn't leave. Whatever I did in adopting all of Father Van's boys—in giving them what money I could afford and in raising more money at a benefit I arranged with other Indian movie stars in Calcutta—was such a drop in the bucket compared to the overwhelming futility of the problem.

Father Van said most foreigners had such horrible nightmares after having been in Calcutta for a few days that they couldn't bear to stay. He continually asked me if Calcutta made me sick, and when I said No he said that I had accepted that dehumanization was *life* in Calcutta. In accepting it rather than being emotionally repelled by it I could then be of some help. It was an important thing to learn, he said, because dehumanization has no geographical boundaries. And if the spectacle of thousands and millions of hungry, diseased, faceless people with absolutely nothing made me sick and repelled me then I would be absolutely no good to any of them or even to myself.

The short walk from my hotel to the nearest shopping center or to the Sarkeeses' apartment was a walk into another world. My prior frames of reference lost their meaning. I found myself framing new values. I had to. The swarms of near-skeletal figures, the bloated silent children stunned me so that I felt terrifyingly bewildered most of the time. Bewildered at how this could happen. I had had no preparation, no identification, no gut-level comprehension of what it was like.

Bodies of half-dead human beings, who didn't seem human at all, lay sprawled half in and half out of the gutters, waiting for the next life to take them. I couldn't tell the difference between the bodies that were male and those that were female. In half-death they lost their gender. Sometimes the figures groaned but usually they made no sound. The welcomed death was silent. Apathetically, perfectly still, they lay, their eyes staring straight ahead.

When one is immersed in the staggering experience of Calcutta it finally becomes absolutely necessary to explore and probe inside one's own self. In Calcutta it is impossible to remain uninvolved. And to evaluate the meaning of the soul-shattering involvement requires an inner evaluation of oneself.

To me it was no accident that I became interested in

spiritual meditation after having lived and breathed Calcutta. I simply had to. I had to explore my own inner self since I was more aware of its existence in Calcutta than in any place I had ever been in the world.

Fifteen

MARTIN AND FATHER VAN arranged for lessons in Yoga for me.

"The ultimate aim of Yoga," my instructor said, "is the liberation of the spirit, the union of the soul with the universe. Yoga is the Sanskrit word for union, or concentration, its purpose being to bring man to the highest level physically, mentally, and spiritually. In all of us there is something greater hidden under the surface. Very few people find it. I want you to learn self-discovery. There is no reason why you or anyone else who makes an effort cannot conquer those things that restrict growth and comfort. You can conquer hatred, fear, and pain through concentration on the inner self. Find your inner self. You have more internal power than you realize."

I began my meditation exercises in half-hour periods at first—relaxing and allowing my senses to melt into the nature around me. Often I would sit quietly in the rice field adjacent to Father Van's Boys Town. It was heavenly to feel the breeze sifting over paddies of rice onto my face. "We are all part of nature," the instructor said, "not separate from it, any more than we are separate from each other. Nature has a purpose; part of her purpose is human life—if we cut ourselves off from nature we in effect cut ourselves off from the purpose of life. We humans have become so self-important in our own eyes that it no longer occurs to us that we are intertwined with the will of nature. For nature does have a will and a harmony that are ever so much more consistent than we expect them to be. We humans have decided our schemes and projects—

we have manufactured what is important in our life cycle with our scrambling and competition and material desires and struggling for fame and fortune and reverence for 'things.'

"We ignore how we were spawned. And it is folly and stupid, because nature will work her quiet and silent will inevitably. It would therefore be easier and more pleasant for us to cooperate with nature. If we would make an effort to blend with nature, our individual competitive ambitions would become happier aspirations, and we would find life not only easier but miraculous."

The instructor continually admonished me for what he called "my Western speed." I never took time for anything. I was too eager to get on with the "next experience," or to continue on the "treadmill of learning things."

"Patience," he quoted an old Arab proverb, "is the key to joy. Haste is the key to sorrow."

"Humans say that time passes," he quoted a Himalayan proverb. "Time says that humans pass."

After a few weeks of meditational exercises my instructor advised me that if I truly wanted to pursue the search for my inner self I should leave the din and clatter of the lowlands and try the mountains.

He said he himself had traveled on horseback into the mountains for days, looking for a place of serenity where his mind and body could be free to experience the dictates of the surroundings. He had found his place and for three months had lived in solitude except for a servant whom he brought with him to cook his meals. Every day he would wake and walk to a small clearing, where he said he had made friends with an ancient tree and a crow who spoke with him incessantly. He said the tree had been suspicious of him at first but gradually began to trust his long and peaceful silences. The instructor spoke as though he were part of the tree, and when he felt fused with everything around him it was possible for him to sit on "a blanket of soft fallen leaves and turn my thoughts inward."

He said he had flashes of his inner truth often during his life in the lowlands, but in the mountain sanctuary he saw the truth continually and with startling clarity.

"I don't understand this science of the mind and the inner self," Martin said to me. "I have enough trouble just walking around. But if that's what you are interested in, the instructor is right: India isn't the place to find it. It's only the low country, the first rung on the ladder to higher understanding. If you want the top, go to the roof of India, to the Himalayas. Not to Kashmir, Nepal, or Sikkim. Too many others have contaminated those places. Go to Bhutan. Hardly any Westerner has ever been there, only three Americans. It's a kingdom of primitive isolation, and its rulers mean to keep it that way."

The mountains were one thing; even the Himalayas were difficult for me to imagine seeing. But Bhutan!! People spoke of Bhutan with awe. It seemed to be regarded as a lost kingdom, as though it existed in the imagination; and, in fact, only a few could prove otherwise. Some even spoke in whispers when the subject came up. And it came up often because everyone was intrigued by Bhutan even though they seemed secretly afraid.

A tiny kingdom nestled high in a valley in the Himalayas, it is bordered by China on the north and the east, Assam on the south, Sikkim and Tibet on the west. An autonomous state, it is almost entirely mountainous. And out of the kingdom in the great mountains came the legends of the mystics.

"Perhaps you could go to Bhutan for this science of mind and for Himalayan Buddhism," said Martin Sarkees. "I have arranged lunch with prime minister Dorji of Bhutan. He is my friend and he is in Calcutta."

The prospect of actually being with one of the titular heads of Himalayan Buddhism was awesome. I knew that the Dorji Family was powerful not only in Bhutan but throughout the Himalayas. Llendhup Dorji's brother Rimp was revered among informed Buddhists as *the* reincarnation of the original Dalai Lama—the pope of Buddhism. I was sure that he would have a calm, all-knowing serenity that would unnerve me, and in my searching, unsure frame of mind I wouldn't know how to behave. I pictured him sitting, wrapped in saffron robes, in the traditional lotus position, meditating. My greeting would destroy his concentration. He would tolerantly raise his hand for silence, and I would be mortified. But when I arrived at the Blue Fox Restaurant in Calcutta (the spot chosen for the meeting), the restaurant was dark and quiet and Dorji was late. Martin, Bhulu, and I sipped lime and soda. Everyone knew that he was coming. Even the waiters seemed tense. "Don't be nervous. You'll like him. He's not what you think," Martin said as the door opened and sun splashed across the dark restaurant.

A tall, slim Mongol of about twenty-eight walked toward the table. He was dressed in black mohair trousers that fit so tightly he might have been born in them. His sports jacket was bright red and a matching vest peeked through. A black silk tie stood out on his shirt like an exclamation point. His handmade Italian shoes had pointed toes and were highly polished. He was chewing betelnut and smoking a cigarette as he swaggered up to the table and thrust out his hand. If I had been surprised at his appearance, that surprise was secondary to my reaction when he began to talk.

"Hi, there, my name is Lenny."

I choked on a piece of ice and shook hands. "It's an honor for me to meet you, Mr. Dorji. I've been looking forward to it."

"Same here," he said. "You're a gas in the flicks, especially the ones with the guys—Frankie and Dino. That clan really swings, eh?" He laughed and sat down, looking around. "That Glenda, Jesus, she's always late. Where is she? The hairdresser's again?"

Bhulu nodded. Glenda was Dorji's wife.

"Well, let's drink up while we wait." He snapped his fingers, and a waiter bounded to our table.

After the waiter left there was a moment of silence. Dorji blinked, and a smile came up like a tide. Everything softened around the edges, and his flip manner bore a trace of sadness.

"I went to school in the States, slept in Grand Central Station for two weeks—easy on the pocketbook but hard on the backside—finally got a room in Greenwich Village. For the longest time everyone thought I was a Chinese laundryman. How do you explain Bhutan to Americans? I wasn't going to try." He paused. "Do you really know New York? I know you've probably been there, but do you really know it?

I shook my head.

"Cruel city, isn't it?" He went on: "For the longest time I thought New York was America until a buddy and I hitchhiked across the country. No, New York is a place you stay in if you're born there, and a place to visit if you're not. But never could it be a place to live in if you're not born there. What part of the States were you born in?"

Martin hadn't prepared me for any of what was happening. I was thrown off guard completely. This Bhutanese Chief of State had slept in Grand Central Station, and people had thought he was a Chinese laundryman? I guess it was no more incongruous than an American movie star who wanted to experiment with her inner self in the Himalayas.

"You started as a ballet dancer, didn't you? And I read in a movie magazine that when you were a chorus girl you hated being in a long-run hit."

Had he been reading *Photoplay* and *Modern Screen* in the wilds of the Himalayas?

"I can also tell you at what point the stock market closed on Wall Street today or how the Dodgers are doing," he said. "I'm interested in all things. I can't afford not to be. Don't let my flip talk and flashy clothes fool you. I want to stay young as long as possible, that's all."

Dorji's wife, Glenda, walked to the table. She had dark lacquered hair and was beautiful. With an air of delicate grace, she scarcely smiled when we were introduced. "Pardon my tardiness," she said, "but I was feeding my babies."

Dorji got up from the table. "Now let's split this scene and dig the races."

The proprietor and employees of the Blue Fox Restaurant stood at attention as we filed out and piled into Lenny's new European sports car and sped away, leaving the sidewalk inhabitants of Calcutta staring at the flag of Bhutan that flew from the hood.

Lenny was the subject of much after-dinner gossip in the upper strata of Calcutta society. His fast life and compulsive gambling met with disapproval in many quarters. He was aware of it; his real friends made certain of that. It made no difference to him.

He said that after the wild regions of Bhutan, which he claimed were still in the Bronze Age, he needed the city life of Calcutta. He said that there was one telephone switchboard in Bhutan and it was located at the border town of Phuncholing. Electricity was unheard of, and except for the Indian industrial engineers who arrived in jeeps, the people of Bhutan did not even have the wheel.

Potatoes, rice (grown at fourteen thousand feet), and red hot chili peppers were the mainstays of the Bhutanese diet. Everything was flavored with rancid yak butter. Although yak meat was eaten now and then, meat was not a favorite dish in the Buddhist land. Dorji's newest son was only six months old, and Lenny feared for his health, which was left to the gods of Bhutan. Hospitals and doctors didn't exist there. The predominant reason for the high infant-mortality rate was the custom of feeding newborn babies the hot peppers in order to "keep them warm." The government and the royal family had not been successful in their attempts to stop the practice.

Cholera was rampant in Bhutan, and had nearly wiped out the 6,000,000 population in the late nineteenth century. Now only 850,000 people remained. Syphilis and leprosy were common, and one out of three persons suffered from goiter, as a result of the low iodine content in the diet.

"Yet, even at our primitive level," Lenny said "our people have enough to eat and are spiritually content."

"We need medical aid badly, but there are always too many strings attached. We won't trade our souls for a vial of penicillin. Look at Nepal and Sikkim now—they're nothing but India's satellites. That's not going to happen to us. But it is difficult. We are a buffer between India and China, and they both want to infiltrate and control us. What they don't understand is that we see no reason to be afraid of China just because everyone else is. China never hurt us, and she probably won't. No one would be crazy enough to invade our mountains. Besides all that, we have much more affinity with the Chinese than we do with the Indians. After all, we are Mongols. Do you understand?"

"I understand," I said breathlessly between frugs. Lenny had taken us to the Grand Hotel night club for dancing. He was sounding more like a prime minister, but he frugged on enthusiastically. I guessed he didn't want to talk in front of the others at the table.

"I hear from Martin you're interested in Buddhism. I notice you wear a Buddha charm around your neck? Why?"

The chain was twisted and tangled three times. I clawed at it self-consciously. It swung up and hit me in the teeth.

"Well . . ." I sputtered, "I'm not really a Buddhist; not yet anyway. I mean I think Nirvana would be very nice, but that's difficult to attain in Hollywood. I do think the Buddhist philosophy of never hurting your neighbor is more realistic than loving him."

He made no comment.

"You travel a lot, don't you?

"Yes, I travel a great deal. I think now it is more than a hobby. It has become my avocation. I think I make movies just to pay for the plane tickets."

The music had subsided in tempo, but I was getting cramps from his frug. He went on with his questions.

"Do you find that you accept the things you see on their own terms?" he asked.

"Yes, I think I do."

"Could you accept an industrially backward society with all its discomforts and still see the beauty in its simplicity?"

The question was full of fearful pride. Why was he so hesitant to expose the truth of his country? What possible comparison could there be between the naked hills of Bhutan, and the primitiveness of his people's lives, and the wall-to-wall plush and hot and cold running water of a Hilton hotel? Comfort was a relative term.

"Lenny," I answered, "I'm not a tourist; I'm a traveler."

He took my hand as he led me off the dance floor,

and announced as we sat down, "She is a strange girl. Are you sure she's American?"

Martin leaned forward. "She lives in Tokyo a lot, you know. I guess more than a little of Asia has rubbed off on her." Men of the East have a way of discussing women as though they weren't present.

"Yes, I will arrange for her interline permit tomorrow morning, but she must return to New Delhi for final confirmation with the Indian government. They are usually extremely reluctant, but I will use pressure and a very persuasive hatchet man. She will leave immediately after. I depart for Switzerland tomorrow to confer with the king. He left Bhutan last week. He has not been feeling well and is seeing his doctor, so I must pay my respects."

"Now to our apartment, a Bhutanese breakfast, and your introduction to Bhalla," said Lenny as we rose and ended the long evening of talk.

Sixteen

THE THIRD FLOOR OF the prime minister's Calcutta residence was heavily fortified with servants. Clad in heavy Bhutanese robes, they roused themselves from sleep in the hallways to bow and prostrate themselves before the young man, who went directly to his jazz record collection. Calling for more betelnut, Dorji motioned us to sit. Never turning their backs on their master, the servants bowed and left. Dorji had consumed ten of the intoxicating concoctions of raw betelnut wrapped in a thick, bitter leaf smeared with lime paste. Called *pan,* it is said that one serving has an effect similar to that of several shots of Scotch. I could see why it was so popular.

On a long table were curries and mounds of freshly boiled, steaming rice. Bowls of crimson chilis were placed in strategic positions.

Glenda retired to feed the babies. We swept past the table to sit in overstuffed modern chairs in the sitting room. Hand-painted Bhutanese designs of the royal family crest decorated the walls.

The front door opened and a smallish, dark-skinned young Indian with bowed legs moved uncertainly into the presence of his prime minister. He wore a mussed, unbuttoned double-breasted pin-striped suit with a tee shirt underneath. The tops of his worn black shoes were scuffed and navy-blue sweat socks drooped around his ankles. A cigarette dangled from his purplish lips, giving the impression that he was a busy man in transit.

"Sit down, Bhalla," said Dorji. "This is Mrs. Parker, whom you shall accompany to Bhutan."

We shook hands and Bhalla seated himself on the edge of a stuffed chair with his legs neither crossed nor jacked-up, but drawn together at attention, waiting for further orders from Dorji.

In all but his clothing, Bhalla was a dignified young man and during the weeks that followed I came to know his curious mixture of humor and solemnity. He had been born in Calcutta, but his love was for Bhutan, a kingdom where he felt a man's soul belonged to himself. He loved her natural, unharnessed forces, her defiance of human conquest. "They seem to have an answer they will not easily share," he said of the looming hills he had come to call his brothers. From the squalor of the low country he had dared to reach out and touch a little of hereafter. "Mountains make me feel immortal and that I have already lived forever." He spoke poetic English as though his initiation to the language had been through Rudyard Kipling. "Here I linger somewhere between my imagination and reality, and that gives me hope."

On the streets of Calcutta he had been hopelessly lost in the futility of his life. A small fire of cow dung was the focus of his existence, its ashes his only possessions. "You agree my flashing white teeth are beautiful, eh?" he would say. "Ashes were my toothpaste."

But this proud Indian boy had dared to change his destiny. In joining the human race he had escaped the misery of India's masses, of whom it was better not to think, and for whom only the euphoria brought on by starvation enabled them to tolerate life without suffering. "It must be nature's way to accommodate the sufferer with a narcotic—a drug made within one's own body," Bhalla said. "Sleep, for example: I never slept as much as I did when I was starving." In the nick of time he had forced himself to think, to fight off the sleep of apathy. He had rejected the religions of the ages, "The meek shall inherit the earth—it is written. . . . Atone for the sins of mankind and later in another life. . . ." Thinking had been his salvation, his motivation, his reality. It was as though his mind stood beside him, propelling him to stand up and walk, to pull his feet through and out of the muck that had been his only inheritance.

In making this choice he found that it was only the first of many choices one must make when one thinks. Since Bhalla's emancipation from misery, his life had progressed through many other choices. Neutrality didn't exist for him—he was a man who had to belong to something. And with fierce loyalty he had taken up his cause, Bhutan.

"Mrs. Parker will travel to New Delhi tomorrow for Indian confirmation of the interline permit," Dorji said to Bhalla. "She will return to Calcutta the following day to prepare for the journey to the high country. Arrange a government plane from Baghdogra to Hasimara, and have a jeep waiting when you land. See that she has warm clothing and boots from the army." Then with a twinkle in his eye he said, "She digs chocolate. Martin knows a good bakery here in Calcutta. Tell them to whip up a chocolate cake and make it heart-shaped as greeting to Mary MacDonald. She won't mind sharing it."

Bhalla nodded and rose from the chair, which had dwarfed him. Dorji looked long and deeply into his eyes. "There's no need to tell you to be careful."

In a day or so, the bureaucratic circles of New Delhi were alive with rumors that I had been granted permission to travel to Bhutan.

"Your invitation seems legitimate," said Mr. Raskothra, the Indian authority in charge of Bhutanese affairs. "I have no choice but to grant permission since it came from Dorji, but I would appreciate your keeping this to yourself. There are too many others residing here in India for years who have requested the same permission, which I have found it necessary to refuse."

I said nothing to anyone. However, typical of India, news of my trip was in every newspaper by the time I left New Delhi.

On my return to Calcutta the sweltering bazaars seemed an incongruous place to purchase wool socks, sweaters, long underwear, and scarves. The high, snowy Bhutanese Himalayas seemed light years away. Brown urchins darted about during my shopping tour, spreading word that the memsahib of blue eyes had money. How could I resist the cries of children, who were unable to believe that there wouldn't be something for them? But there wouldn't be; I knew the pitfalls of street charity, and my fear of a chain reaction of mounting demands was too real. How their eyes burned with envious anticipation on the doorstep of the tiny grocery shop. "Out, out," warned the bargaining proprietor. "Nuisance, nuisances," he joked, although there was deep resentment of me in his eyes. I pulled cans of Del Monte, Heinz, and boxes of Kleenex from the shelves. Years of dust swirled in the shop as the items came down for the first time. An Indian could never afford them, and a foreigner would take his meals in reputable restaurants.

"Sweets, do you want sweets?" Martin asked, holding up stale candy bars and out-of-date Lifesavers. I couldn't bear to buy them, not with the children watching.

Warm clothing for women was unheard of, but now and then the "barbarian Western male" stalked the tiger of Bengal, and for those hunting safaris he needed sweaters for the cool evenings of the jungle. I wanted to buy them all—to provide some economic stability for the proprietor and longer life for the hunted tiger.

I returned to the Dorji residence to express my thanks

and found Lenny packing for his immediate departure
to Switzerland. Engrossed in whispered conversation with
some of his aides, he seemed agitated. I wondered what
it was all about.

"Go in peace and with open mind," Dorji said to me
as he left us abruptly. "Enjoy my country and learn."

Dressed for a mountain safari, Bhalla and I arrived
at Dum-Dum Airport. Martin and Bhulu were there to
see us off. There would be no contact with them or with
the outside world for one month. We all knew it. Steve
sent me a cable:

GO BHUTAN AND LEARN STOP BUT
DON'T FALL OFF MOUNTAIN

Martin winked and said he hoped I'd find a level of higher
enlightenment, and wished me well on my adventure. I
touched the small gold Buddha and ivory hand around
my neck for good luck.

The loudspeaker announced planes leaving for Cairo,
Bangkok, Tahiti, Nairobi, New York, and it touched off
a warm glow inside me when I realized that it is actually
possible to reach such places.

I remembered a fresh new spring morning in Virginia
when I was about six. I was walking to school. The sun
was a warm liquid, and it buoyed me along like a rubber
ball on water. I spread my arms and flapped them like
wings. I skipped with my head thrown back, not bother-
ing to look in front of me. I was too young to know that
that was necessary. And then I saw the butterfly, perched
on the edge of a green bough in a massive, earthbound,
spreading tree. The fluttering rainbow-colored wings
stopped beating for a moment. The butterfly seemed to
drink in everything around its antennae, to feel the sun
and the lilting breeze. It seemed to become one with
the day. Suddenly, with a swoop its wings spread and,
carried by the air, it took off in front of my face. My

six-year-old imagination hopped on its back and soared aloft with the creature that used to be a caterpillar. I was no longer earthbound. I was free.

Bhalla, holding the heart-shaped chocolate cake with tender care, sat next to me. Our first stop would be Baghdogra, a small airport in the district of Darjeeling.

Suddenly my heart leapt. Over the horizon loomed the famous Himalayas—Mount Makalu, Mount Kanchenjunga, and the lord of the mountains, Everest. An hour away they were visible. And beyond the lofty slopes lay China—the Gobi Desert, the grandeur of the Yangtze River, and the millions who could conceivably change the social concept of the world. I wondered how long it would be before I could go there. I pulled my Minox camera from its case.

"Very sorry," said the sari-clad stewardess, "picture taking aboard plane or at airport is strictly forbidden since the Chinese emergency."

"That includes all of India," Bhalla added. "They've frightened us into exaggerated suspicions. Sorry."

I leaned back. If I was going to photograph my first glimpses of the haunting Himalayas, I would have to do it with my mind's eye. That's when I decided to keep a diary. It would be my only record of entering a world inhabited by mystics.

Noisily the plane lumbered to a stop at Baghdogra, where it would have a one-hour layover before returning to Calcutta without us. Bhalla and I were ushered into a small wooden waiting room and met by the private pilot who would fly us to Telepara and then on to Hasimara. He told us there were royal travelers about to board the plane going back to Calcutta.

I looked out the window and there, climbing the gangplank to the DC-3, was a well-dressed Bhutanese family, including a woman, two attendants, and three young children.

"That is the queen and the prince and princesses," said Bhalla in a steady voice.

"Why are they going to India?" I asked. "Why aren't they in Bhutan?"

Bhalla merely shrugged. "I don't know," he said.

At that moment, although we wouldn't know it until much later, the entire royal family and the prime minister were away from Bhutan; the king was in Switzerland and his wife and children on their way to Calcutta.

Our single-engined Cessna climbed until the exquisite valleys and lush tea plantations of Darjeeling were far below us. On and on we went until we reached the green isolation of the Telepara plantations. Our ferocious racket seemed to disturb the tranquillity of centuries as we landed.

Three people emerged from a grass hut. "These are my friends," explained Bhalla. "They heard you were going to pass overhead, and they would like to have their picture taken with you." I hadn't expected this. Hollywood seemed impossibly remote, but movies somehow seemed to reach areas that the people who make the films never even heard of. It always astonished me. And whenever I questioned people about the pictures they liked best, they always talked about the people in them, never the story. They were interested in how the people felt. They tried to identify with the feelings of the foreigners in the films because they couldn't identify with their circumstances. Apparently the same things made people everywhere laugh and cry. If the right chord was struck in Hollywood, it resounded around the world.

The Cessna could seat only two, so the pilot and I sat in front and Bhalla lounged atop the luggage, still clinging to the chocolate cake. Below us the lonely figures, longing for contact and probably another film, waved at us until we were out of sight.

Abruptly, other aircraft broke through the clouds. Jets—German, French, Indian—shattered the granite peace of the surrounding mountains. Fifteen minutes later we were over Hasimara, the air force base closest to China.

"Definitely no pictures here," said Bhalla. I could see what he meant.

We landed in a grassy field some distance from the air base, an obsolete sparrow among the birds of combat. As we left the plane, Bhalla looked around in distress. The jeep that was to meet us was nowhere in sight. I climbed down into the blazing sun to wait, dressed for the snow country. Dust clouds swirled near the burning earth.

Bhalla handed me a Thermos of sizzling water. "You'll need it," he said. "I'm going on foot to get the jeep. The plane has to return to Baghdogra, but you will be fine here. Watch the bags, please. I won't be long." With hunched shoulders, he ambled away through the high grass.

Shaking hands with the pilot, I thanked him and watched as he climbed aboard the small plane. Evidently a man with schedules to keep, he took off, tipped his wings, and disappeared beyond the mountains.

I sat down on the luggage. Hot gusts of wind rippled through the tall grass. My mind raced a little and my heart began to pound. It was such delicious pleasure to be uncertain of what might happen next. The feeling had always excited me. I didn't like being sure of tomorrow, or even of the next minute. That was the kind of security I never wanted.

It seemed incongruous that I should feel this way, given the background that had molded me, where you "looked before you leapt" into anything.

I thought of the warnings I had heard about Bhutan. "Strange things happen there. . . . Don't go. You will be robbed of your soul. . . . The mystics will steal you from yourself. . . . It's not like our world; it's too different to understand. . . . You will never return the same, provided you return at all."

And yet, as I sat on my suitcase alone in the wild grass hearing the strange sounds of the mountain people, my only emotion was the excitement of the unknown.

Seventeen

A JEEP roared toward me out of the tall grass. A thin, wiry young Bhutanese was driving. Bhalla sat beside him. They looked haggard.

"We landed on the wrong side of the mountain," said Bhalla. "Meet Larry Llamo, another of Lenny's assistants."

We shook hands. His grip was strong and his manner direct. "We are expected at the rest house in Phuncholing for lunch. We must go now."

We crossed the bamboo border fifty yards away and entered the kingdom of Bhutan. Immediately the atmosphere changed. Four suspicious border guards checked and rechecked our passports and interline permits, while two sentries rummaged through our suitcases, gazing suspiciously at the heart-shaped chocolate cake. Guns hung from their shoulders and colorful robes covered chests made massive by living in high altitudes.

Bhalla, Larry, and I sat quietly in the front of the jeep. Lush palm foliage swayed nearby, against the backdrop of ice-capped mountains above. On both sides of the road there were swampy rice paddies smelling of excrement, to remind us that we were still in Asia. But there would be an immediate transition in terrain, customs, and thinking. India, only one mile behind us, was a world away.

Phuncholing was a loose conglomeration of huts rather than a village. In fact, in Bhutan there are no villages, towns, or cities as we know them. The 850,000 inhabitants are isolated from one another; 2,000 live in the wide area called Phuncholing.

The rest house stood in wild contrast to the antiquity around it. It was a square, modern prefabricated structure, painted white and surrounded by a picket fence. Wild flowers grew around the front porch. A rocking chair by the front door moved in the breeze. The scene needed only a crap game going on on the front steps to resemble something Dorji must have passed on his hitchhiking tour of the United States. In fact it looked like a street in the San Fernando Valley.

"You are pleasantly impressed with the Western influence?" Bhalla asked proudly. He had never been out of India but he had looked at lots of picture magazines. "And we have beer also, from the pubs of London—warm and authentic and very delicious—with our stew."

He was right. How the thick Bhutanese stew, made with potatoes, yak meat, and turnips, and spiced with hot chili peppers, could be so appetizing in the heat of the lowlands was a mystery. But then, so were the fiery curries of India, sometimes eaten when the temperature was 116 degrees.

The stew lay heavy in our stomachs but it was fortification for the incredible trip ahead. Bhalla and Larry talked happily together, exchanging news from remote corners of their beloved land. "Dorji has left." "Conflict in high places." "The main palace residence in Paro is closed." "The queen and children were recalled to Calcutta." And the most significant communiqué of all: "The Paro-Phuncholing road is safe for travel."

The road linked Phuncholing to the royal residence in Paro Valley in the mountains one hundred and five miles away. Before it was built very little communication had been possible among the Bhutanese. Now the road was the country's lifeline. It was a tribute to ingenuity and physical endurance.

Begun in 1962 immediately after the Chinese invasion of Tibet, it was carved into the sides of mountains. More than a thousand people had perished during the three years it had taken to build the road. Landslides caused by blasting had carried jeeps, bulldozers, and vehicles of all descriptions over the side to destruction thousands of feet below. And during every monsoon season parts of the road disintegrated, making it an impassable, swampy stream. During the last monsoon a construction worker had been trapped in a jeep for two weeks before he was rescued.

We began to climb. The road was crowded with laborers. Men, women with babies on their backs, and even children pounded rocks into gravel, which they then placed in neat piles ready to be packed into the dirt road, making travel possible during the next monsoon. As they pounded, the adults puffed at the cigarettes dangling from their blue lips.

Most of the laborers were imported from Nepal by the Bhutanese government. They earned about three rupees a day (fifteen cents), and paid for their own meager food and housing, and after a year and a half of toil returned to Nepal about fifty dollars to the good. They were mountain people, accustomed to strenuous work in high altitudes, and were traditionally friendly with their Bhutanese neighbors.

When I got out of the jeep, the laborers, fascinated by my pale skin and round blue eyes, stared, gaped, and smoked at me, while I managed to keep a tenuous hold on the cliffs. I felt lightheaded. My breath began to come in short gasps because of the altitude. How could they smoke continually in such a rarefied atmosphere?

I looked up. Giant mountain walls climbed to the sky above me. Mist curled about my feet. With two more days of climbing ahead I was already standing on a cloud! We moved on. It was November and at four o'clock the Himalayan sunset splashed the sky with a mixture of colors so vivid and startling that it was difficult to relate them to the simple colors I had known on the earth below.

Five hours and thirty-six miles later we arrived in a tiny village, where we spent the night in another pre-fabricated rest house. More Bhutanese stew with chilis and a wood fire were welcome after the drastic drop in temperature.

The luggage, stashed in the back of the jeep, was covered with dust, including the chocolate cake. I longed to eat it that night, but I would save it for Mary. I fell fast asleep. The bouncing had numbed my back and back-side. Paro Valley was another two days and seventy miles further into the mountains.

Dawn broke early, the yawning mountains forcing their way through a sky of apricot and magenta. Buddhist prayer flags rippled in elongated squares. The cries of children could be heard, and trails of smoke wafted into the cold sky. And then the pounding on the road began. The road, always the road—it seemed to consume the life of every human being.

After a breakfast of chilis and rice we were on our way again, the chocolate cake intact and the dusty luggage cleaned. Our next stop was Chasilakha, the Indian indus-trial headquarters for the Paro-Phuncholing road construc-tion.

The farther we climbed, the more treacherous the road became, sometimes narrowing to the width of the jeep. The surefooted mountain people pranced along without shoes, unmindful of the jagged rocks and the potential death below. Larry was driving. Bhalla nodded in light sleep in the center of the front seat, and I was a package of frayed nerves on the outside, attempting to read. Only

the sound of our jeep broke the silence and the repose of
the hills.

Then we heard the thunder of shifting earth, cascad-
ing rocks, crackling branches, and screams. We rounded
a curve in the road, and Larry slammed on the brakes
just in time. Bhalla sat bolt upright. I nearly fainted. Right
in front of us was a gaping hole twenty feet wide. Part of
the mountain had fallen four thousand feet into the chasm
below and had taken a section of the road with it.

I tried to swallow. Sweat trickled down my neck. Who
would ever know if we had gone over? Life on the road
was expendable.

I didn't move. My eyes shifted from the gaping hole
to the rock chasm below. A squashed yellow bulldozer
lay in a cloud of fresh dust. Larry and Bhalla leaped
from the jeep. The laborers stood stunned. Another road
comrade had been scratched from the race against the
elements.

There was no way of rescuing the driver, or even
finding out if he was alive, though there wasn't much
chance of that. At least it had happened quickly.

The laborers returned to their pounding with impassive
faces, looking up at what remained of the mountain with
what seemed to be a mixture of awe and private hostility.

Our jeep straddled the narrow road. There was no
room on either side. It was impossible to turn around
and go back.

"Transshipment is the only possible answer," Bhalla
said. He was used to disaster. I wondered if he ever became agitated, upset, or frightened and, if so, whether
he showed it.

Calling across the chasm, Bhalla gave orders for someone to walk to Chasilakha and bring back a truck to meet
us and our belongings on the other side of the gap in
the road.

Some of the laborers dropped their work to help us with the heavy load. I put my suitcase on my back and started up. My calf muscles bulged with the strain and my heart pounded against my chest. A Sherpa hacked a jagged footpath before us, clearing away some of the dense mountain underbrush with a machete. The path was narrow and straight up; it was like climbing rocky stairs to an attic. The Sherpa and his laborers, wearing no shoes, maneuvered deftly on the rocks, never looking down, always up.

Sharp stones slashed at my tennis shoes but the big problem was balance. I couldn't hold on to anything without dropping the suitcase, and the only way to balance the heavy suitcase was to climb in hunched-over position. My thick yellow sweater suffocated me. I couldn't look down for fear I would lose what little confidence I had managed to muster.

Branches scratched our shoulders and faces. Our arms were too busy to protect our eyes. Stinging nettles lodged in the underbrush penetrated our clothing and produced an acute itching that we couldn't scratch. We were lucky in one respect. At any other time of year the foliage would have been infested with leeches. Human beings and animals alike are prey to the black, curved mounds of slime. The only way to get rid of them is to cut them out, skin and all. In the cold weather of November, thank goodness, the brush was leechless.

Up and up we went. In Bhutan it seemed impossible even to reach the top. I wanted pictures of our trek. I set the light exposure and the distance gauge on the Minox, handed it to one of the laborers (who had never seen a camera before), dropped my suitcase, and raced ahead to get in the picture. When I said, "Now," he pushed the magic button, only to be disappointed when nothing happened—no explosion, no noise, no magic, no nothing. He returned the camera, wondering why I'd gone to so much trouble.

We trekked for three hours. My breath held up and my legs became used to the strain, but my skin still smarted from the sting of the nettles and my shoulders ached from the heavy load of my suitcase. It was my first lesson in adjusting to a new and wonderful land. If it was raw nature I was after, unspoiled and undeveloped by man, I was certainly going to get it. One had to move through the Himalayas with trust because you are totally at the mercy of nature. Every day pilgrims, Sherpas, people who know the region well lose their lives through landslides suddenly tearing away part of a well-worn path and hurling them through space to their deaths below. It is part of life in the great mountains. My mind flashed back to a Hollywood party with jewels and hot and cold running profiles—I laughed out loud. Bhalla looked at me and winked.

The truck was waiting for us on the other side. It was a rattletrap, barely functioning, but at least we could rest. We collapsed in the back as it chugged to Chasilakha, two hours away.

Chasilakha is a busy construction center, the first I had seen in Bhutan. It was a community of about a hundred men who loaded dirt, mixed crude cement, hand-sewed two-by-fours—all with the inevitable cigarette hanging from their lips. An Indian overseer was their boss.

Beside a pile of dirt, with their backs to the road, sat two of the most unusual women I'd ever seen. They were tall and solid, and moved with broad and brazen gestures as they combed their long, thick black hair. They were obviously Indian and I wondered if they were employed to keep Chasilakha men happy. But strangely, one by one, Bhutanese or Nepalese laborers would come before them, seeming to report on the progress of building and respectfully awaiting their reactions. I was fascinated.

The women rolled their luxuriant hair into buns atop their heads. They stood up, plucked turbans from their pockets, and put them on. No wonder they had seemed unusual; they weren't women at all. They were Sikhs from the Punjab. Tall, arrogant men—I had seen them before, but never with turbans off.

The road-building authorities were all young; thirty seemed to be the maximum age. Some of them had been on the road for two years, never having come off the mountaintops in that time. They lived in wooden dormitories stocked with movie magazines, cases of rum, beer, Scotch, bourbon, and brandy—and American jazz records that were played on battery-powered phonographs. The music and magazines kept them sane; the liquor kept them warm.

Larry, Bhalla, and I sat down to another meal of Bhutanese stew and chilis in the canvas tent that served as a mess hall. A card table supported the liquor that began to flow like the Ganges. The workers from Tibet, India, Nepal, and Bhutan came in and sat down. They observed me with interest, staring silently. Then they began to eat. Bhalla watched them carefully. The fact that I was traveling alone with Bhalla and Larry baffled the Chasilakha workers. Some smirked in anticipation, others just ate and looked, and one Sikh must have been thinking that two years was long enough. He sidled over to me and, taking me by the arm, suggested that I spend the night in the barracks.

With a warning glance at the Sikh Bhalla said, "Dorji's orders were to continue immediately from Chasilakha." At the mention of the prime minister's name the Sikh dropped my arm and the drinking stopped. "We will take flash snapshots with Mrs. Parker, if you want, but then we push on."

The sun had set and the temperature had dropped
below freezing. A chilling rain fell outside. The Sikh
climbed onto the running board of our jeep. Clinging to
the window frame he began shouting frustrated admoni-
tions. Bhalla reached over and shoved him into the mud.
His turban fell off, and his black hair spilled to his waist.

The cold, wet air sobered Bhalla and Larry enough
to drive, as we pulled out of Chasilakha, but the road
was a frightening mess. Mud streams ran under the
chained wheels. We picked our way along the slick passes
for two hours, our eyes straining and tense. It was too
dark to see the chasm thousands of feet below.

Icy gusts of wind howled down the canyons. I wondered if there would be warmth when we reached Paro.
The rest houses along the road had not had any heat.

The Paro River spilled from a gigantic waterfall a
few miles further on. I hobbled up and wondered what
masses of drifting snows and melting glaciers were responsible for the icy, frosty waterfall. Thirsty from the rum
we had consumed, I took off my shoes and waded in for
a drink. The water was icy and fresh. Bhalla and Larry
sipped warm coffee from a Thermos. I leaned over, stepping on a rock for support. The water rushed by and
neatly toppled me face down. I came up freezing, spurting,
and coughing, my decision made: it was the last bath I
would take in Bhutan.

Forty-five shivery minutes later we arrived in Paro
Valley. It had taken two and a half days to travel a
hundred and five miles.

Eighteen ❧

PARO VALLEY belongs in the high, dry, re-
cesses of the imagination. It could have been the blueprint
for *Lost Horizon,* just as everyone had said. It is a sanctuary nestled in the arms of the great mountains, providing refuge for mortals intimidated by the Himalayas. With
such solid walls of granite I could understand why the
outside world leaves it alone, knowing that farther above
and beyond is a blizzard-swept world of deep crevasses,
glaciers, and massive hanging ice blocks no one could
conquer.

Wild flowers peeked through the light layer of snow
which covered the mountain grass. Eerie shadows played
on the rocks and rills of the valley floor, sending a superstitious chill through me. The stars shone like zircons
close enough to reach out and pluck.

The palace was closed. The guest houses about one
mile away were reserved for us. The walls of the stark
wooden structures were decorated with the royal Bhutanese crest. Each of the isolated guest houses had a front
porch with two wooden steps leading inside. Against the
mountains they looked like miniature doll houses. I would
occupy one house and Larry and Bhalla another. The rest
of the doll houses stood empty, dark, and waiting in the
shrill wind.

Bhalla showed me into what would be my home for
the length of my stay in Bhutan. An Indian army cot
made up with a sheet and a thin khaki blanket was the
only furniture in the rectangular room. Adjacent was
another smaller room with a cement floor. A wooden box

covered a pot inserted in a hole in the cement—the toilet. A white porcelain sink was attached to the wall. Icy water ran through a pipe and trickled outside to the ground. There was no light and no heat. Chips of orange paint flaked from the hand-painted designs on the walls onto the khaki blanket. Sliding wooden shutters covered un-glassed windows. The mountain wind blew through the room over my wet clothes.

Bhalla flicked off his flashlight.

"Across the way is the community room for guests, where there is a fire going," he reassured me. "Come and dry off."

Outside stooped Sherpas peered at us around corners of the guest house. Their faces and arms were covered with layers of the charcoal they burned inside their thatched huts. An invader—me—with boxed belongings had arrived, and the next day a storage place would have to be found.

The door of the community house was ajar. A roaring fire of blazing tree trunks in an immense pit seemed to be playing tricks on my eyes. If not, then a Japanese couple dressed in ceremonial kimonos waited on the steps of the community house.

"*Irashaimas,*" they greeted me. "We were told you were coming and wished to welcome you on your first visit to Paro Valley," they said in Japanese.

Japan swept over me—the cadence of the language, the smell of the woman's floral-scented perfume, the gay brocade of the kimonos, the graceful, considerate, physical manifestations of their traditional courtesies.

Mr. and Mrs. Nishioka had been recruited by the Bhutanese government to help with horticulture, planting, and agricultural programs. Nishioka-san had been doing the same thing for Nepal for a year before he had been called to Bhutan. Now he would spread further the respect that all Asians seemed to have for the Japanese.

Beside the fire pit Nishioka-san made paper doves. Japanese hands are never idle. Concentrating on pieces of torn paper, he fashioned works of art out of trash. Oksan watched silently. The talk waned, and I was warm when I bade them goodnight. I had come a long way and needed sleep.

Undressing down to my long johns in about thirty seconds, I leapt into the paint-flaked cot, hoping the warmth from the fire would stay with me until I fell asleep. It was no use. The cold was like an ice pick jabbing through me. I didn't know how I would get through the night. I had always suffered in cold weather, and this was the coldest I'd ever been in. My teeth chattered and my insides tied themselves in knots. I lay wondering how to conquer it—I would have to. I couldn't go on like this night after night.

I am not cold, I am not cold, I thought. But the cold had already engulfed me. I was operating from negative thoughts. I would have to control the *fear* of being cold. I would have to use that inner self the Yoga instructor in Calcutta had urged me to find. "Be effortless in your concentration," he had said. "The point is not to be something, the point is simply 'to be.'" "Relax when you are pained or uncomfortable. You will mold into your surroundings and its dictates and therefore become comfortably fused with it."

I tried relaxing my muscles and controlling my chattering teeth.

Then I remembered the orange circle.

"You have a center in your mind," the instructor had said. "It is the source from which all your thoughts spring. It is your nucleus, the center of your universe. Find it. Concentrate. It will come. Relax with it. That is meditation. Allow nothing to divert your conscious or unconscious attention. Not fear. Not pain. Sorrow. Cold. Nothing. Stare into your interior. You will see it. It will look like a tiny sun. The sun is the center of every solar system and the reason for all life on all planets in all universes. So it is with yours."

I closed my eyes, searching for the center of my mind. If only I could find that tiny sun. I will concentrate on the real sun, I thought, the sun I know, the sun I have seen. I will find that in my mind, and it will be hot.

The room left me. I felt my knotted muscles begin to relax. The freezing room and the windy granite mountains outside began to drift out of my conscious mind.

Slowly in the center of my mind's eye a tiny round ball appeared. I stared and stared at it. Then I felt I *became* the orange ball. Slowly, slowly the center grew. It seemed to generate heat and light. The heat spread down through my neck and arms and finally lodged in my stomach. I felt droplets of perspiration on my midriff and forehead. The light grew brighter and brighter until finally I sat up on the cot with a start and opened my eyes, expecting to find that someone had turned on a light. Perspiring all over, I was stunned to find the room dark. I lay back. I felt as though I were glowing. Still perspiring, I fell asleep. The instructor was right; hidden beneath the surface there was something greater than my outer self.

If only I could find it and use it more often.

Nineteen

THE BHUTANESE MORNING shimmered cold and crisp, but I was still fairly warm. In the mountain air the slightest sound could be heard miles away. It was as though sound was borne on the rays of the sun.

Four sooty Bhutanese faces stared down at me. With a curious open honesty, they watched me open my eyes and yawn. I smiled up at them. They didn't smile back, but gazed instead at the untouched suitcase on the floor and then at the picture of Steve and Sachie propped up beside my cot.

Dressed in Bhutanese boots and robes covered with soot, they walked to the suitcase. I sat up in bed and gestured for them to open it. A youngish man opened it gently and began to rummage through it. Blinking with confusion, the four men touched each foreign object: toothbrush, toothpaste, Minox camera, bras, panties, clothespins, Kleenex, Kotex, aspirin, hair curlers—objects from another planet as far as they were concerned. The hill people live in such close association with nature that they are totally unaware of intellectual and material concepts. They don't know what "things" are or, more important, what point there is in possessing "things." One of the reasons their leaders have forbidden the influx of foreigners into the kingdom is that they regard foreigners as bearers of materialism, which is antipathetic to their own philosophy and therefore dangerous to their own power.

The men spied the dust-covered heart-shaped chocolate cake mashed out of the corners of its box in the corner.

"No, that's for Mary," I said, shaking my head. With that slight indication of disapproval on my part, they left the room. One returned immediately with yak-butter tea for my breakfast.

The sound of rock pounding ricocheted through the hills. Mountain trails were dotted with trudging Sherpas and Tibetan laborers, who lived higher in the mountains and trekked to Paro every day for employment on the road. The Himalayas rose like triumphant giants all around— domineering and all consuming. Their monstrous bodies gave me a profound sense of insignificance. How could I relate to something so overpowering? How could any- one feel life was important, even one's own life, in the shadow of such crushing strength? The sense was over- whelming. It semed irrelevant to concern oneself with one's individuality. It simply didn't exist. Had the moun- tain people come to terms with the giants? They had seemed awed by them on the road to Paro, but it was a friendly awe—as though they knew the mountains would remain forever and were therefore not mysterious.

The secret, then, would be to accept one's insignifi- cance. Perhaps that was enlightenment, true happiness, Nirvana. Perhaps that's what the lamas and yogis meant by achieving a sense of "nothingness." Perhaps serenity and harmony come from the realization that one is actually meaningless. Perhaps internal conflict is the result of trying to prove otherwise.

But to look at the painstakingly painted hut–doll houses nestled in the arms of the great mountains it seemed that the mountain people themselves hadn't totally ac- cepted their insignificance. The tiny structures were ex- quisite proof of individual expression. Hand-carved wooden roofs curled upward on the edges, reaching for the low-flying clouds. The prayer flags that rippled in the sunny mist were meant to remind the Almighty One of the life-long wishes of those who flew them. And they never doubted that their prayers would be answered.

The mountain people might rot of disease, lose the battle against the elements, die in total ignorance of civilization, and even succumb to the superstition of their own beliefs from time to time, but they seemed to have a driving compulsion to express themselves while accepting the insignificance of their lives.

After a breakfast of eggs cooked and served in yak oil washed down with yak-butter tea, Bhalla pulled a jeep to a stop in front of the community house.

"Mary is away in Ha Valley," he said. "As Dorji's secretary, she has been sent to hear the Oracle's predictions for the coming year. She is due to return tonight."

The Oracle in Ha is a Buddhist priest through whom it is believed a deity speaks. He is regarded with awe and is totally obeyed. The Oracle predicted the assassination of the former prime minister the year before. I asked Bhalla how Mary had traveled to the Oracle.

"She walked," he said. "Ha Valley is far above Paro on the Chinese border and only accessible by foot. No animals could negotiate the trails."

"She must be quite a girl," I said.

"You will see."

The dust swirled around our faces and laid scarves of powder on our hair as we drove off. I waved to Nishioka-san, who stooped over his rice crop on the floor of the dry, dusty valley. He was going to prove that fertility was a question of relativity.

Leaving the jeep on flat ground, we proceeded on foot across a narrow planked bridge to the stone gates of the dzong (monastery). Buddhist monks greeted us and silently led us into the courtyard.

The walled dzong was the religious and civic seat of Paro Valley, where priests and secular authorities ruled jointly. The massive stone buildings of the dzong were whitewashed and trimmed in crimson. Beneath the complex there was a dungeon, where prisoners never saw the light of day.

No one spoke as we entered the stone courtyard. The priests and lamas walked about in bare feet, swathed in musty-smelling thick brown robes. The only sound was of muffled cymbals clashed together by an old lama seated cross-legged on the cobblestones. In front of him were twenty-six lamas rehearsing their masked dances to the accompaniment of the eerie, muted sound. The dances centered around the temptations of the devil; the arm and leg movements warded off the invasion of evil. Their bare feet slapped the cobblestones, and their breathing became heavy, as the evil temptations mounted. The older lamas looked on with formidable poker faces, as one by one the younger men sank to the ground, either having conquered evil or succumbed to it, I wasn't sure which.

In the monastery's long classroom, small boys (future lamas) chanted prayers in high-pitched, singsong voices, bowing in unison over their scriptures. Towering directly above them was a bronze statue of Buddha, looking serenely down, surrounded by Hindu gods.

The ceilings, twenty-five feet high, were supported by massive beams, and wooden staircases rose from the cavernous dungeons to the lofty rooftop, wrought and fitted by hand with magnificent brass decorations.

The high priest led us through each chapel of the monastery, prostrating himself before each replica of Lord Buddha, and directing us to follow suit. Lavishly decorated Hindu gods seemed to smile from carved niches in the walls as we paid our respects to the Buddha who, though he was born a Hindu prince, had endured the self-imposed rigors of the eightfold path to Nirvana.

In the silence of the rectory we were served tea mixed with rice and yak butter and flavored with sugar. Because I was a foreign guest, the high priest waited for me to finish my tea before he started on his own.

Tea is a ceremonial exercise throughout Asia. There is a legend about the origin of tea. It is said that a South Indian sage named Bodhidharma journeyed into China in about the sixth century to meditate. He used to meditate before a blank wall. During one of his meditational periods he became annoyed with himself because he felt drowsy—so annoyed that he cut off his eyelids, so that he would never fall asleep again, and threw them away. They supposedly took root on the spot and became a plant which until that time was unknown—tea—and the leaves of the plant were useful in keeping one awake.

The tea plant did originate in South China and the sage Bodhidharma developed the philosophy of Zen, whose followers even today sip tea as they meditate.

I drank all of the tea. Bhalla and I bowed and took our leave of the high priest and attending lamas. The high-pitched singsonging resounded loud and clear through the open classroom, and the lamas began their masked dances again.

Bhalla and I walked from the dzong. Leaving the jeep behind, we tramped over the wooded terrain of the mountains. We forded narrow streams in our bare feet, straining to see the source of the icy water somewhere above us. The air was so clear and pure it felt like a regenerative current going through me. On the mountain path little animals darted about, and in the wooded outskirts the wild bear and leopard waited for evening. Higher up the mountain we encountered the lepers of Bhutan. Eyes, noses, hands, and parts of faces were eaten away, while others in earlier stages of the disease had only a

look of anticipated horror in their eyes. They excommu-
nicated themselves from society and never came close to
the village, preferring to avoid the stares of those they
frightened.

In the Paro village area, primitive stalls displayed
Bhutanese boots made from well-chewed yak skins, hand-
loomed strips of heavy colorful material, flour made from
corn husks, charcoal for hut fires, potatoes, and chilis. In
one or two stalls hung clothing, sweaters, and wool head-
coverings. Since the mountain people wear only one set
of clothes, in which they live, sleep, eat, work, and die,
sales were slow.

Old women sat, hunched over, savoring betelnut and
dipping pan leaves into lime paste. Circular bushel baskets
beside them were laden with the delicacy, ready to be
sold for practically nothing. The Bhutanese citizen does
not want for means of intoxication; there was plenty for
everyone.

Coins are not round and flat, designed to be easily
deposited in pockets, for Bhutanese robes have no pockets,
but are made of thick, twisted pieces of steel and are
heavy and lumpy. Dating back to the sixteenth century,
the coins looked more like roughly hewn pieces of jewelry
than money. Food or belongings are carried in straw
dishes in the overlapping folds of the robes.

The huts of the villages are built on stilts, the family's
animals living underneath. Mountain flies and insects
swarm in straw on which the horses and chickens sleep,
and above, inside the huts, are the continual charcoal
fires, always built in the middle of the living and sleeping
area. There are no facilities for sewage or running water.

There are no hospitals in Bhutan, no doctors, and no
medicine. Local medicine men treat disease with superstitious rituals, much of the time successful, because faith

plays a great part in any case. But with leprosy, syphilis, cholera, and typhoid, the medicine men were sadly ineffective.

In Calcutta, Dorji had explained the reluctance of Bhutan's leaders to introduce the modern age into their medieval kingdom. It wasn't simply materialism they rejected. They didn't want industrialization, machines, or other modern equipment. It would destroy the tranquillity of centuries, he said, and disturb the peace of the people. They wanted no foreign trade—there were too many strings attached, and Bhutan wanted to remain independent. But Dorji's heart ached at Bhutan's refusal of medical aid and knowledge. His people might be happy enough but they were sick also. Help was needed. As it was the country was underpopulated. Lives must be nourished and spared, he felt. But the rulers had refused. Even doctors, they felt, would be an influence from the outside to contaminate the citizens.

So the Bhutanese citizen would have to wait before entering the age of modern civilization. Faith made his life bearable. He would accept any adversity delivered by nature or circumstances until his rulers decided it was time. And yet, in spite of the filth, disease, and illiteracy, and though the children played in dung piles, and adults walked in snow and ice without shoes, the citizens of Bhutan seemed serene and full of joy in life. Each individual, eyes shining and manner tranquil, seemed to possess an inner calm.

The sun set at about four o'clock every day, abruptly plunging the valley into cold darkness. The fire pit of the community house was always welcome. One evening Bhalla, Nishioka-san and Oksan, and I sat quietly beside the fire pit. The door of the community house was ajar, and I gazed out at the low-flung stars.

Suddenly one of the stars sprouted legs and floated

toward me. It was a woman, one of the most exquisite I
had ever seen. Perhaps she was one of the mysterious
"hollow-backed beauties" who, the superstitious mountain
people say, lurk along paths to tempt the men of the
mountains. Their beauty is irresistible, but should a man
indulge himself, he dies at daybreak. At night the rocks
and tree-lined cliffs belong to ghosts and spirits. Mortals
flee to the shelter of caves and huts made of rock and
yak hide to wait for the safety of sunrise. Even the rea-
sonable, the well-educated, and the intelligent dare not
disbelieve. There is evidence—much evidence. Blood-red
gargoyles have been *seen* dining on human hearts; invisible yetti leave scratches across the chests of sinners, producing a fever and hysteria so complex that modern
Western medicine has yet to solve the riddle. Only recently
a Western-oriented prince had refused to believe the superstition of the Festival of Lights. It was said that a dead
king resided in the massive tree adjoining the royal palace.
In deference to him and for fear of disturbing his sleep
during the festival, the tree was not adorned with lights.
The prince scoffed and kicked the tree to show his scorn.
By dawn his leg was swollen and crippled and he was
unable to move. He remained in this inexplicable condition for days, until a Buddhist priest was summoned to
extract an apology from him. The instant the prince asked
forgiveness of the dead king, his leg became normal. It is
said that the event was witnessed by a most jaded intellectual who ultimately fled in fear of the unanswered
questions of the Himalayas.

Clearly, I too was succumbing to the mountains. They
were beginning to mesmerize me and I longed to believe
that reality didn't exist.

The raven-haired beauty was at the door. She wore
the traditional Bhutanese dress and coral beads about her
neck. Faint pools of water twinkled in her hair, where

only minutes before there had been snowflakes. A tightly woven cummerbund around her waist revealed a perfect silhouette beneath. She puffed crystal breaths as she approached us. Her arms were bare and she wore only sandals. She was about twenty-three years old, and had eyes like black olives and skin of tan satin. She put out her hand and introduced herself in English.

"How do you do? I'm Mary MacDonald, Llendhup Dorji's Paro Valley secretary, and you are my favorite actress. Is Jack Lemmon as funny in real life as he is in the films?"

"Oh, no," I thought. "Not again." I hadn't come twenty-four thousand miles around the world and into the Himalayas to talk about the picture business. I toppled from my illusion and said Yes.

Mary had walked fourteen miles through deep snow high on the Tibetan border to hear the pronouncements of the Oracle. She was a Christian, but when it came to Bhutan she was steeped in the superstitions of centuries. The Bhutanese believe that if the Oracle is completely drunk when he makes his pronouncements he will have no conscious control over his predictions, thereby enabling the deity to speak through him with no interference. So, Mary told us, the Oracle had been given liquor for forty-eight hours before he entered the prayer circle that had been cleared for him.

On this occasion, he entered the circle, looked around at his audience, and became enraged when he realized that no members of the royal family were present. Shouting wildly, he flailed at the prayer flags and uprooted them. The audience, believing that the gods were truly angry, shrank in horror.

Attendants replaced the flags and the Oracle began once more. Shaking uncontrollably and babbling incoherently, he lunged again at the prayer flags. Suddenly he regained control of himself and screamed a warning: the royal family should be more aware of the activity at the monastery in Thimphu (the capital of Bhutan). He reminded the onlookers that, eighteen months before it was sent, he had predicted the anonymous letter from the monastery at Thimphu that had threatened the assassination of Jigme Dorji, Llendhup's brother. It had come to pass. The Dorjis should take his warnings seriously.

Mary had rushed from the scene in Ha Valley to report the incident to the royal family. The news that the royal family had already gone worried her. Mary wasn't an easily intimidated person. Her direct, level manner communicated a sense of security. And her natural laughter dispelled fear. But now Mary was uneasy.

She began to consult the horoscopes intently. Mary described herself as a Himalayan cocktail because she had Indian, Bhutanese, Scotch, and Irish blood in her. She had been raised as a Catholic by two old maid aunties in Kalimpong, which had once been a part of Bhutan but had been ceded to India by an English-made treaty. Even though she had been brought up a Christian, in times of stress, she reverted instinctively to Asian superstitions. Bhalla sat quietly, staring into the fire. The sooty royal servants, who were not paid for their services—they considered it their duty to serve royalty—drifted in and around the table set for dinner.

Larry Llamo dashed into the room wearing several sweaters under a parka and high boots.

"I've received a commiqué from Phuncholing to return immediately," he announced. "Probably road trouble."

Mary and Bhalla exchanged private looks but said nothing. Larry clearly thought he should be businesslike. "Sorry I couldn't be with you longer." His sense of duty prevailed. He could be depended upon, even when he was in love.

And Larry *was* in love with Mary.

She rose brightly. Her words of parting to Larry sounded like a mother's careful pat on the head before her son's departure on a dangerous journey. Bhalla told me that Mary had never been kissed and that every wife whose husband knew Mary was jealous of her. Bhalla turned on the portable phonograph and "Come Fly with Me" blasted forth tinnily as Larry left.

We ate our Bhutanese stew. A treat in the form of an Indian condiment had been brought from Phuncholing. I took a huge tablespoonful. It was delicious. Mary and Bhalla feasted on the familiar chilis. We laughed and joked. Mary's appetite defied her figure. She downed three helpings of the thick stew and topped them with two giant chocolate bars we had brought from Calcutta. The heart-shaped chocolate cake, dust-covered and probably stale, lay on the floor in my room. Leaving the table, I made my way across the frozen grass to fetch it.

The icy air stabbed my nose, and my ears began to ring. Suddenly the world spun around . . . and around. I broke out in dripping perspiration and my stomach turned over in violent nausea. Right ahead I could dimly see my room. It was blurred around the edges. The ringing in my ears grew louder and louder in rhythm with my pulse, which galloped at a frightening rate. My heart pounded and nausea rose and fell until in one final wave it rose to the surface. I fell into the room toward the hole in the cement, just in time.

My vomit and the bile that came with it were black. I retched and felt as though I were turning inside out. I was terrified. I hadn't had a proper cholera shot before entering Bhutan. There hadn't been time for the two-week series, but the doctors hadn't seemed concerned because the shot did not immunize one against the disease anyway; it only prevented a fatality. The only immunization against cholera was to stay out of contagious areas.

The symptoms were there: high fever, intense vomiting, dehydration, blurred vision, dizziness, *black* vomit, and unbearable nausea. I collapsed on the skimpy cot. A fleck of yellow paint from the ceiling fell into my eye.

Mary and Bhalla swam in and out of my consciousness. "Don't know what it is—bring cold towels—she's retching again—don't let her fall—wants to be alone." The palace servants looked down at me with impassive and cruelly impersonal expressions.

Mary and Bhalla held me up, kept me from falling, as time after time I retched into the hole in the floor. I was dehydrated and devastatingly thirsty. I imagined that the smell of yellow paint was choking me.

I was overcome with fear and overwhelmingly lonely. What was I doing so alone? Why? What was I doing vomiting black bile at the top of the Himalayas?

Waves of longing for something I couldn't quite touch swept over me. I wanted to climb higher and higher into the mountains to look for something farther and farther away—not to renounce the earth below but to embrace new worlds above so that I could be part of all there was.

Everything smelled sick. I wrapped my arms around my stomach, trying to control the nausea. I thought of the Masai woman rocking back and forth holding her stomach, not even realizing she was giving birth.

I wondered if people really were a part of each other, intertwined and related in the struggle of being alive. If I really learned more about myself, would it really help me to know others and vice versa? When did the searching stop? Would I know when I knew? Was I trying to find my identity or lose it? I didn't know.

The wind howling outside filtered through the cracks in the sliding window. I thought of Sachie and what she would do if anything happened to me. And of Steve who had always endorsed my trips and my searching. Was I being selfish in living my life the way that made me happiest? Would it be better to restrict my longings and my spirit—better for everyone including myself? Freedom seemed so lonely so much of the time anyway. Yet when I thought of Sachie I wished freedom for her. Freedom, with her front windows open and unlocked, with breezes and challenges blowing in. I wished that she would know herself through freedom. And I wished that underneath she would understand that there is no such thing as being safe—that there are no safe havens for anyone who wants to know the TRUTH, *whatever* it is, about himself or others. . . . I hoped she would feel that life is important enough to be lived fully and that she would learn that in the last analysis you only have yourself to live with and inside of, and you have no choice but to be true to that inside self. . . .

I thought of many things but finally nothing mattered except my stomach. I would have traded anything for an easy, quiet stomach. It was all so simple; nothing but feeling good again meant anything to me—not Steve, not Sachi, not my life or my ideas, not movies I would make or trips I would take. It all boiled down to one thing—I didn't want to throw up any more.

Finally I was so exhausted I fell into a deep sleep, I didn't care if I vomited in the bed—I had to rest.

Days seemed to pass. I lost my sense of time. Gradually, gradually I realized I was feeling better. The nausea had subsided, and when finally I opened my eyes wide I felt absolutely euphoric because I wasn't sick any more and my temperature was normal.

Mary and Bhalla opened the sliding windows. A cold breeze blew across my face. I tried to describe to them how exquisitely happy I felt.

They helped me out of bed. My balance was completely shot. They brought me tea and fresh spring water. Looking out the window, I craved sunshine and fresh mountain air. I wanted to walk on the mountaintops outside. For a few days I sat on the steps of the rest house soaking up everything around me. Slowly I got my strength back. I had been sick a few times in my life— once when my appendix burst and once when my fever rose to 106 degrees with the Asian flu—but this time it had been different—not because I may or may not have had a fatal disease called cholera but simply because no one could help me. The feeling of facing something terrifying totally alone was worse than the sickness itself.

I felt as though I'd been on a long journey through myself. I was moved more than ever to search for the "phenomena" of the mountain people. Now that I was well I wanted to visit the lamas—the mystic lamas and their monasteries, higher up, carved into the sides of the great mountains of Bhutan.

And so one morning Bhalla, Mary, and I rose at five-thirty to climb fourteen thousand feet to the Monastery of Taksang. Mary, as always, was wearing a colorful Bhutanese dress and simple sandals on her uncovered feet. I, as usual, was freezing. The orange-circle technique only worked for me during the nights when I was by myself and could concentrate. The rest of the time, unless the sun shone, I was cold. My mind seemed to be too cluttered, too diverted, to relax with the coldness and thereby overcome the feeling of being afraid of it.

Smiling, Mary handed me a hot-water bottle. Her hair was wringing wet. "I've just washed it in the mountain stream," she said. Clutching the hot-water bottle I envied her as much as it was possible to envy anyone. "Don't worry, the sun will be up soon," she said. "You will be warmer and my hair will get dry."

Shivering and shaking, I climbed onto the bony horse,

belonging to one of the Sherpas. I tucked my diary under the saddle. My fingers were too cramped to write anyway.

Picking our way along the narrow mountain paths I thought how ridiculous some would think it was that we literally trusted our lives to the mountain horses, which had no control whatsoever over the paths that broke away under us every few yards. I thought of the two Buddhist nuns who had gone over the side just two weeks before, almost unnoticed because trippings on the trails was commonplace in the mountains.

We stopped beside a mountain pond. Above us a few thousand feet a monastery jutted out over the mountain in the clouds.

"The lama who worships there has spent his entire life meditating silently," Bhalla said. "It is customary for a villager to bring him food twice a week. That is the only contact he has with other human beings and the only food the lama can depend on. But so revered is he that he will never want for anything. The hill people believe their gods live on in the lamas."

The lama appeared on the mountain trail above us. He looked down. As though he didn't recognize we were there, he began to glide toward us. His feet didn't seem to touch the path. He actually seemed to skim as he moved, his saffron robes blowing behind him.

We stood beside the pond. The lama glided toward the water and, with a stick, cracked a hole in the icy pond. He then gently lowered himself into the water until he was submerged up to his neck. His expression never changed. For fifteen minutes he remained immobile surrounded by ice. The three of us didn't move. Then the lama came out of the water and stood on the bank, silent and motionless as though in a trance.

Bhalla nudged me. Steam began to rise from the lama's body and in no time he began to perspire profusely. He returned quietly and retired to his monastery.

Bhalla winked. "There is another lama in these hills who performs an unbelievable trick. Sitting on a straw mat, legs crossed one over the other in the lotus position, hands resting lightly on his knees, he suddenly, *from* the lotus position, can jump three feet into the air. I have seen it. It's a mystery to me how he can defy gravity."

I had wanted to ask the next question ever since I arrived. "Bhalla, I want to see levitation. Is it really so that people can levitate? My instructor in Calcutta told me that reversal of the poles of gravity within oneself is possible if you can project enough psychic concentration to another planet above you. He said that it's a question of mental energy, which in effect becomes magnetized, and through concentration you can actually bring yourself into the gravitational pull of another planet and therefore repel the gravity on earth and rise off the ground."

"Many people say they have seen it," said Mary. "They say that one can accomplish that early on in the stages of higher enlightenment. But I don't know if they have *actually* seen it or they *believe* they have seen it. As far as accomplishing it is concerned, I have the same reservation. It's quite common in the atmosphere of meditation to feel you are floating above the earth. Lots of people say they have felt that, when they reach a certain mental state of relaxation and peace, they are no longer only part of the earth but become one with everything, including the sky above them. I tend to believe it's a feeling instead of a fact. In the Himalayas it's hard to distinguish the difference. For instance, I know of a tribe of mountain people higher in the Himalayas who supposedly only eat a few times a month. Instead of food, which is scarce in high altitudes, they have learned to live on the ultraviolet rays of the sun. It's not inconceivable, given all the vitamin and energy quotient of the sun's rays. And there are cer-

tain valley people protected from the outside by geographical location who are totally devoid of disease and sickness, living to be one hundred and fifty and older sometimes. There is so much we don't understand but we must
believe because it gives us hope."

We remounted our horses and continued to climb the
mountain trails toward Taksang.

It is said that a thousand years ago a lama riding on a
tiger stopped on the cliff where the Taksang Monastery
now stands and claimed it as his dwelling place. He medi-
tated there alone for twenty years, and after him there
came a succession of followers, each meditating for
twenty years, until the cliff came to be called Tiger's Nest.
A lama lived there now keeping the same vigil. According
to custom, his food was brought to him by a local villager.

The monastery, carved into the side of the mountain
fourteen thousand feet up, was accessible only by a long,
winding trail that approached it from the rear. The trails
were twelve inches wide, and even though our horses
moved with caution and were accustomed to the rocks,
they tripped and fell to their knees occasionally, drenched
with sweat. On steep inclines they stopped every few feet,
puffed hard, and waited before going on. We rode for six
hours. The sun finally blazed down on us.

Mary raised her arm and we stopped. We were beside
a waterfall. Silently we dismounted. The water was sil-
very and mountain birds played in and out of its spray.
The sun rays looked as though they dripped from the
birds' feathers onto the water and the mountain rocks. No
one spoke. I was beginning to feel strange. I sat down and
ate a piece of bread. It wasn't the altitude that made me
feel dizzy. I had been in high altitudes before. Something
was happening in my mind. It was more psychic than
physical.

The Sherpas led the horses back to the bottom of the

mountain. We would climb on foot the rest of the way up
the rock cliff to the monastery.

Taksang Monastery was about a thousand feet above
us. The mountain air filled my lungs. Bhalla stopped
smoking. We began the climb. My rubber-soled tennis
shoes held securely to the rock cliffs. Mary took off her
sandals. Bhalla did the best he could with his scuffed,
pointed Italian models. About fifty feet below the crest,
the rock mountain became carved stone steps. We
pressed our feet into them. Then the stone steps stopped.
Thick wooden planks stretched across the rocks: the
stairs leading to the monastery itself. We looked above us
—straight up. The lama of the monastery, his brown
robes beating against him in the mountain wind, waited
for us at the top. Etched against the sky, he bowed to us
as we finished the last of the climb. We had approached
his monastery from behind. No one had told him we were
coming, and he couldn't have seen us. Yet he greeted us
as though he had known of our visit all along.

I stood up straight. The wind felt as though it were
circulating *through* my mind, not around the outside of
my head. I stared at the mountains around me and the
valley below me. But I wasn't looking at the spectacle. I
was the spectacle. I sat down dumbfounded on a rock. My
eyes felt as though they were swaying with mountain
trees. I felt as though I had *become* the flowing mountain
streams and the silver waterfall below me. I had an overwhelming desire to leap from the cliffs and try to fly. I
was positive I could do it. I lost my grip on reality. It was
as though my spirit, independent of my body, was soaring
aloft over the earth *with* the wind; swirling with it, dipping and playing in rhythm with the gusts, bending with
it to and fro. I felt disengaged from myself. I wasn't
surprised when the wind changed direction because I was
with it to the instant. I *was* the wind.

I was beginning to understand. It was as though the wind that I was was a language. I couldn't understand all the nuances, but the meaning was becoming clear. I felt fused and part of all things. It felt as though I wasn't only me any longer—I was everything.

Was this the phenomenon everyone spoke about? Was this what those who were frightened meant by "soul robbing?"

I looked over at Mary and Bhalla. They both seemed mesmerized. They were staring, unblinking, eyes half closed, over everything below us. They too seemed disengaged from their bodies and were willing to ebb and flow with whatever was happening inside their own minds.

I glanced at the lama. He was watching me. He seemed to understand yet at the same time he was impassive, almost detached, as though he had been the wind for the twenty years he had lived on top of the mountain. He was no longer human. He was everything. His face was lined and creviced but he seemed very, very young.

The lama touched my arm, then Mary's and Bhalla's. They got up, eyes still half closed, and helped me up. The lama led us to his receiving chapel, where the correct number of places had been set for yak-butter tea. He blessed us. In silence we sat down and drank the tea.

The wind raced and bounced through the corridors of the monastery. It stopped for a while and caressed and slapped up against the sides of the hand-hewn walls.

A massive figure of Buddha loomed over us, smiling down with an expression of detached wisdom, as though the Buddha had achieved a sense of complete and serene harmony with all things surrounding him.

There were eight chapels in the silent, windy monastery, built by hand and decorated by the lama. He worshiped three times a day in each chapel. He was engaged in carving others from the sides of the mountain as further proof of his dedication to his belief. The lama led us through his chapels. Inside the mountain, thick, steep planked stairs joined one to another. Silently before each altar we assumed prone positions, our heads touching the floor, and paid our respects with prayers and offerings of coins. Myriad colorful Hindu gods hovered above the altars of Buddha, as the sunlight shafted through high, tiny wooden-barred windows. The mountain fell away beneath the windows as though the monastery hung suspended in midair. I felt my conscious mind was suspended with the monastery.

The lama left us in front of Buddha in one of the chapels. He returned a few moments later with saffron cloth spilling through his fingers.

"These will protect you." The lama opened his hands and offered us small strips of the cloth. "They have been blessed. Wear them about your necks until they disintegrate."

The cloth was rough and scratchy. I tied it obediently around my neck. In this sanctuary, the concept of protection didn't seem to exist. In fact, nothing had any meaning as I had known it. There was no such thing as good or bad, right or wrong. Fear didn't exist. There was nothing to be afraid of because of the feeling of being all things. All prior frames of reference seemed to float aloft with the wind.

Magenta, orange, and purple clouds hung low over the monastery. With the sunset, it was time to leave. The monastery would hover in a sea of starlit mist in an hour. We would descend most of the mountain in darkness.

The lama bowed good-by from his rocky heights as we descended the stone steps and sheer cliff. The descent was faster. On the loose rock inclines, I relaxed and slid for hundreds of feet, loose pebbles scurrying after me. Shadows played through the overhanging cliffs and trees.

I was smiling so much inside myself that I felt I didn't even need to breathe. We skimmed in silence. Suddenly Bhalla stopped. From a distance, perhaps maybe halfway down the mountain, came a series of whistles. High, sharp whistles served as a language of communication for the mountain people.

Mary grabbed my hand.

"Light a match for each of us," said Bhalla as he handed me the box.

"A leopard," said Bhalla. "The whistles are warning us. Walk calmly as though nothing is wrong. The flames will frighten him."

Mary clutched her saffron strip of cloth. Bhalla led the way.

The whistles changed pitch and moved in different directions. Down and down we walked, feigning nonchalance, lighting and relighting matches. Flat open ground appeared ahead of us. We broke into a run and made for our horses.

The Sherpas were nowhere in sight. Bhalla whistled up the mountain. There was no answer. "Build a big fire with some of the dead timber," Bhalla directed us. "I'm going back up the mountain. I'll be all right with a fire behind me." Mary and I built the fire and waited by the horses. We heard the whistles again, followed by raucous shouting, and out of the darkness Bhalla and the Sherpas charged toward the safety of the open fire. The Sherpas had baited the leopard from different directions to divert him from our route, and had lost each other in the darkness. They sat on their haunches beside the fire and asked for chocolate.

Each of us absorbed in his own thoughts, we mounted the horses to return to Paro Valley. Fires flickered in mountain caves, dotting the soft darkness along the way . . . again the mesmerizing silences . . . I felt the stars resting on my head . . . again I *was* the stars . . . I was everything.

As we rode, the lead Sherpa began to chant a Buddhist prayer. Soon the others chanted with him. Their voices slapped and echoed against the cliffs as the black mountains seemed to come out and sigh in the night. The deep fire pit of the community house glowed through the open door in the distance.

The sight was welcome but I wasn't cold any more. It was probably the coldest of all the nights but I wasn't cold—because I *was* the cold. I didn't feel afraid of it. My insides no longer knotted together, my teeth didn't chatter, and I didn't run to the community house all shivering and miserable. I could have loped along on the flea-bitten horse the rest of the night. The night wind began to howl around me. But again it was inside me not outside me. I didn't even think of the orange circle. It was no longer necessary. It was as though the orange circle had been the first step in using the power inside myself and the next step had something to do with relaxing and being part of everything instead of devising techniques to conquer those feelings that made me uncomfortable. The final step must be complete and total acceptance—acceptance to the ultimate. Acceptance of everything there is and everything there would be. That would be harmony.

Twenty

INSIDE, hovering over the fire pit, I heard Mary and Bhalla whispering in the corner of the rest house, hunched over a piece of paper. The fire illuminated their faces. They looked worried. Finally Mary stood up.

"There is proposed dynamite blasting tomorrow," she said simply, "and also for the weeks to follow. We must leave Paro Valley immediately—at daybreak."

Leave?

I didn't want to ask any questions. But I knew it was more than dynamite blasting. Only the day before, I had been granted a longer stay on my interline permit.

So it was over, I thought. Just when I was beginning to understand. And just as I had begun to feel a sense of harmony and fusion with everything—with everything around me, not just with nature but with people too. I was beginning to feel that I truly knew and understood Bhalla and Mary with my new perceptions. My feelings surged with theirs, and at times I had little pockets of feeling that I *was* each of them.

The morning sun rose over the ice and frost. There were no fires. The hills were silent. No Sherpas trudged the mountain trails. The rock pounding had not begun. The rest-house servants had disappeared.

We loaded our luggage into two jeeps. Mary and I rode with a driver. Bhalla drove the other jeep alone. We pulled away from the palace rest houses without a last look, without good-bys, without a reflective moment. Nothing. We just left. As though it were commonplace for me to have visited Shangri-la and now it was time for the tourist to leave and get on with the tour.

Mary stared straight ahead as the dust cloud from Bhalla's jeep covered our windshield and irritated our eyes, noses, and throats. Her eyes were red-rimmed and little pools of tears spilled down the edges, streaking through the dust on her cheeks. She reached into her robes and pulled out the paper I had seen her poring over the night before. It was from Larry Llamo and in his handwriting.

Mary dearest, leave Bhutan with the guest immediately. Many people being arrested. Everyone confused. Come now. Whatever happens to me believe this note and that I love you.   *Larry*

Mary wiped her cheeks and sighed. "There is so much we don't understand," she said at last, "and haven't understood since the former prime minister's assassination. They caught the assassin but no one knows whether he worked alone or was the instrument of a conspiracy. He never revealed anything."

"What has that to do with what's happening now?" I asked.

"Because Dorji's followers are the people being arrested," she answered simply.

"Who's arresting them?" I asked.

"In our kingdom there are many questions without answers. Sometimes conflict has nothing to do with political opposition. Sometimes it is a palace intrigue involving family jealousies, relationships, wives, mistresses, and phobias. We once had a king who was completely under the influence of his mistress. She was said to be administering a powerful love potion to him while she plotted his destruction. The mistress was in cahoots with the king's mother, who actually desired the power for herself."

"Is the royal family directing the arrests?" I asked.

"I don't know. We know that Dorji went to Switzerland to talk with the king. We know there have been some differences between them, but we know nothing of the outcome of the talks, or why the arrests are being made in Phuncholing and on the road."

I thought of the strategic location of the kingdom. It is one of India's buffer states against China, like Sikkim and Nepal. And for China it is a jumping-off point to India and Southern Asia. Topographically, it is more suited to the Chinese because they are Mongolian mountain people themselves.

"Mary," I asked, "are there many Chinese in Bhutan?"
She looked ahead. "I know nothing about that."

"The Bhutanese feel antagonistic toward the Indians, don't they?"

"Yes," said Mary. "We want to be Bhutanese. We resent India's controlling influence."

I thought of the American consul in Calcutta who had asked me to keep my eyes and ears open. I wondered what he meant. Had a coup been planned to coincide with Dorji's departure from Bhutan? Were the Americans involved? Were there Chinese in Thimphu, the capital of Bhutan, and further north toward the Chinese border? Was my stay cut short because we were scheduled to visit Thimphu the next week? Had I been given an interline permit from New Delhi just to allay any fears Dorji might have had that trouble was brewing in his kingdom? Had the king ordered arrests from Switzerland? And were we going to be arrested too? If so, why?

Mary said she knew nothing. It was all conjecture until we reached Phuncholing. And we would have to make the rigorous trip in one day.

Two hours out of Paro Valley the road-construction crews carried on their work as though news of the trouble hadn't reached them: men smoked, women pounded rocks, and children lolled in back porches. To them it was just another day on the Lost Horizon.

Then we heard the sound of motors from overhead. The rock pounding stopped and all heads turned upward. Two helicopters shadowed the face of the sun.

Bhalla ran to us from his jeep.

"The royal helicopters," he said. "They're on their way to Paro Valley. Maybe Dorji is with the king. Do you think we should return to Paro?"

Mary glanced at the note from Larry. "I trust Larry's warning," she answered. "Perhaps he couldn't explain his reason, but I believe we must leave Bhutan immediately."

Mary was a young woman of certitude. When the chips were down she was clearly the boss. Despite her exquisite beauty she was more of a man than most of the men she knew. To her, men were people with whom one was honest, forthright, level, and brotherly. They were not people at whom one waved the flirtatious wand of femininity. Her reactions to pressure were decisive and she didn't complicate the issue with feminine emotion.

Bhalla didn't question her decision. He returned to his jeep and we continued.

Mary gazed wistfully into the dust clouds. Something seemed to be passing before her eyes.

"I wonder if I will ever marry," she said suddenly.

"Why?" I asked.

"Because I've always done what my aunties wanted. They never knew any men and thought that I shouldn't either."

"So I devoted myself to the 'consequential aspects of life,'" she explained. "You know, languages [she spoke six fluently], 'events,' studies, 'ways' of people, and so forth. My aunties sent me to London to study because I was attracted to Lenny Dorji's brother Rimp. And by the time

I returned to Kalimpong he had married someone else."

"Did you love him?" I asked.

"How do I know?" she said. "I've not known men well enough to decide. Anyway my aunties will probably arrange a marriage for me soon. At least then I'll be kissed."

She fell silent and stared straight ahead again. I picked dust from my nose, my ears, and my lips. My lungs ached with the dust from each breath. Traveling as fast as possible on the pitted, bumpy road, we lurched along, our arms and fingers cramped from trying to hang on securely. Just outside Chasilakha there was a dynamite blast. Ahead of us, tumbling rocks and hillside fell onto the road. We didn't stop. Bhalla accelerated and rode over the slide. The road underneath remained solid. We followed without giving ourselves time to think, lurching and tipping to safety on the other side of the slip.

We reached Chasilakha in six hours. The construction engineers and the arrogant Sikh were gone. Chasilakha was quiet. We found boiled water and cold potatoes in the rest-house kitchen. Mary and Bhalla munched chilis as we pressed on.

Down and down the dusty dry mountainsides we bumped. The bones in our backsides felt as though they were coming through the skin. It was strange to remember the mud and torrential rains of a few weeks before. Now only the dynamite blasting would prevent passage. Perhaps whatever was occurring below had been delayed purposely until the weather assured passage by road. Darkness came. The temperature dropped abruptly and we reduced our speed around the curves.

Suddenly the headlights of a jeep caravan appeared on the road below; it was coming toward us.

"Get down!" Mary shoved me out of sight. Our driver pulled over to make way for the caravan. He waved as the jeeps passed. "Armed soldiers, guarding civilian prisoners," he announced impassively.

I saw Mary's eyes searching each jeep. Although she had no way of knowing it then, we learned later that Larry Llamo was in one of those very jeeps, handcuffed and gagged, on his way to the dzong prison in Thimphu, where he was chained by his hands and feet and tortured for two weeks in an effort to force him to admit that Dorji had attempted to overthrow the king. The note he had sent Mary warning us to leave the country had been one of his final acts before he was taken prisoner.

When the last jeep had passed, we resumed our trip, rushing headlong toward Phuncholing, the gateway that would lead us from Bhutan back over the border into India. We reached Phuncholing seventeen hours after leaving Paro Valley. From then on it was a nightmare.

As we approached the village, we found the road blocked by armed guards, some in the khaki uniforms of Indian soldiers and some in Bhutanese robes, all swaggering with self-importance and fairly bristling with guns and ammunition.

When they motioned us to halt, Mary sprang from the jeep and confronted an Indian officer, who seemed to be in charge. "What's the meaning of this?" she demanded.

"Who is with you?" he countered.

"A foreign guest from America . . ." Mary hesitated. ". . . and Bhalla, the prime minister's aide, who was assigned to accompany her."

At the mention of Bhalla's name the officer's eyes grew bright. "That's Bhalla in the other jeep?" he asked.

Mary didn't answer directly. "Where is Prime Minister Dorji?"

The officer smiled faintly. "You will receive your instructions at the rest house," he said.

Surrounded by armed guards, we were led to the rest house. Once a haven, it now resembled a barracks or a guardhouse. Soldiers milled about outside. Flashlight beams sliced the darkness, directing us inside the white picket fence which had looked so quaint on our way into Bhutan. Wildflowers in the garden had been trampled, and an armed sentry stood watch on the front porch.

Bhalla nervously brushed dust from his trousers, drew the collar of his leather jacket firmly about his neck, and climbed the steps, moving past the sentry and on into the living room. Mary and I followed. The sentry stared straight ahead, not acknowledging our presence.

We found the rest-house servants cowering in the kitchen. No one greeted us. No one spoke. Bhalla approached one of the servants. "What's happened?" he asked. "What's going on?" Edging fearfully away, the servant pushed open the screen door and slipped from the kitchen. Gently Bhalla questioned another, but he too left, followed quickly by all the others. Bhalla went after them and I could hear muffled conversation as he questioned them behind the building. Mary and I waited, sitting on wooden chairs at a table—set for three. The screen door swung open, and Bhalla returned, shaken.

"They think Dorji is still in Europe," he said. "Some of his followers escaped in time. The others have been arrested." Bhalla looked at Mary and then at his feet. "Larry was in one of those jeeps that passed us on the road."

Mary winced, and then she was on her feet, eyes flashing. "We must leave the country at once," she said. "We can't wait until morning. Come on."

Trying to appear casual, we walked out to the front porch and down the path, headed for our jeeps. At once armed guards with fixed bayonets loomed from the darkness. In one almost choreographed movement, they surrounded us, bayonets jabbing close to our bodies. I sucked in my stomach. The peace of the great mountains seemed far away. I touched the scratchy saffron strip of cloth the old lama had given me.

One flashing blade arched imperiously past our faces and over our heads. Its meaning was clear. We were being ordered to return to the rest house.

We obeyed.

Twenty-one 🌸

IT WAS LIKE a bad movie, with a script calling for me to be taken prisoner in the Himalayas with two characters named Mary and Bhalla. But there was no director and there were no cameras. It was all real, and there I was, squeezed somehow between the opposing factions in some crazy coup, some political intrigue that I didn't understand and which even Mary and Bhalla didn't seem to understand.

In the dining room of the rest house, the three of us sat in the straight-backed wooden chairs. Fine dust covered our Sherpa jackets and crusted our hair and eyelashes. Our shoes were shredded from the jagged rocks of the mountains. Our stomachs rumbled in harmony as we sat waiting—hungry, thirsty, and dog tired.

There was a heavy tread on the front porch. The door opened, and a guard strode into the dining room. Mary recognized him. "Hello, Wanchuk," she said.

He confronted us, standing with legs apart. His bulging calves were adorned with hand-knit socks and they grew like woolen trees out of his chewed-yak leather boots. His hands were on his hips. A black, yellow, and red hand-loomed robe was wound about his body to just below thigh level. A machine gun swung from his shoulder.

"Why have we been arrested?" Mary demanded in Bhutanese.

"You will be detained here," he said.

"But why?" Mary persisted.

He ignored her.

Bhalla, hunched forward in his leather jacket, said nothing.

"How long must we stay here?" I asked.

Wanchuk's pop eyes peered through thick glasses that perched on his Mongolian nose. Ignoring me, he turned to Bhalla. "You are assistant to the deposed prime minister," he said, and it was an accusation, not a question. Bhalla's leather jacket squeaked as he made a slight movement. He stared at his scuffed shoes, and then raised his eyes to Wanchuk.

"Come with me," Wanchuk said.

Bhalla sat where he was.

Mary stood up, translated what Wanchuk had said, tossed her hair over her shoulder, pulled a comb from her sash and, turning to me, feigned concern for her appearance. Her eyes bore into mine. Leaning close, she whispered, "Don't let them take him, even for a minute."

I had been worried before. Now I was plain scared. *Deposed* prime minister? Dorji?

Uncertainly I got to my feet, with Mary translating for me, I asked, "Why do you want Mr. Bhalla to go with you?"

Wanchuk answered in chiseled tones. "I have communication from his royal highness in Paro Valley."

"You mean the *king* ordered us to be arrested?" I asked.

Wanchuk stared through me, not replying.

"Couldn't you speak with Mr. Bhalla here, please?" I asked. "Instead of taking him away. Because we would like our permits to leave Bhutan immediately and Mr. Bhalla is my escort."

Wanchuk grunted.

With a glance at Bhalla, Mary said firmly, "You realize, don't you, Wanchuk, who this lady is? You know, of course, that if any harm comes to her, or if she is detained, there could be unfortunate repercussions in America for our country."

For a moment longer Wanchuk stared at me impassively. Then he swept up his robes, turned and left, slamming the door.

The three of us let out a sigh. I sat there trying to absorb what was happening. "What is it, Mary?" I asked. "What's it all about?"

Mary's face was genuinely concerned. She shook her head. "Eighteen months ago," she said, "I sat in this very room playing cards with Jigme, the former prime minister —Dorji's brother." She crossed the room and pointed to a chair. "Jigme sat right here. The door to the kitchen was open. Jigme had just won a pot, with a royal flush, and he was laughing when a shot was fired through the doorway and hit him. I held him in my lap. He lay in my lap, bleeding. There was no way to give him a blood transfusion, not here. If we could only have given him blood, he might not have died. . . ."

Mary paused. Her eyes were clouded. "How about the assassin?" I asked. "Was he caught?"

"Yes, later, but he never talked, never told whether he did it on his own or whether he was directed. The king was horrified. He appointed Dorji acting prime minister." Mary shook her head sadly. "Jigme died in my arms. His last words were 'Serve the king well.' That's all I know.

I tried to find some meaning in what she had told me and in the little I had been able to find out about the Bhutanese political regime. Wanchuk, when warned by Mary of repercussions to Bhutan, had seemed stolidly unimpressed, and I was confident that neither he nor the other guards outside had the slightest notion of "who I was" and I doubted very much that they cared. Yet I couldn't really believe that I was in any personal danger.

If it was true that Dorji had been deposed, then it was also true that I was his friend and that my trip had been made under his auspices, but this seemed hardly enough to make me an enemy of the state or of any of its see-sawing factions. Bhalla, on the other hand, was a close friend and follower of Dorji, and in any political upheaval he would be suspect. It was Bhalla they were after, Bhalla who was in danger.

All this seemed perfectly clear when, a few minutes later, a guard entered and placed three official-looking documents on the table before us.

Two were departure permits, one for Mary and one for me.

The third was a demand that Bhalla be "handed over to the authorities."

We sat there reading them, and then looking help-lessly at one another. Servants appeared from the kitchen with food. Silently they placed potatoes, chilis, and stew before us. Ice clinked in a pitcher of fresh cold water.

Wanchuk appeared, pointed at the food, ordered us to eat, and left again.

Bhalla shook his head. "We mustn't eat or drink," he said in a low voice. "The food has been drugged or poi-soned, I'm sure of it."

My mind reeled. If he was right, then all my nice theories about not being in danger were just wishful thinking. But by now I was no longer thinking of myself. I knew that Bhalla was in danger, and that was enough. The three of us were in it together, and the three of us had to get out. And it seemed clear that what we did would have to be done quickly.

Mary offered a plan. "Where is our jeep driver?" she asked Bhalla guardedly.

"Behind the house," Bhalla said. "He's scared. He won't even talk to me."

"Get him," Mary said.

Bhalla obeyed.

Cowering like a reprimanded dog, the driver entered the dining room.

"You still work for our prime minister," Mary said crisply. "Exchange clothes with Bhalla."

The driver's eyes jerked upward. He twitched.

"Do as I say," Mary demanded. "And now."

The driver slouched into the bathroom, where he gave Bhalla his turtleneck sweater and a knit hat that covered all but the eyes. Putting them on, Bhalla slipped out the bathroom window.

The driver sat down with us, wearing Bhalla's leather jacket.

Mary's plan was quite simple and might work. We knew that the jeeps were parked at the side of the rest house, toward the rear. Posing as our driver, Bhalla would simply take the wheel and we would all three cross the border. There was no time to transfer more than a few essentials. The servants were occupied with food as Mary and I passed through the kitchen and left by the back door. No one stopped us. All the guards were out front. I grabbed my hand piece, which contained my passport, diary, pictures, camera, and money. The nine-by-twelve leather-framed photograph of Steve and Sachie was stashed at the bottom of my big suitcase. It had been around the world with me three times and had been company in the loneliness of hotel rooms, native huts, and wooden lean-tos in the Himalayas. Now I would have to leave it behind. I checked the saffron scarf again and the good-luck trinkets that I wore about my neck.

Bhalla was waiting in the jeep. Mary and I loaded our small pieces into the back and got in. We pulled away and circled toward the front of the rest house. The guards on the front porch let us pass. They knew that Mary and I had departure permits, and they thought, just as we hoped they would think, that our driver was taking us to the border.

We had gone no more than a hundred feet or so when Bhalla slammed on the brakes. "It won't work," he said. "Wanchuk is at the gate. He'll recognize me. You two create a diversion at the gate while I hide under the luggage in the back. One of you will have to drive the jeep across the border."

Mary and I leapt from the jeep and rushed up to the gate, screaming insults at Wanchuk, the guards, the bayonets, and the audacity of anyone who dared demand we leave without Bhalla.

"When we get to India," I screamed, "you will answer for Bhalla's disappearance."

Wanchuk and the gate guards stood stock-still. Other guards rushed up from the rest house to see what the disturbance was all about, leaving the jeep unobserved. I took out my camera and popped flash bulbs very close to their faces. The flashes startled them. They flinched, trying to brush the bright spots from their eyes. I had been out of film for a week, but the hot flashes were enough.

Glancing over our shoulders, we could guess that Bhalla by now was safely hidden under the luggage.

Still sputtering with feminine indignation, Mary and I sashayed back to the jeep. My knees trembled. Wanchuk and the other guards, still seeing spots before their eyes and confused by our outburst, let us pass. Mary took the wheel and let out the clutch. We lurched forward.

The quarter-mile ride to the checkpoint was a numb dream. Violence hung in the starless night. I wondered where it might come from, and my concern above all else was to avoid it. I heard Bhalla, beneath the luggage, call hoarsely, "If they stop you at the border, crash right on through the bamboo pole." A shiver went through me.

Mary glanced skeptically back toward Bhalla. He was panic-stricken. The soft-spoken Indian from the dung fires of Calcutta's streets was determined to hang on to what he had made of his life, regardless of the consequences.

We rolled on and I began to see myself with a strange detachment, as though I were watching myself ride through the darkness, and hearing the decisions and counter-decisions that ticked off in my brain. I couldn't brush Steve and Sachie from my mind. They hung there in my mind's eye, saying, "Be careful." Aloud, I said to Steve, "What would *you* do?"

Mary answered. "We'll see," she said.

Something in her voice alarmed me. If she panicked at the last moment, how could I stop her from jamming the gas pedal to the floor? And if she crashed through the pole, what then? There was little doubt in my mind that there would be gunfire. I could jump from the jeep, of course, and the worst I would suffer would be a few broken bones. I was sorry I hadn't taken the wheel myself. At least then I would have been in control of my own destiny.

The bamboo-poled border was a few feet ahead of us. Mary trained the headlights on it. Palm trees swayed on either side of the road. Beneath the trees, with guns and bayonets poised, the border guards stepped across the road and blocked our passage.

Bhalla gasped under the luggage.

"Crash through, crash through," he said.

I whirled to look at Mary. Would she do it? My heart pounded so hard I couldn't breathe. Oh, if only I was in control of the jeep! I hated being at the mercy of someone else's panic. Mary turned around.

"Quiet, Bhalla," she said. "I can't crash through. They'd shoot the three of us, you know that. I'm stopping." She brought the jeep to a halt and stopped the engine. When I heard the motor die I breathed again. Bhalla didn't move.

In full force, the military guards surrounded the jeep and peered in at us. I tried to smile. They didn't react. The guard in charge shouted an order at Mary.

"He says Bhalla is missing. We must return to the rest house," Mary translated.

"Well, let's turn around and go," I said, grateful that at least we had avoided violence.

Mary hesitated. Oh, no, I thought, maybe now she'll make a break for it. She turned on the ignition and shoved in the clutch. The guards dispersed.

I didn't know then, and I don't know now what was in Mary's mind at that moment, or what her intention was, because in a flash everything changed.

The guard in charge shouted something very loud and very angry. Mary froze. Before I could ask what was happening, the guards rushed toward the jeep again. Suddenly two pieces of luggage hit me in the head and fell into my lap. With a sharp cry Bhalla tossed the suitcases from his shoulders, and leapt out of the back end of the jeep. He fell to his knees in the rice field and rolled out of sight into the dark, shadowy dung.

I screamed, "Bhalla, come back!" I was afraid they would shoot him.

Another jeep screeched to a stop. Wanchuk bounded from it. An angry flush covered his face. He was apoplectic. He screamed something at Mary. He screamed again at the guards. They readied their bayonets and rifles and ran through the rice field. The hunt was on.

Flashlights reflecting on steel bayonets swept across the field; shouts and sounds of running soldiers, heavy breathing, and scuffed dirt kicked into the flashlights' rays.

I watched the spectacle in disbelief. The guards went after their prey with long predatory strides, perspiration dripping from their foreheads and chins. They were supposed to be Buddhists, people of a higher understanding. Why were they acting like animals?

A chorus of excited shouts came from the darkness. Guards shuffled on top of something. Bhalla cried out. The quarry had been bagged. The hunt was over.

Surrounded by guards carrying bayonets and rifles, Bhalla was dragged ahead of the pack. His face and arms smeared with dung, he was gagged with a gray rag and handcuffed. His black eyes burned with fear—an animal caught in a trap, afraid to die but preferring that to what might come instead. He made nervous, jerky movements with his arched head. His body caved in at the waist as if the trap had caught him in the mid-section. I could almost feel the thud of his heart. His handcuffed wrists bounded against his thighs as the guards prodded him on.

Looking up he saw Mary and me standing beside the jeep. He straightened his body. His eyes were full of the knowledge that he had gambled and lost, but the most overwhelming degradation was his loss of dignity. With a shrug and an embarrassed half smile, he raised his bound arms in front of him as though he wanted to shake hands and say good-by.

I couldn't bear it. I forgot about myself, the guards, the reasons they might have for the arrest, Wanchuk—everything. Tearing my scarf from my head, I ran to Bhalla and tied myself to his wrists.

Wanchuk stood open-mouthed and stunned.

"If you arrest Mr. Bhalla and take him to prison, then you'll have to do the same with me," I said. "I'm not leaving Bhutan without him."

Mary stood next to the jeep, lending support. "I agree," she said.

Tears welled up in Bhalla's eyes. No one made a move to separate us. Wanchuk stood motionless, his cheek twitching. His expression was that of a man who needed time to think. Casting about for an appropriate order, he fell back upon his old standby. "You will return to the rest house," he barked.

"I want to make a telephone call to Calcutta," I said. "If you're going to keep me here, then I have a right to tell someone that I'm safe."

"You are free to go," Wanchuk intoned.

"I am not free to go *alone*," I replied. "Prime Minister Dorji instructed Bhalla to accompany me in and *out* of Bhutan. As far as I'm concerned, Dorji is still prime minister—and Bhalla is still my escort."

Wanchuk looked at me and blinked.

We made our way back to the rest house, and found it empty. Bhalla relaxed as, still bound by the scarf, we sat side by side in two of the stiff wooden chairs. The stew and potatoes cooled on the table and ice melted in the pitcher of water. We stared at it. The stiff wooden chairs dug into the small of our backs. We were too tired to sit up straight.

Mary stood by the door, looking out. No one spoke. Bhalla's silence was filled with more than he could express.

Twenty-two

IT WAS THREE IN THE MORNING before we were permitted to leave the rest house to make the telephone call. Across a rice field pitted with gullies, Mary, Bhalla, and I followed two armed guards to the one telephone switchboard in all Bhutan. Dust spiraled in the dry wind about the isolated telephone hut. Rocks, tall swamp grass, and thorned bushes surrounded the one telephone pole that rose high over the hut, its wires extending across southern Bhutan, across Assam, East Bengal, Pakistan, and into India, where in Calcutta I hoped to reach Martin and Bhulu, or perhaps Glenda Dorji.

With loud knocks, we roused two soundly sleeping Indian telephone operators. They opened the door, shivering as the cold blast of night air swept into the hut.

"We want to make a telephone call to Calcutta," Mary said sternly.

The guards followed us in, sitting impassively on bamboo cots, saying nothing to the telephone operators. The place smelled of machinery and sweat. A crudely constructed headset lay on a dusty table near the switchboard, and one of the operators placed it to his ear. "The line is out of order," he said, removing the earphones. Mary walked to the table and picked them up. She plugged in a line and I heard the comforting sound of a dial tone.

"What do you mean, 'out of order'?" she demanded. "This line works."

"That's the line to Paro Palace," the operator said. "You wanted Calcutta."

"Get us Calcutta, if you please, and immediately," Mary said.

The operator expertly crossed wires and plugs and waited. "There is conversation on the line," he said. "It's busy."

"We'll wait," Mary said. We sat down. The guards stood up stiffly, and the operators reclined on the cots. They showed no interest. After fifteen minutes, Mary lifted the headset and demanded they try again.

"Conversation on the line," the operator repeated.

An hour and a half passed. When there wasn't conversation on the line, the operators reported out-of-order or busy signals. Twice they connected us with Thimphu and once to Chasilakha, just to make it look as though they were trying. The guards fidgeted. The game was ridiculous. Finally I got up and Bhalla lurched to his feet beside me. I had forgotten we were still tied together.

What I wanted to do was to try making the connection myself. Untying the scarf, I left Bhalla and walked to the switchboard. To my amazement, one of the operators helped me plug in the correct line, and I heard the Calcutta operator. As I gave her Martin and Bhulu's number, I heard a scuffle behind me. The guards, waiting patiently until my attention was diverted, had gagged Bhalla again and were dragging him from the hut. Mary was screaming. I dropped the headset and rushed outside, grabbing the back of Bhalla's turtleneck sweater. The guards released him.

We filed back into the hut—guards, operators, and prisoners. No one stopped me as I picked up the line again and repeated the number to the Calcutta operator. The guards smoked. Mary stood between them and Bhalla. Bhalla, once again tied to my wrist, pulled the gag from his mouth and stuck out his tongue at the guards. He was regaining his confidence. The guards blew smoke in his face.

The number kept ringing. There was no answer. Pulling the plug, I started again.

"You've made your call," one of the guards said. "That's enough."

"Just one more?" I tried to ask it nicely. "I only want to tell them I'm all right." The guard turned away, and I gave the operator Glenda Dorji's number. This time I got an answer.

"Glenda?"

"Shirley!"

"Yes, can you help—" The line went dead. One of the guards had pulled the plug. I looked at him, and he smiled. My blood ran cold.

Mary leaned toward me and began speaking in low tones. The widow of Jigme Dorji had lived alone in Phuncholling since her husband's assassination—and still didn't know who was responsible for his death or why he had been murdered. Mary seemed to feel that Tess, or Tess-ala as she was called in the Bhutanese form of endearment, might help us.

"The foreign guest wants to see the former prime minister's wife," Mary told the guards. They did not object, and after we met Tess I understood why.

At five o'clock in the morning we were led across a wind-swept field to her small house. Mary tapped on the bedroom window. No answer. She tapped again, finally calling Tess-ala's name, whereupon a curtain parted slightly. Tess looked out. "What is it?" she asked. "What do you want?"

"Can you help us please, Tess-ala?" Mary spoke calmly.

"No."

The answer obviously shocked Mary. "May we talk to you for a moment? We know we're disturbing your sleep, but we haven't slept for two days."

"No."

"Please, Tess-ala. Please. Or they will take us to the dzong."

Seeing Tess withdraw from the window, we went around to the front door to wait. Fifteen minutes passed, and fifteen more. Nothing. We heard voices coming from the rear of the house but when Mary started to investigate, the guards barred her way. It was then that the front door was finally opened and with obvious annoyance Tess gestured us to enter. We saw Wanchuk at the back door.

"Now what is it you've wakened me for?" Tess asked in English. She was a slim, rather attractive woman of about thirty-five, cultured in her manner, and wearing a nightgown that was obviously European.

Mary explained what had happened. Tess sucked in her breath, as though with surprise. "I know nothing of what you say," she said.

"But Wanchuk must have told you something just now," Mary said. "Can't you request that Bhalla be given an exit permit?"

Tess opened a cabinet door. "Would you like some fruit?" she asked, bringing out a bowl of oranges and apples. Slowly she peeled an orange, letting the twisted peelings fall to the lap of her nightgown, never looking up. What could she be thinking? Bhalla had been one of her husband's trusted associates, and since the assassination he had been just as close to Llendhup Dorji, her brother-in-law. So Tess knew full well who Bhalla was and must have known the danger he was in now.

Her head tilted in an attitude of Oriental feminine innocence. "I can't understand why the authorities have done what you claim," she said, looking into Mary's eyes, indicating with a gesture that as far as she was concerned the discussion was over.

Taking a deep breath, Mary crossed the small cluttered living room and sat next to Tess. She seemed to find it hard to control herself. Forcing Tess to look at her, she spoke intensely in Bhutanese. Tess listened, casually eating the orange. Then Mary began to cry. Taking Tess gently by the hand, she led her into the bedroom. I could hear an emotional discussion going on. Once Mary left Tess, walked to the back room and stood there, sobbing. Bhalla winced and stared at his shoes. The guards by now were waiting outside.

When Mary returned to the living room, dawn was breaking. She looked totally defeated. "Let's go," she said. When I asked her what had happened, she wouldn't discuss it. She said that sometimes she was thoroughly ashamed of the ruling hierarchy of the kingdom she loved. That was all.

Exhausted, we returned once more to the rest house. Even the guards were tired, and Wanchuk, I was pleased to note, seemed out on his feet.

The bedroom of the rest house had two cots, with no bedclothes or blankets, but it was a place to collapse. The guards were stationed in the dining room, where they fell asleep. Mary and I took the cots, while Bhalla stretched out on the floor.

Phuncholing was quiet. The Bhutanese coup d'état hung in limbo, like an Asian chess game, until morning. The only sound I heard was the rumble of my own stomach. We hadn't eaten for a long, long time.

I can't recall exactly what I was dreaming. I only remember *feeling* that I wasn't alone. I opened my eyes.

Two guards stood over Bhalla, prodding him with bayonets, while another held his mouth closed. Two more were dragging him from the bedroom. The scene was too

ludicrous to be true. What I would have done had I
bothered to think, I don't know. As it was I reacted instinctively. Jumping from the bed I rushed at the guards,
waving my arms like the Wicked Witch of the North, my
eyes crossed and tongue flapping like an insane vampire
and screamed, *"Bahhhhhhhhhhhhhh!"* The guards looked
up at me in dumbfounded astonishment, dropped poor
Bhalla with a clunk, and fled. Bhalla looked at me and
collapsed with laughter. "That," he said, laughing, "is
what they call paper-tiger tactics."

Loud shouts came from the hallway. Mary sat up in
bed. Someone flung open the door. Two guards rushed in
screaming and yelling. "Get up from the floor," said Mary.
"That's what they're screaming. They're telling us to get
up and get out—all three of us. They're furious but they
say we're free and Wanchuk wants to see us at his headquarters."

It was all happening so fast. Smells of cooking came
from the kitchen; the servants were in attendance again.
I asked if I could use the bathroom. "No." Bhalla wanted
to wash some of the dung from his clothing. "No." We
were taken out of the rest house into the open air. The
morning was cold and crisp. Birds fluttered in the trees
and the flower garden seemed to come alive again.

"Let's transfer our luggage now while we have the
chance, and before they change their minds," said Mary.
We piled our belongings into one jeep. The guards
watched every move impatiently. We were starving, dying
for the food we smelled, but it was better to obey the
guards and report to Wanchuk immediately.

Wanchuk's fury was unbridled as we were brought
before him. His face was flushed again. "The queen has
given orders for your release. You will proceed to the
checkpoint."

"The three of us?" I asked.

He leapt up from his desk and screamed. "Yes, yes, yes, the three of you . . . now go . . . gooooo immediately!" He pointed in Bhalla's direction.

Bhalla shuffled toward the door, turned around, sucked in his breath, and with his right arm gestured a Bhutanese "up yours" to Wanchuk.

Yes, he had certainly regained his confidence. So much so that what he did looked almost dignified. Mary blushed a bit. We laughed and ran to our jeep outside. Bhalla got behind the wheel, shoved the jeep into gear, and we raced for the bamboo border. The guards didn't even stop us to examine our passports. They lifted the bamboo pole and waved us over.

Phuncholing receded behind us as we bounced along, Buddhist prayer flags rippling in the misty clouds over the village huts.

We stopped laughing. No one spoke. On and on we bounced into the heat of Assam. The pungent smells of the lowlands filtered back again. Into the princely state of Cooch Behar, the foliage of the rain trees, pepul trees, and mango trees covering thousands of incessantly chattering birds that sounded like high-pitched musical instruments. As we moved farther and farther south, green pigeons buried themselves in the branches of the red berry trees. Lagoons surrounded by rice paddies were dotted with splashing brown and shiny children. Millions of voices seemed to be talking at once as I heard the sounds of India again. Far behind and above us lay Paro Valley. Finally Bhalla turned to me. "I want to thank you," he said in a quick voice. "I will probably not have the opportunity to see you again, after you leave India, but thank you for my life. It belongs to you, for always." His black eyes filled as he stopped talking abruptly.

I looked out at the countryside. The sun was beginning to set. A hot wind came up, swirling down from the great mountains behind us. I didn't want to cry. I couldn't assimilate all that had happened. It didn't matter that I didn't understand the reasons for any of it. What somehow mattered more was how close I felt to Mary and Bhalla. I felt that awful twinge that comes from knowing you'll soon say good-by to people you love very much. I didn't want the experience of having known them to end. I didn't want the experience of having known more of myself to end. They were part of me now and I of them—for always, I guess—whether I ever saw them again or not.

I felt the wind playing tag in my head again, as it had in the mountains. What was it saying? I felt I could almost grasp it. It whispered about touching everything and everyone, because wind goes everywhere. It reminded me that all human beings would always be part of each other—that we are inextricably intertwined whether we meet and make contact or not. The wind swirls and moves and caresses all things and when it moves on it never turns back—there is so much out there ahead of it. I thought of the places I had been—the people I had come to know and understand and love—the Masai in Africa, the gutter babies in India, the whores in Paris, the moviemakers in Hollywood, the Japanese, the blacks in Mississippi, my own mother and father in Virginia, and my husband and daughter, who like myself seemed to be everywhere.

I looked over at Mary and Bhalla. The pain of leaving those you grow to love is only the prelude to an understanding of yourself and others.

Mary reached over and touched my hand. I put my arm around Bhalla's shoulder. The wind roared on ahead of us and I wondered if I'd ever catch up.